a sheep's faith journal

J. "Frog" Roberts
A Sheep's Faith Journal

Published by Spines
ISBN 979-8-89691-635-2

a sheep's faith journal

"ORDERED STEPS"

J. "FROG" ROBERTS

contents

This book is dedicated to Sheila V. Roberts, who God lent to me for 137 Seasons, 413 months. She was the heartbeat of my love, the rhythm of my pulse, and the Gift God overwhelmed me with. The woman God pointed out to me in a liquor house, and in no uncertain terms, proclaiming in an audible voice: "There is your Wife" as she walked by with a hairstyle that I wasn't feeling. So, I immediately retorted back with a beer in my hands: "I ain't looking for a wife." And again, that voice declared to me with sublime authority, "THERE IS YOUR WIFE." One month and twenty-five days later, we were married at the Justice of the Peace. She was my Wife for 34 and half years.

And even though she was called home on June 29th, 2024, she will always be 'is' in the present and will never be 'was' in the past tense. She was indeed my Wife and the apple of my eye. She was the stone on which God crushed me, shaping me into the image of Christ as I pressed toward the mark of the Husband made for her. She was surely in Christ, the tool that showed me the way to manhood. So that as her man, I learned to break free of my childish ways. This Book is a glimpse into my journey, not only as a servant of God but that of a man learning how to become one in the Spirit with his rib, a wife just for me. Yes, Sheila was indeed bone of my bone and flesh of my flesh, and without her, this testimony of our 'faith walk' as One, would not be possible, and this true story, "A Sheep's Faith Journal" would not be told.

Sheila V. Roberts: Married – January 5, 1990 / Called to Glory – June 29, 2024

The Foundational Cornerstones for this Book: In the pages of this Book, I have copied my own spiritual thoughts, discernments and other nuggets that have helped me through, and in the now of my faith walk home, as I make my way through "the valley of shadows and death." Always contending for my faith, as I press toward the eternal glory of Life in Christ. In this Book, there are two "foundational scriptures" that I deem to be the two pillars, or the true "Cornerstones" that give structure and support to all that is comprised within its pages. It is for me, a Book of prayers, poetry, psalms and supplications. And as well, it is a compilation of many scripturally discerned interventions that have aided me along the way and to this day continue to assist me in my faith walk, as I press onward to know more intimately the Father. And in this testimony of my journey, there are Spiritual insights revealed to me that still have not manifested nor divulged unto me their mystery, hence I have concluded that they are more than likely things that may sooner avail themselves to you, the reader, even before they appear to me for my good. Yet, I do not measure what has helped me, as some new doctrine of God, but only the tools that have allowed me to remain faithful to the cause of Christ. No, they may not be on the same level as were revealed by the Holy-Spirit in the equipping of the Saints with the Word of God, which was given to Holy Men as the Word declares. (2Peter 1:20)

Knowing this first, that no prophecy of the scripture is of any private interpretation —For the prophecy came not in old time <u>by the will of</u> <u>man</u>: but "Holy Men of God" spoke as they were moved by the Holy Ghost. And so the reason that I am led to write this Book of; 'My Faith Walk' as a sheep, is so that whatever I've received of the Lord to my benefit, and or to the benefit of the reader can be exhausted unto the exploitation of the goodness of God in the life of the believer.

"They that hath an ear, let him hear what the Spirit saith;" (Rev 2:11)

the foundational stones

CORNER STONE NUMBER I

2 Timothy 3:16,17 – All Scripture is given by inspiration of God, and is profitable for Doctrine, for Reproof, for Correction, for Instruction in Righteousness, that the man or Woman of God may be Perfect, thoroughly equipped for every good work—

CORNER STONE NUMBER II

Deuteronomy 29:29 – The Secret things belong to the Lord our God, but those things which are revealed belong to Us and to our Children forever, that we may do all the Words of this Law. *A Sheep's Faith Journal.*

"My sheep hear my voice, and I know them, and they follow me:

— And I give unto them eternal Life;"

light, the life of men

St John 1:1-5 - In the beginning was the Word, the Word was with God, the Word was God, the same (*and they were One and the same*) was in the beginning with God. All things were created by Him (*the Word*), and without Him (Jesus), nothing was created. In Him was Life, and the Life was the Light (*Spiritually illuminated Life giving Force*) of men. And the Light shown into the darkness, and the darkness comprehended it not... (*the darkness could not absorb it, the light was too brilliant to behold*).

Genesis 1:1-5 - In the beginning God created the heaven and the earth. And the earth was without form, and darkness was upon the face of the deep. And the Spirit of God moved upon the face of the waters (*and the Light of God penetrated the darkness of the waters*). And God said let there be Light (*as he declared it by way of His Word, which is Christ*). (*and the Light of His dear Son lit up the universe, illuminating the very darkness in His brightness – Rev 21:23*) and God saw that it was good.

Now, as we see the creative force of Light in its Spiritual prowess, we see it at work demonstrated by the Word of God. So let us define the word "Light", not only in its natural force but more important for us as Believers, let's understand its Spiritual meaning. We will start out with Webster's New World Dictionary, and progress from there.

Webster's New World Dictionary –

Light *(n)* 1. the form of energy that acts on the eyes so that one can see... 5. helpful information or knowledge. 7. the way something is **seen; aspect. (*v*) 4. to guide by giving light**

THE LIGHT OF SEEING

Light (n) 1. the form of energy that acts on the eyes so one can see —

(Spiritual Insight from the book of Luke 10:23,24 – and He turned to His disciples and said privately, Blessed are the eyes which see the things that you see: for I tell you that many prophets and kings have desired to see those things which you see, and have not seen them; and to hear those things which you hear; and have not heard them).

Now, in this statement made by *Jesus*, we see that the *light* of revelation has opened up unto the disciples a clear path to understanding what had never been revealed or seen by neither King nor Prophet. And because of their appointed position in "the fulness of time" (*Gal 4:4*) the *light* of revelation revealed the plan of God unto babes (*Matt 11:35*) And so now we see "in the disciples" for the first time, the *Kingdom* of God being Spiritually comprehended by regular laymen unlearned and intellectually inferior to any scholar of the day.

And now, because of the opening of their eyes by *Jesus* in revealing to them the mysteries of the *Kingdom,* we who are centuries removed from the distant calling of those first *"Twelve"* have now also attained access to that same *light* of revelation, showing unto us the mysteries of the Kingdom. And so we, like the twelve (*in plain language*), now have access to that self-same *light-anointing* that opened up their understanding, access to the same information and knowledge that is still necessary to the success of our own upward calling into the Glory of the Son, as we began to understand by wisdom how to apply all the vital and different aspects of **walking with God**. As we strive to live in Christ by all that is revealed in the *light of the knowledge of Christ (2Cor 4:6)*

As the Book of Acts so eloquently states in *Chapter 26:18 - to open their eyes and to turn them from darkness to light, and from the power of Satan to God — that they may receive forgiveness of sins and an inheritance among those who are Sanctified by Me (Christ).*

Guidance by Discernment

The Light of Guidance

Light (v) 4. To guide by giving light....

Acts 9:3 - 5 - (*6 - So he [Saul], trembling and astonished, said 'Lord, what do you want me to do'? And the Lord said to him, "Arise and go into the city and you will be told what you must do"*)

Acts 9:10, (*11 - And the Lord said unto him (Ananias). Arise and go into the street which is called 'Straight' and inquire in the house of Judas for one called Saul, of Tarsus: for behold he prayeth*).

Commentary of Acts 9:6 & 11, 12

In these two verses of scripture, we see the *Lord* guiding two individuals from two socially diverse backgrounds, one a Jew and the other a Greek. And though Ananias was a Greek, it was obvious that he was 'born-again.' And of course, Saul, who would later use his Roman name "Paul", who having been conquered by the bright Light of Jesus, found himself vulnerable and being led to the house of this Greek, which as an unconverted Jew would have never been seen in the company of such a person, but God by a strong hand led him out of that now 'defunct law ' ...made so by the fulfillment of it in Christ. —*So,* the *Lord* guided a blinded Saul to a city called *'Damascus'* ...and placed him in the hands of a Gentile he did not know. —*And* after being without sight three days, neither eating nor drinking [*vs-9*]. Then the *Lord* said to Ananias *"Arise and go into the street called* Straight, *and enquire in the house of Judas for one called Saul of Tarsus: for behold he prayeth,* —*And hath seen in a vision a man named Ananias coming in, and putting his hand on him, that he might receive his sight* [*vs-11,12*].

And so, we see in this *'Scene'*, a once waster of the Church having hands, laid on him by a man (Ananias), who in the flesh (and without discernment), greatly feared this man called Saul. —But *God,* by His own grace, had filled Ananias with the *Holy Spirit,* hence he was well able to discern that his orders to free Saul came straight from the will of God.

THE NEED FOR LIGHT

Ps 27:1 – *The Lord is my **Light** and my Salvation; whom shall I fear?*

Ps 36:9 – *For with thee (Christ), is the fountain of Life; in thy **Light** shall we see (discern) **Light** (Truth)...*

Ps 119:105 – *Thy **Word** is a lamp (guide) unto my feet, and a **Light** unto my path (direction)*₁

There may be many interpretations of the *'Light of God'*, its purpose and impact in and on the *life* of a Christian. But a believer's duty and individual responsibility is to search out for his or her own purpose in the **light** of Spiritual discernment and revelation (*Deut 29:29*). They must also allow the **light** of their discernment to shine into the hidden places of their own lives, in order that the purging of sin and other hindrances might be exposed, removing all leaven from their lives. So that the **life** of

Christ in them can show forth unto victory in their everyday walk. And in doing so, the pureness of their motives is shown openly to the glory of the *Father* in *Christ Jesus,* hence allowing for their individual gifts and talents to show forth for the work of the Ministry, desiring always to let their **light** shine *(Mt 5:16),* that people may see their good works and *glorify* the *Father.*

St John 8:12 – *Then spake Jesus again unto them, saying,* **I am the light of the world: he that follows me shall not walk in darkness, but shall have the light of life (which is the Word)**

John 1:5 - 7 – *This then is the message which we have heard of* **Him,** *and declare unto you, that God is* **light,** *and in* **Him** *is no darkness at all. If we say we have fellowship with* **Him,** *and walk in darkness, we lie, and do not know the Truth. But if we walk in the* **light** *as* **He** *is in the* **light,** *we* have *fellowship one with another — and the* **"blood of Jesus Christ His Son"** *cleanses us from all sin.*

Eph 5:14 – *Wherefore* **He** *says, awake thou that sleep. And arise from the dead, and* **Christ** *shall give you* **light...**

Cor 4:6 – *For* **God** *who commanded the* **light** *to shine out of darkness, has shined in our hearts, to give the* **light** *(revelation) of the knowledge of the* **glory of God** *in the face of* **Jesus Christ...(be ye separated, come out from among them** *[2Cor 6:17]...***don't live, do, or be as the world... Light has no fellowship with darkness** *[Eph 5:11]* **"the worlds way of living")...**

Rev 21:23 – *And the City had no need of the Sun, neither of the Moon to shine in it — for the* **glory of God** *lighten it. And the* **Lamb** *is the* **light** *thereof (the Lamb, Christ is the glory of the Father) ...*

Rev 22:5 – *And there shall be no night there; and they need no candle, neither light of the Sun —for the* **Lord God** *gives them* **light...**

**Light Meditation — *Selah!*

So, here at this juncture, let us take time to meditate, and reflect on what has been said, just to allow the light from them to penetrate all the places of our spiritual need. And of course, we know that what has been written to this point is for the Born Again Christian first, and for those who are seeking to find their higher place in the plan and calling of God. So let us allow time for absorption and for the leading of the Holy Spirit on how we might benefit from His Holy Scripture and the confirming revelations from them that have blessed me and are still blessing my life today. And so, I chose the word "meditation" which means *(v) 1. To pass some time thinking in a quiet way; reflect. 2. To plan or consider* [to *meditate* making a change]. And to use this word with the spiritual revelation on the importance of the *light*, I believe shows us how to fully absorb and utilize the splendor of walking by Faith. You with the *light* of *meditation,* I believe we're better equipped and more able to discern the area of our walk we need to pay more attention to.

[Joshua 1:8]– *This book of the Law shall not depart out of your mouth; but thou shall meditate therein day and night, that thou may observe to do according to all that is written therein* (Note: in the book of Matthews, Chapter 22:37 thru 40, Jesus fulfills God's plan, and capsulizes the Old Testament Laws into *the* 'New Commandments', and establishes that on these two hang all the Old Laws and the ministry of the Prophets).

So you see, by the *light of meditation,* we have a tool that will allow us to walk out our walk of faith in a more efficient way, as it makes way for us to be better equipped to focus on those areas in our lives that need more attention, those areas that tend to have more distractions. Distractions in simple matters that really are not as important as our natural senses and reactions would have you believe. Issues like "Did I pay that bill today?" "I meant to pick up some detergent," etc. and of course, if you had your 'Bills' scheduled, that question wouldn't invade your quiet time, or if you'd written a 'grocery list' you wouldn't have to have your prayer time interrupted. These are of course simple examples, but you get the picture. We all deal with those kinds of leavened minutiae that can make us miss hearing or discerning a serious word or insight from the Holy Spirit. You see, I know these types of distractions, to some, may not seem to be such a big deal, and you might even call me a bit fanatical, and that may very well be, but when you've been distracted by something that you can't even remember that clearly, and you drive eleven miles to a 'job' get ready to unlock the door, and quickly realize that you left the key's at home, suddenly that natural distraction becomes a 'spiritual' battle within. A spiritual battle, which may accuse the Holy Spirit of not looking out for you and reminding you not to walk out the door without your keys.

Yes, I'm guilty...that's a real-life example, one that, as a twenty-five plus year Christian, I am not proud to admit. My point in all of this so-called dexterous minutiae, is to show how easily we can lose our focus in this faith journey, it doesn't take much: but as we mature using every weapon at our disposal, including *meditation* —we will be better able to carry out the plan of God for our lives with more succinct understanding of application in the things of God meant to lead us to a less stressful life.

A life more adapts to listening and carrying out the plan of God amid our everyday life. For indeed, we ought to know at some point in our growth, what the plan of God involves, not just about our needs, but what the greater need and purpose of the Kingdom of Heaven has come down to accomplish, for the Kingdom of God is indeed with them who believe, as Jesus declares (*Luke 17:20,21 –, The kingdom of God comes not with <u>observation</u>: Neither shall they say, Lo here! or, lo there! for behold: **the kingdom of God is within you**)*. Hence! He has given us the tool of meditation by way of the Holy Spirit so that we are more able to walk in a greater cohesiveness, with a better level of understanding of how to utilize our *faith* according to the will of God in our daily walk.

And so, as we familiarize ourselves with the usefulness of **meditating** on scripture delicacies such as, *"Habakkuk 2:4 - but the just shall live by his faith"*. For me, the light of these types of scriptures will always work to strengthen our faith walk as we meditate upon them.

Also, study: (Romans 1:17 / Galatians 3:11 / Hebrews 10:38). Now let's take a closer look at the essence of *Hebrews 11:6 - but without faith it's impossible to please Him... for he who comes to God must believe that He is, and that He is a rewarder of them that diligently seek Him...* And so, we see in these two verses, pulled from two different dispensations, a strong line of agreement, and through the light of **meditation,** I believe, and am totally convinced (by experience), that we can hear more astutely what the Spirit is saying to us, in our situation. Therefore, discerning more clearly how to walk by faith, both in our daily lives while carrying out those things that have been revealed to us, for us, and for the lives of others, and especially of those connected to us who are of the household of faith. And so, I believe that without meditating on the **word** of God in a way that is conducive to our spiritual needs, we will not fully be able to access those things we so desperately need in the nurturing of a more dependent relationship with the Father. A relationship based on complete surrender to the sacrifice that was made at Calvary. Yes, indeed we will increase in wisdom and stature as we meditate on His **word**... and then we will truly be able to take ownership of: *Deuteronomy 29:29* as it declares with promise —*The secret **things** belong unto the Lord our God: but those things which are revealed belong unto us and to our children forever, that we may do all the words of this Law.* Now, of course, this promise was made under the Law, pertaining to those who were under the Law... but by revelation and understanding, we can claim all the Spiritual ramification and power of that **word**... And again, for me, through the **light of meditation,** I can get revelation on what I can glean from the "Old" to apply in the "New". And I get just such a clarity of the importance of **meditation** when I read (Joshua 1:8), in it God tells His servant Joshua that he should *"meditate day and night"*, *"and observe to do all that is written"*, and by doing so *"then he would prosper and have good success"* Now as a lay-person, by permission, I will say it another way: Because the Father has given us the Holy-Spirit, we now have tools that not only give us guidance in the **truth**, but also gives us strength in our faith to stand, and by doing so the responsibility to stand is on us.

And as well, it is our responsibility to seek out scripture, to meditate on those scriptures that are allotted to us for our own personal growth, in the *"renewing of our minds"* as we live out our daily lives, so that we may be able to receive, perceive and understand how to apply all that is revealed. Hence, by the **light of meditation**, I'm learning how to more keenly focus on and grow in the kind of faith that pleases the **Father** in doing my part for the **Kingdom**. Selah!

NOW FAITH:

In the Light of *"Now"* —*Faith is what*?

<u>Webster's New World Dictionary</u> –

Faith **n. 1.** belief or trust that does not question or ask for proof **2.** belief in God and religion [**Job kept his faith in spite of his troubles**]

<u>Me (John Roberts inspired interpretation; by the Holy Spirit)</u> –

Faith - the future established in the immediacy of <u>**Now**</u> — future events called into being on behalf of what is hoped for and is accepted Now. Though not yet manifested into the desired reality, but is in the production line of the **Kingdom**, as ordered goods: in other words, your blessing is on the way...(*Romans 4:17 - as it is written, I've made you a father of many nations)... before Him whom he believed, even God, who quickens the dead, and call those things which be not as though they were.*

<u>Oxford University Press Dictionary</u> –

Now ***adv.*** **1.** at the present time. **2.** at or from this precise moment, *Hebrews 11:1 -* <u>**Now**</u> *faith is the substance of things hoped for, the evidence of things not seen.*

<u>Me (John Roberts inspired interpretation:</u>

Substance - the invisible or Spiritual material needed to produce what is desired or hoped for in the material world. — Evidence - the reality of the invisible power of what or who you believe can bring to pass the thing your faith has produced.

What Now is to Faith

Now, pertaining to our faith: it eliminates the possibility, or the probability of us ever receiving from the *Kingdom*, what we want or need in our life today. You might ask how. Well, simply put you can't use whatever is distracting you today as an excuse to believe in what you want today, tomorrow. Because what you want today by faith is always a future need, and to put it off for tomorrow because of your distraction today will more than likely push what you needed by faith today further down the road.

That's why faith is always established in the realm of ***now*** and not later. And so, ***now,*** at this very moment...is the immediate time you must make your request known to *Heaven*, regarding your future desire. You see, I believe that the Kingdom can only begin the process of shipping your ordered need or desire: First, based on the *will* of the Father, and second, that what you've ordered is God's will for your individual life. Because from my life experience with Christ, all of God's will for our lives is somewhat allotted to our individual circumstances. In other words, the thing that's meant for you according to God's will may not be the thing that's pertinent to my need. [Example: A pastor with a thousand members and a budget to reach the masses will always have a different set of needs and obligations than little ole me. Cause I may only be called to witness in my community and be a good father to my two children, with a lifestyle budget to match our needs, hence our faith must believe in very different things. So, to sum it all up – *now* is always in the <u>present</u>, it will never and can never exist in the hopes of waiting for tomorrow, to seal what you need to hope for *now* (today), this very second. Because in the *now of faith* is your future destiny, for person, place or thing. Again, as God's *word declares: [Hebrews 11:1 - 'Now' faith is the substance of things hoped for] [and your faith is the evidence that you believe God for the thing not seen]*

Of course we can describe it *now* another way: *Now* is always established in the present I say always the 'present', why? Simple, because *now* can never operate from yesterday's desire, nor can it be postponed into tomorrow's plan. Or, we can say it like this: What you desired earlier is never the same if you desire it *now* because each thing that is desired at the time it is desired will have its own salvation to work out in order to manifest into what it is hoped for. In the same way, you can't put off for later, the thing you hope for now, it has to all be hoped for and believed for in the *now* of our <u>*faith*</u>. Now, you might be saying to yourself, this is complicated stuff when it should all just be established on the fact that I'm trusting God to take care of me, after all, I am His Child. And if that is your thought, then let me say it a simpler way. *Now,* always starts the working of our *faith for all our future desires and needs!*

So, our Faith is Now

Jesus said in Matthew, Chapter 9 v 29 - According to your faith be it unto you. So, this book on *faith* is one in which I hope you will be able to study at your own convenience the things in it that may highlight what you're experiencing or searching to understand. I hope and believe that if received, it will be a book in your library from which you're able to glean and learn from, like many other books glorifying our Savior and Lord, Jesus Christ. I hope it will become for you a Spiritual delicacy in your appetite to consume Christ, as the scriptures declare: (*Ps 34:8 - O taste and see that the Lord is good*). So, because of the way this '*book* is structured, there's intentionally no set format as to how each person may study, absorb, and digest what is needed for their daily walk of faith.

FAITH STUDY:

The Spiritual Nature and the Power of Faith—

Faith Breadth Lesson –- *What does this mean?* It means that we should exhaust every *scripture* and verse on **faith** that the Holy-Spirit reveals to us, until our understanding has been received. We must stay *hungry* for the power and operation of faith in our lives. For example, let's read in reverse (***Eph. 3:20 back to 16***), together (**20.** *Now unto Him that is able to do exceedingly abundantly above all that we ask or think, according to the power that worketh in us.*

Faith is Now:

Ephesians 3:20 — 16 (reverse reading continues)

19. *And to know the love of Christ, which passeth knowledge, that ye might be filled with all the fulness of God. –* **18.** *[and] may be able to comprehend with all saints what is the* breadth, *and* length, *and* depth, *and* height. – **17.** *[so] That Christ may dwell in your hearts by* **'faith'***; that ye, being rooted and grounded in* **love,** *–* **16.** *[and] That He would grant you, according to the riches of His glory, to be strengthened with might by His Spirit in the inner man.* —

Now, when I read this forward and then was led to read it backwards, what I received from doing so was only *faith* illuminated, hence showing me that the substance all we hope to be, have, and achieve in Christ can only be accomplished through the fellowship of our *faith*, and by no other means. Faith is that 'power' working in us, strengthening our 'Inner Man' so that we're able to comprehend the place we need to be in our Spiritual lives where *love* is concerned because love is the catalyst that allows our *faith* to move mountains, and any other obstacle to the plan and **will** of God for our lives.

And so, for those of us [*though it may only be a few of us*], who think that we can be a Christian or have Christ in any form without having *faith* and being led by it, we deceive ourselves because you can't have the God kind of faith operating in your life without a proper relationship with Christ established by faith and strengthened in the Holy-Spirit. [*Now we will discuss in future pages, more about the Holy Spirit*]. But let me simply state: "It is by way of the Holy Spirit of God that we have the *Spiritual* **power** to call by *faith* (in Christ) those things that be not, into the realm of Now, establishing what we want according to His will for our *__individual lives__*. Amen!

Faith is Now

In these Lessons on *'faith,'* you will discover **3-Pillars** associated with the *strength* of our *faith*...as you will learn, they are *vital.*

Faith Depth Lesson: [Word Application]

Pillar # 1 – St Matthew 9:20 - 22 ... 27 - 29 [*Based on 2nd Timothy 2:15 - study to show thy self-approved unto God, a workman that need not to be ashamed, rightly dividing the Word of Truth*]

9:20 - 22 Thy *faith* has made you whole: (sometimes it's as if we, as His children, act as if our shame is enough to keep Jesus away, since we really don't deserve whatever, it is we're seeking to get from God. So, we stay in our sickness, addiction, and many other hindrances because of the lack of revelation concerning our positioning in God. But if we profess to be the children of God, we must also confess our boldness to touch the hem of His garment, as Apostle Paul declares by the Holy-Spirit in— *Hebrews, chapter 4 vs 16 - let us therefore come boldly unto the throne of grace, that we may obtain mercy, and find grace to help in time of need*). 9:27 - 29 According to your *faith* be it unto you: (so, if we know who we are in Christ, then we have the confidence to stand on that place, and believe with assurance that whatever we ask according to God's will for our individual lives, will be granted; yes indeed, according to my faith be it unto me). You see, where our faith is concerned, we must desire to go and grow deeper in the things our <u>relationship</u> with Christ requires. We cannot remain on the surface of any relationship if we expect a deeper intimacy than what the shallow ground can produce, as *Jesus* states in the Book of *Matthew, chapter 13:23 - But he that received seed into the good ground is he that <u>hears</u> the word, and <u>understands it</u>; which also bears fruit, and brings forth, some a hundredfold, some sixty, some thirty*). So, we see that the measure of our *faith* will always be increased by the measure of how deeply we want to take our relationship in Christ and on what level of intimacy. For me, it's as deep as I can go.

FAITH HEIGHT LESSON – THE MIND OF CHRIST

Pillar # 2 - St Matthew - 8:5 - 13 and Philippians - 3:9 - 10 [*Based on Colossians 3:2 - Set your affection on things above, rather than things on the earth.*]

Matthew 8:5 - 13 - And when *Jesus* was entered into Capernaum, there came unto *him* a centurion *(a gentile)*, beseeching *(pleading)* **him**, *(to heal his servant from a grievously tormenting* disease) ... And *Jesus* said unto the centurion. *Go your way; and as you have believed, so be it done unto you.* (Here we get a glimpse into the faith of a gentile, and one who, because of his position in the Roman military, and obvious belief in the Messiah of Israel, who also being a man of authority — *" and of course, this could've only come by revelation, because Spiritually speaking the authority he had, and the authority Christ had was as different as night– from day. Nevertheless, he'd received an awesome revelation because of the simplicity of his faith in Christ".* As Christ admonished those who were following **him** just for *his* power to manifest bread *(food)*, how they might work the works [St John 6:24 - 29]. But what we'll see in further study of this group of Jews is the reason *Jesus* warned them. They weren't believers; hence they had no revelation of who Jesus was. — And so, for me, the lesson in this is plain, *you* must be born-again, as the centurion obviously was by the evidence of his **faith** and belief in the one God sent. Therefore, he was able to work the works).

Philippians 3:9 – 10 - And be found in **him**, not having mine own righteousness, which is of the law, but that which is through the **faith** of *Christ* the *(only)* righteousness which is of God by **faith.** That I may <u>know</u> *him*.

Know *verb* 7. **archaic** *(ancient language) have sexual intercourse with (past* **knew** *- past of* <u>know</u>*)-*PHRASES **be in the** <u>know</u> *- be aware of something known only to a few people.* <u>**Know**</u> **no bounds** *- have no* *limits* **Oxford University Press)** *[Genesis 4:1-And Adam* **knew** *Eve his wife (had sexual intercourse).]*

Know - *v.* **4.** To be **_acquainted_** with [*I know your brother well*]

Acquaint -*v.* **2.** *to cause to* **know** *personally; make familiar with*

Familiar -*adj.* **1.** *friendly; well* **_acquainted_**; *intimate* **2.** *–;* **_intimate_** *in a bold way* **3.** *knowing about; acquainted with* **4.** *well,* **known;**

Intimate - *adj.* **2.** *very close or* **_familiar_** *[an intimate friend].* **deep** *and thorough [an intimate knowledge of* **physics]** **(Interpretation by Me: an intimate but limited knowledge of God on a need-to-know basis) (Webster's New World Dictionary)**

Strong's Exhaustive Concordance: Hebrew, Chaldee & Greek

Hebrew:

Know = **"Yada"** - *a primary root; to* **know** *(prop. To ascertain by seeing) Used in a great variety of senses: figurative, literal, euphemistic.*

Figurative - for Adam and Eve to bear children, they must first **know** *(have sexual intercourse with)* each other to produce offspring.

literal - the literal meaning of the statement in: *[Genesis 4:1 And Adam* **knew** *(past tense of* **know***) Eve his wife and she* conceived*], And Adam had **sexual intercourse** with Eve, and she conceived.*

Euphemism - to acquaint oneself with God, is to know him: (acquaint - **1.** to give knowledge of; inform [*He* **_acquainted_** *himself with all the facts.*] **2.** to cause to know personally; make familiar with [*Are you acquainted with Sarah?*]

Scripture Context: (English) know (knew) — (Hebrew) yada....

Euphemism *(Philippians 3:10 - That I may* **know** *Him, and the power of His* **resurrection***, and the fellowship of His sufferings, being made*

*conformable unto His death.) [That I might be acquainted with Him...
Job 22:21 - Acquaint now thyself with Him, and be at peace:]*

<u>Literal</u> *(Genesis 4:1 - And Adam **knew** Eve his wife; and she conceived.) [And Adam yada Eve his wife, and she conceived]*

Note: This is a simple exercise in getting to know a few words related to comprehending the importance of understanding the necessity of how certain simple words apply themselves to how we live our daily lives with respect to carrying out our responsibility in the nourishing of our *faith*.

FAITH LENGTH LESSON

Pillar # 3 - Job 12:12 - With the Ancient is *wisdom*, and in length of days is understanding [*Reference: Isaiah 45:21 and Daniel 7:9 - 22*]

[***Based on: Acts - 1:6-8*** > *When they therefore had come together, they asked of Him, saying. — Lord wilt thou at this time restore again the kingdom of Israel?* And He said unto them: ***It is not for you to know the times or the seasons, which the Father hath put in his own power — But you shall receive power, after that the Holy Ghost is come upon you: and you shall be witnesses unto me both in Jerusalem and in all Judea, and in Samaria, and unto the uttermost part of the earth.***]

Note: The insight that I have been given in this message is that: our *faith* is eternal, and the *length* of our learning and increasing in it, and all that it entails is unmeasurable. Hence as the scripture proclaims, pertaining to the glory of the Lord as it continually works in us, changing our spirit by our *faith,* perpetually from *glory* to *glory.(2 Cor 3:17)* And yet, in that constant place of change, it is not for us to know whether or not we have arrived at that appointed place, seeing that we are still earthbound until the purpose of God is fulfilled. And if we are spiritually discerning in our quest to **know** the *truth* concerning our spiritual walk of faith, we will understand by the writings in that great book called the *"Word of God "* no one ever had a retirement plan for living out their life as a *believer,* both Old and New Testaments, no they continued their journey from *glory to glory,* until they split the seams of eternity: and for the Old Testament *Saints* it was *Father* Abraham's bosom —but for the **Church**, our retirement plan is to transfer from death to life. *[2 Cor 5:7,8 For we **walk by faith, not by sight:**] —We are confident, I say, and willing rather to be absent from the body, and to be present with the Lord Glory n. 4. great beauty, power, or splendor*

Conclusion: The longer you live as a servant of the highest God, the more evident it should be that the power of His love is openly operating in your life, hence showing more evidence of His beauty in you, as the power of His splendor is exuded from the very pores of your service to Him on behalf of the Father. Amen!

Lesson Summary: *Zechariah 4:1-(5,6)-7* (Paraphrase: *Not my might —**Nor** my Power — but by His Spirit*) - *Then the Angel that talked with me answered and said unto me. Knowest thou not what these things be? And I said, no my lord. Then he answered and spake unto me, saying: This is the "Word of the Lord unto Zerubbabel", saying. Not by might, not by power, but by my Spirit (Holy-Ghost), saith the Lord of hosts* (Webster Dictionary: *Host - n. 2. an army*).

And so we see, here with *Zerubbabel,* that the power of God is always demonstrated by the Spirit of God, which in this instance and all those situational instances following the Old Testament examples, leading up to the day of *Pentecost,* and just as important, in our present day *now* – we see the necessity of the Holy-Spirit or *Holy-Ghost,* [whichever you feel comfortable with], operating in our everyday walk of *faith.* Yes indeed, if we surrender to our need for the Holy-Spirit to freely operate in our lives, we will then have all the power we need to grow *spiritually,* and with purpose, we will begin to activate that same **'dunamis - power'** that was demonstrated in the life of our *Savior,* the Apostles, and all of those who desire victory in their lives. We must desire to have that kind of *power,* a power that gives us strength to lift up the *'feeble knees'* — *(Job 4:4),* helping us to reconstruct our lives out from under our mount of defeat into a victorious and glorious place of *triumph.* So, just as God reveals to Zerubbabel, it is only by way of the Holy-Spirit, who is our *Comforter,* do we have the fellowship not only of strength but of *joy, unspeakable joy* as we come to understand that through our sufferings unto victory do we have true fellowship with our Lord. Our Lord who being conformed in the likeness of sin and paying the price, not only for our salvation but for the **faith** that we must have to endure our own *cross,* a cross that can only be taken up by us, in the strength of *the* Holy Spirit, who is our precious *gift* in this battle called life. For as the *word* of *life* gives confirmation of *Zechariah 4:6* in *Acts 1:8 - But you shall receive Power, after that the Holy Ghost is come upon you:* we further see our **faith** in action, as we increase in the knowledge of Christ, and in the *power* of the Holy Ghost. So, let us praise the Father even more for not only saving us through the *cross of Christ* but also equipping us with that **Dunamis - power** that we might be conformed day by day into the expressed image of his dear *Son,* who was triumphant in His cause of obedience, by the power of that selfsame *Spirit,* that was provided for the success of Zerubbabel against his enemies, even as for ours now. *Amen!*

Glory #1 - A Testimony Break [*Testimonial Confirmation Date: 12/28/05*] ***Zech 4:6 –But by my Spirit saith the Lord***

On December 19th, 2005, I was terminated from my job as a *'Courtesy Bus Driver'* at Hertz Rental Car Agency, located at Charlotte Douglas International Airport, Charlotte, NC. It was a position I'd held since I was hired in April 2002... and indeed, it was one I enjoyed, as touching and relating to the many varied customers that I served, I also enjoyed my fellow employees, and it is because of them, and my relationship with Christ *(and after explaining it to my wife, who was not for it, nor against it, yet nevertheless because of the Godly wife that she is, accepted my decision)*, that I accepted the invitation by one of the other leaders, Mr. Kenneth *(who was, and still is my brother and friend in Christ)*. It was somewhere around October that I had decided to completely give myself over to the fight to be represented by the Local Teamster Union, and with a made-up mind and no regrets, we began to engage our fellow disgruntled employees of *'Counter Sales and Bus drivers'*. And our effort soon began to pay off – as more and more employees joined our ranks, and a successful campaign was on the way. –Now, just a flashback to the position I held when I was approached by Mr. Kenneth and the Teamster Rep to become one of the spearheads of our fight to be represented by a Union; I was a Lead Bus Driver, but in title only. Because none of my recommendations were recognized or accepted even though my position was to help improve the service to our customers, and to tighten up our Route efficiency. So, the obvious cause for this testimony is my disappointment with the Company. Because their inaction became the reason for my resignation from the Lead Position. Therefore, I joined my coworkers in our struggle for a Union Contract. Hence, that decision brings us to December 19th and my abrupt firing! *(Now of course, my joining the Union they say, was not the reason they'd decided to terminate me — but that story is for a different testimony)* December 19th was on a Wednesday —six days prior to Christmas, which for them in their evil scheme to eliminate me from the fight, was a perfect time. *(Of course, this part is all speculation for me, but it seemed to me to be an obvious and curious time to terminate someone, and for very suspect reasoning)*

ON MY BED

It was now the 28th of December 2005, the ninth day of my firing, as I lay in bed with eyes wide open, contemplating my next move and speaking to the Lord about our newly created unemployed status. Without the second income, we so desperately needed...As I spoke with *Him*, trying to stay in a positive place spiritually, my mind reflected on the last words I spoke to the City Manager, before being escorted out, *saying* to him— **"remember this day: the same way I'm being escorted out is the same way you will be"** --- Now as I thought on these things, I begin to wonder to myself, how will this situation bring *glory* to the **Father** —and how He might show *himself strong* Suddenly I heard the Lord speaking very clearly in my *spirit* as I communed with *Him*. And He began to speak in my spirit to the strength of my soul, *saying:* **"Not by Might, nor by power —but by My Spirit"**!

So, after those words had resounded in my ear, I began to rehearse them for my reassurance over and over again, for my own spiritual strength and encouragement. And as I did, the *Holy Ghost* began to rehearse **those words with me**, and we rehearsed them until I was moved in the spirit to get out of bed. And as I did, I immediately fell on my knees in worship. When I finally got up, it was around 6:00 am, and the Spirit of the Lord was on me very fiercely, and I began to declare with much power in the *Holy Ghost* out of my own mouth, not only the **words** in **(Zechariah 4:6)** but also the confirmation of those **words** by Apostle Paul in **(Romans 12:19 –for it is written, Vengeance is mine; I will repay, saith the Lord)** ...and for over fifteen more minutes, these two verses were repeated in concert until I got off of my knees in *prayer*.

SCRIPTURE REF: Zech 4:6 / Rom 12:19 / Phil 4:13.

Testimonial Conclusion

Twenty-one days after my termination, and according to the word of the Lord, I stood in faith, and by *His **Spirit** ...* favor was shown to me. I was hired at Bank of America by way of a seed I'd sown in the *life* of one of my former managers at Hertz. Now let me regress back for a moment, just to fill you in on how this miraculous event unfolded, an event which you will learn is the <u>*first*</u> confirmation of what God spoke to me on the morning of **January 28th** in regards to the *"Spirit of God"* –*(Zechariah 4:6)*, and later in the **<u>Book</u>**; I will reveal the <u>*second*</u> confirmation in *(Romans 12:19)* on *"Vengeance is Mine: I will repay saith the Lord."* But first, let me describe to you how the miracle of Aaron Orr happened. A man of God whom the *Lord* once used to speak into my life.

It was in 2003, the month of November, while on break, I began sharing with him the dream I'd had the night before, a dream that was more like a nightmare. Before I could complete the last sentence of my dream, the Holy Ghost fell on him, and he wasn't quite prepared as he excitedly began to interpret my dream, while I stood there in awestruck amazement at the interpretation the Lord gave to him as it bears witness in my *spirit*. So much that before the day was over, the $40.00 I still had as a seed to the Lord, the Holy Ghost impressed upon me to sow it into Aaron's life. And I obeyed.

So, now it's January 2006, I've been terminated from Hertz, and Mr. Orr is no longer at Hertz, and I'd only spoken with him a few times since he'd left Hertz in 2004, which was well over a year, or more, and he was nowhere in my thoughts nor on my mind. *(but God)*. Then, suddenly, out of the blue — the next Monday *(exactly seven days after my departure from Hertz)*, Lord dropped him in my *spirit*. And the Holy-Spirit spurred me on to call him, and then I remembered, the last time we spoke, he'd told me of his new position with a staffing agent; I couldn't remember the name of the Agency, but I still had Aaron's phone number. I thumbed through my old address book and found his number. I immediately gave him a call, no answer —so I left him a message, to please return my call as soon as possible, and that was that. The next day, sure enough, he returned my call. After the excitement of our greeting, he asked how everything was — and without hesitation, I told him that Hertz had fired me. *(Aaron wasn't surprised, he knew firsthand how they worked.)* After filling him in on more of the details of my termination, I let him know that the Lord prompted me to give him a call. *(Now of course not knowing the mind of God, I assumed that Aaron was still working as a recruiter for the Temp Staffing Agency, and that was the reason why the Lord had me call him, but of course it was just an assumption. I was wrong. Aaron quickly let me know it was not a problem and that he was glad to hear from me. So how can I help you, Bro? Aaron, I need a job, and I was hoping you might be able to hook me up. Well, Bro... I'm no longer with the Temp Agency, but I might be able to help you out. As I am now with Bank of America, and we're looking to hire in the Check Sorting division.)* My immediate reaction was a shout for joy, a hallelujah, and Amen. Just like that, God had moved on our behalf.

So, after having me do a preliminary phone application, Aaron scheduled my appointment with HR. And within one week of my initial telephone conversation with Aaron, a new direction was on the horizon. — And on January 9th, I was hired, just 21 days following my unjust termination. Two days later, I began my new job with Bank of America as a *'check sorter'*... [**To God Be The Glory**]. Not only did God bless me with a job, but He also gave me a $1.86 cent raise. I went from 12.50 per hour to $14.36 cents... Amen! And so, for me to clearly hear the **voice** of the Lord in such a succinct and concise tone "saying: **'call Aaron'** without a doubt brought **(Psalms 75:6,7)** to Life, quote:

"For promotions cometh neither from the east, nor from the west, nor from the south. But God is the judge: He puts down one and sets up another. Hallelujah. Amen"

So, at this Juncture... I'm moved for you and me to give *Praise* to the Lord for all that *he* has done. So let us lift *him* with a *poem,* a poem that was specifically given to me after I had vanquished the plan of the enemy at another place and time in my walk when afterward a celebration of our *victory* was necessary for magnifying the Lord:

Walking in the Spirit

My Lord said to me — "You have my blessing and my Authority To cast into that Lake of shame — those demons, and princes of False-Hood-fame.

— Now Children, do you understand, there's Power only in One Name — JESUS

press on in faith

FAITH LESSONS AND NUGGETS:

Hebrews 11:1 *thru* 40 **(Heroes by Faith)**

1 Peter 2:9 **(Who we are in Faith)**

Philippians 3:14 - I *press* toward the *mark* for the *prize* of the high calling of God in Christ *Jesus.* —

The 'Mark' (the Bull's Eye of our Faith)

When we began our *life* of *faith* in Christ, most of us didn't understand or had not yet received revelation of, is that for us all, the **mark** that God set for us to reach in Christ is the highest calling that we can *all* obtain. That is to say —the **Cross.** You see, beyond a shadow of a doubt, I believe that without the **Cross of Calvary** and the sacrifice that was made there, we have no *victory*, hence no Christ. But because of the obedience of Christ there and the sacrifice he became on behalf of the Father, we now have an established precedent for victory. Thus, it behooves us to **"fight the good fight of faith take up our own cross unto** *victory"* and to never relinquish at any time the authority we now have by way of our own *cross* in the duty of our daily sacrifice. A sacrifice of the flesh and all of its dastardly wicked deeds. O, we must not be deceived. If we ever hope to reach that **mark**, then we must understand that to accomplish that feat can only be done daily, upon the *cross* of our own obedience, so that we to can declare the works of our obedience finished for that day as it leads us every day, into a stronger place of faith as we move upward, and on to our objective which is our heavenly call. [*Refer to these scriptures on the Cross and the Mark : Ph 3:14 / Lk 23:33 / Ph 2:8 / Col 2:14 / Mt 10:38 / Heb 12:2 / Lk 9:23*]......

Philippians 3:15 — Let us therefore as many as be *perfect* [holy], be thus minded: and if in anything you be otherwise *minded,* God shall reveal even this [the *mark*] unto you. —

So now, we can begin again to receive in our spirits the evidence of our pressing forward, in our upward pursuit of the **mark**, and what that press means to the *household of faith*. And special as a lesson of study to all of us who are not yet able to receive in ourselves the fullness of what the word of God means in regard to our reaching out in *perfection,* or by our *holiness,* which is perfection... in our pursuit to obtain the *prize.* And so, it is now obvious to me that as we struggle in the learning process, we learn to eat the meat of the *word of* God in small bites, if necessary; so that we can chew and receive, in due course, the substance of what we can digest, or comprehend as we run our **race by faith** to *win* the Prize. Yes, in due season, we shall reap if we faint not **(Gal 6:9).** For the race is never to the swift **(Ecl 9:11),** but rather to the one who endures **(Mt 24:13),** hence let us run with patience the race that is set before us, looking unto Jesus; who for the joy that was set before him endured the **cross (Heb 12:1,2).** And in doing so obtained the *prize* of the Father, whose prize we are: —If we hold fast <u>the</u> *confidence* **(Heb 3:6):**

That *he* who has begun a good work in us will *perform* it *(Ph 1:6)* until the day we reach our **mark**, which is for us the **prize**: —our calling and our position in Christ *(Ph 3:14)*.

Therefore, we must find ourselves in *him*, and never at any time in our own *righteousness*, always allowing the Holy Ghost to speak to our hearts all things pertaining to Godliness, never being discouraged as we press on in our upward <u>*faith journey*</u>, hearing our Lord, as *he* commands us always forward.

And so, as we press toward perfection, establishing our testimony of hope, and overcoming daily in the spotlight of success, we by our *faith do* vanquish the enemy on the cross of our daily crucifixion *(Lk 9:23, 24)*.

So, in closing, we see that our objective is always to pursue the **mark**, which we define clearly by our identification as a servant of God. Servants not only of the receipt of **his** bountiful blessings but also of *his* sufferings *(Ph 3:10 -12)*. So let us please remember as we march on into the infinity of the glory that's set before us, in regard to our **targeted mark**, and that *is this* **"We cannot bear today's cross tomorrow, we must bear it today, every day, in the presence of that day's Now, which is after all what** <u>**faith is**</u>**"**. We Press On!

Faith is still —*Now*....

—*We cannot bear today's* <u>**Cross**</u> *tomorrow* —

—*We must bear it* <u>*Today*</u> *in the* **Now** *of our Faith*—

So now, let us return once more to chew on and absorb, by the sponge of our *spirit,* a few of the nourishing ingredients in the "now" power of our *faith.* Defining the meat, or the importance of understanding why we need to recognize that understanding what goes into the compound makeup of the "<u>now</u>" in our *faith,* should be just as important to our *spiritual* well-being as knowing the nutritional value of the food we buy at the grocery store. So, with that train of thought, let us define this word "*now*" with its other defining ingredients, or words that are derived from the natural mind's need to appeal to our senses, and then see what we can glean from them in regard to the build-up of our most *holy-faith.* Making palatable to our spiritual reasoning, the fierce urgency of *Now* —.

Webster's New World Dictionary —1973 **Student Handbook Edition**

Now **adv.** 1. *At this moment, at the present time.* —**n.** *this moment,* *Instant* **adj.** 1. *With no delay; immediate* [an *instant* response].

Present **adj.** 2. *Of or at this time; for now; not past or future*

Immediate **adj.** 1. *Without delay; happening at once* [the medicine had an *immediate* effect] [Me: our faith has an *immediate* effect if we believe it]

Today **n.** 1. *This day* —2. *The present time...*

Now, you may think to your natural self, what does knowing the different ways of expressing **now** have to do with *our faith.* Well, consider this. If your perspective on faith is built on the Theology of — 'God's timing' to deliver unto you the thing you believe **him** for in the *'present now'* or *'instantly'* in the *'immediate-now'* —for example: If I don't have this *'bill'* paid by 5:00 pm on Friday, (and it is now Monday, and I don't have any money to pay it), I will be evicted, if God don't come through. — .

So, my question to you is, which one of these words fits in your *spiritual* mind, the *urgency* of your need. Now for me, it would more than likely be the word "*today*'. Why? Because what I need by Friday has to be settled.

You see, I believe that whatever my need is, and the urgency of that need has to be settled *immediately*, not tomorrow, but right *now*! Okay, so you might say: 'Wait just a minute,' are you trying to say that we can make God move on our behalf, even if *he* doesn't want to?' Well, my answer to that question is, let's see what the **word** of God says. *(Mt 9:20 -22. And behold, a woman, which was diseased with an issue of blood 12 years, came behind Jesus, and touched the hem of his garment. For she said within herself, if I may but touch his garment, I shall be whole.*

But Jesus turned himself about, and when he saw her, he said — Daughter, be of good comfort; _thy faith_ hath made you whole. *And the woman was made whole from that hour).* So, in the middle of her _today,_ by the immediacy of her faith in action, she was healed. Now, you might argue: "Yea, but look how long she suffered, over 12 years, where was her faith then?" My response is simple, Christ wasn't available for right **now-faith**, *his* time wasn't yet, and neither was it time for her faith to be on display. And of course, that's just one example, but you can find many more testimonies in the scriptures of how God moved and does move on behalf of *his people*. We simply must ask for more revelation regarding how our faith operates. I personally believe that it operates on the amount of confidence we have in our relationship with God because, without a doubt, it works, always and only in the realm of **now**, no matter which form of 'now' our *faith* takes on; *instant, immediate, present,* or *today*, it will *work*, as long as we believe in the **one** God sent *(Jn 6:28,29)*. And, to know that without the kind of *faith* that says, **"let there be"** and **"it is so"** [which is simply asking for what you need to happen in your life, to be settled in the *heavens* when you leave it at the altar]. If that is not the kind of *faith* in God, then it's impossible for you to truly believe that you will have what you want or need. For the **Father** will reward those who diligently seek *him* **now** *(Heb 11:6)*. As the **word** so urgently states: —**Today if you will hear His voice** (Ps 95:7), Amen!

Now, of course, the things I write while on my journey are not things that I have mastered but am myself endeavoring to absorb by revelation all that is meat for me, and the rest I leave for you, the reader. To seek out, if you so desire, to use what I am in the process of disseminating into all the places of need in my own *spiritual* growth, even as I press toward the target of my own *Salvation*. And so, for me, sometimes it takes an in-depth study into the breakdown of simple words that have a complexity about them, where the application of the **word** of God is utilized in the *life* of a believer. And as a believer who

believes in the power of the **word** by **faith,** is indeed the work, and revelational knowledge on how to apply faith is the **key**!

THE FAITH KEY: REVELATIONAL "INSIGHT" THE *FOUNDATION* OF APPLICATION

Insight - **n.** 1. the ability to understand people and things as they really are. **2.** a clear understanding of some problem or idea.

Deuteronomy 29:29 - *The secret things belong to the Lord our God: but those things which are revealed belong unto us and to our children for ever —that we may do all the **words** of this law. —*

The Book of Deuteronomy is one of the foundational books that list the Commandments of Moses, the Prophets and the Law. It is one of the main instruments of God that leads us into the **now** reality of established truths and revelations of the new Law by which we order our steps of *faith* by the guidance of the *Holy Ghost*, by way of the *New Testament*. It is that spoken word of Old, used as a teaching tool in the *New Testament,* revealing to us, by the *hands* of the Apostles, the *living word* of God to the nourishment of our *faith*, making all things possible if we believe. And **he** is today, still revealing, and confirming to us and in us the same power given to those *twelve men* responsible, according to **Acts 17:6** (saying) —These that have turned the world upside down have come hither also. And just as they operated by the *Holy Ghost,* with revelational insight and knowledge, so to must we as we preach, teach, and proclaim the *good news* from our **Spirit** of witness, which is for us primarily from the *New Testament* of our Lord and *Savior, Jesus the Christ.......*

2 Timothy 2:14, 15 - *Of these things put them in remembrance, charging them before the Lord that they strive not about words to no profit, but to the subverting of the hearers. —Study to show thyself approved unto God a workman that need not be ashamed, rightly dividing the word of truth.* Now, at this **word,** let us put a placeholder here: — Let's take a moment to reflect and understand for ourselves what this really means. I believe it's to be used as a tool when witnessing to those who are not yet of the *household* of **faith,** or to baby Christians. When delivering the **word** as a tool to win the lost or to strengthen the *babe,* we must recognize that we wield the **word** of God as the only weapon of choice for *Spiritual Battle.* And we must use all of the *Spiritual Artillery* at our disposal — **Amen!**

Faith is still — *Now*

Now will always be the *Spiritual Weapon* that destroys, by faith today, the enemies of our destiny. It secures for us today, our hope and aspirations for tomorrow, making irrelevant our past failures. **Now** will always create for us our manifested needs and desires in their season.

Or, let me say it another way: — *[I believed today for a certain miracle or blessing, and by faith, I claimed it in the immediacy of now. — One year later, I received the thing I'd hoped for. So, what happened? Simple, because of what was established in the immediacy of that day one year earlier, my future miracle or blessing was accomplished.*

Repeat — Repeat — Repeat — "The Action of Redundancy"

If there's any consistency, any redundancy in what is read in the pages of this **book** —let it be to the drill of repetition because it's the practice and *professionalism* of what being a successful, blood-bought Christian is all about. Even as we do so in whatever chosen field of profession we have chosen as our livelihood. If a *doctor*, then the best that we can be. And likewise —whether a *Plumber*, *Carpenter* or *Fisherman*. We are to strive to be the best at, even as the **word** of declares: ***"Whatsoever we do, we do it all to the Glory of God (1 Cor 10:31). Therefore, repeat, repeat, repeat.***

Hebrews 11:1 - *Now faith is the substance of things hoped for, the evidence of things not seen* (**Now when we follow Christ, we learn in the 'Book of Romans" what we can do by faith. No different than what Father Abraham did in the 'Book of Genesis, chapters 17 and 22)**

Romans 4:17, 18 [*God speaking to Abraham*] - (*As it is written, I have made thee a father of many nations). Before **him** who he believed, even God, who quicken [**make more alive**] the dead, 'and call those things that be not as though they were.' Who contrary to hope believed in hope, that he might become the father of many nations, according to that which was spoken. So shall thy seed be!* (**That seed was established in the <u>Now</u> of Abraham's faith-reality, propelled through time unto Christ...please Study this Chapter: Romans 4:1 thru 25, in its entirety)**

So let us look at **St John 20:24** *through* **29** in a Paraphrased rendering of its *Spiritual* significance using 'Now' at the beginning of each verse. Listen and meditate on what it means in context with your *spiritual* discernment. See if you can receive (as I have) the urgency of it. Then, be strengthened as your faith is energized.

Here is my inner interpretation of **St John 20:27** [*After the resurrection of our Lord, he appeared unto the doubter, so that he might believe –- (St John 20:27)*]. As you can see, Christ was very concerned and loving toward the doubter. So, listen and see if you can hear where the *now of faith* must be applied and activated in your *walk* as you listen to how it was revealed in *me*:

Now the Ignition of Faith

Now Thomas, put your finger in my hand wound. ***Now*** *thrust your hand into my side; and be not faithless but believing.*

Now Thomas answered and said unto ***him****, my Lord and my God.* **29 - *Then Jesus said to Thomas,*** *now* *because you have seen me, you* ***Now*** *believe: but blessed are they who have not seen* **(me in the Now of their reality)** *and yet have believed* **(in me by the Now of their faith in me Today).** **[So, in these scriptures, I learned that the Now of my faith is more blessed and should be used in at least a more powerful and significant way than Thomas, since he had to see in order that he might believe. This is for me, a simple but great revelation]**

So, let us <u>*examine*</u> how **Now** eliminates the need, the possibility, or even the probability of <u>*next*</u>. *(Next -* **adv. 2.** *- at the first chance, after this).*

Now, to put *next* in its proper context, you might have to see and understand it being used in one of its truest forms, which for me is a word that I am truly familiar with in my own life, the word <u>***procrastination***</u>. Why? Because to procrastinate about what you want to achieve in life and having no plan is like trying to figure out how to get God to bless you, without you ever taking any responsibility in building the relationship with God that is needed for your spiritual growth and *faith* success. *(Procrastination* **v.** *- to put off doing something until later).* **Faith** can't wait, for it to exist in your life, it must be acted on **Now.**

Jude 1:24 - Now to him that is able to keep you from falling, and to present you faultless: **Amen!**

INTERMISSION PART I — FAITH TESTIMONY

The First Strength Test of my *faith* - The Birth Evidence

(Acts 19:2 - Have you received the Holy Ghost since you believed?)

It was March 1991, and I hadn't been home long from my trip to pick up my Article 635-200 Chpt 10 Discharge, *(Character of Service)*, a Discharge under less Than Honorable Conditions *(are as the Army, ever so politely states it)*, "for the good of Service —In Lieu of Court Martial. Now, believe me when I tell you I am in no way proud of that time in my life, but this book won't be distracted by how my life was lived before that moment or after. But for the glory of God, whatever needs to be told will be. Amen!

It was the middle of March, exactly eight months beyond the day of my spiritual birth. The Lord had performed a quick work in my life. ---

From July 1990 till March 1991, with March being the month of my *spiritual* declaration to the demonic world, by way of my mouth that I was free, as I was filled with the *Holy Ghost* on that momentous day. A day that changed the course of my future as I began to speak with *new tongues*. Tongues as Apostle Paul writes in **1 Cor 13:1,** *Though I speak with the tongues of men [languages] and of angels, [spiritual tongues].* As *tongues* began to overflow out of me, I felt the *power of Authority,* a power that I'd never known, and immediately following as I stepped out of my bathroom, facing my hallway wall, I suddenly saw faces emerge visible to me on the surface of the wall. They were demonic spirits with the most hideous monstrosities I'd ever laid eyes on. And with powerful *words of Authority,* I rebuked them in the name of Jesus and immediately they were expelled from their hidden perch.

Faith to receive the Holy Ghost —

Now, before I go further, let me regress back to a point before being filled with *power* from on High. I'd been studying and seeking to know the Lord in a deeper way *(I was hungry for that, that I'd never tasted, and thirsty for such as I'd never consumed)*. Yet, while thirsting and hungering, I was still addicted to the filthy habit of cigarettes. But, mind you now; even though I was a smoking *Christian*, I felt no condemnation but rather a deeper yearning to know *him* better, and because of that, I began to feel that smoking had become an acute hindrance to my spiritual growth, and with that *new sensitivity*, I began to care more about my wife's health.

Now, of course, I didn't quit immediately, nor did it stop any time after my encounter with a *spiritual* conscious regarding my wife's health *(asthma)*. But, because of all the new emotions of consciousness that were now stirring in me, I no longer smoked with the same reckless abandonment. I felt the intensity of that *nasty* habit begin to slowly abdicate or relinquish its position of vice. With careful thought, I relocated my smoking to the outside. My zeal to kick back after a great meal (or any meal) began to diminish over the next seven months, finally climaxing on that day of sudden impact. I was intensely engrossed in the word of God as I delved piercingly into the *spiritual* nature of the **word** of God on a need-to-know, must-have basis. It was absolutely imperative that I get a hold of the thing that had captured my soul's longing. *Then* one night, while sitting quietly watching tv in our bedroom, channel surfing the *(trying not to wake my wife)*, my attention was grabbed and captivated by a very charismatic and fiery preacher, one I'd never heard or seen before yet somehow hearing him speak made my *spirit* leap inside, and I knew I needed to hear more. And as I listened to him with great intensity, it seemed as if every fiber of my being was set on alert. So intense was his message that it began to pierce the deepest recesses of my *soul*, as he, in a demonstrative flare, began to perform to the script of his message, demonstrating to his audience as much as he was able to transfer to us the triumvirate force of authority that Christ revealed when *he* went to hell, triumphantly plundering the dark kingdom of lucifer. As *he* carried out the command of the **Father** —going beneath the earth, to destroy the works of the Devil —snatching from his defeated hands the **keys** of *hell* and the *grave* **(death)**— *(1 John 3:8 - For this purpose the Son of God was <u>manifested</u> that he might destroy the works of the devil) (Rev 1:18 - I am he those lives, and was dead; and, behold, I am alive for evermore,* Amen; *and have the keys of hell and of death)* His name was Rod Parsley [**Pastor Rod Parsley**]. And of course, at that time, I wasn't familiar with many T.V. Evangelists other than the well-known ones, like Billy Graham, Jim Baker, and such. But I'd never heard or seen this fiery man of God before, but the message he *preached* on that night —he spoke directly into my *spirit*, and it ignited my soul with the cleansing fire of heaven. And when it hit me, it sent me into a place of power that before that *night*, I'd never known before. Though I was born-again and delivered from alcohol and drugs on July 15th, 1990 *(a most notable and auspicious day)*. And afterwards I immediately leaped to my feet, tears swelling from my eyes as I began to plead the blood of Jesus. I grabbed my cigarettes and ran to the bathroom, ripping them one by one from the pack, screaming and rebuking them.

I attacked those cigarettes as if they were living creatures. It was as if they knew what was about to happen to them. It appears they had set themselves in array against *me (but unlike previous battles where I'd soon surrender and go in hot pursuit of a pack or find some house tea and roll me a cigarette, just to see the smoke rise as I puffed)*. But that night, I was ready for battle, and because of God's timing in introducing me to Pastor Rod Parsley, this night I would have the *victory* —*on* this night, my soul would rejoice in deliverance, and I'd finally be free of the last vestige of *hells* demonic grip. Because on that night, my *'Spirit-filled-Man'* finally had the strength to standup and defend its soul, my soul, my life. I took those **eleven cigarettes** while rebuking them and pleading the blood of Jesus. I began to methodically rip them apart *(with snot and tears flying all over the place)*. — I thrashed them violently into the cesspool of my toilet and once they were submerged and drowned, I flushed them with tears of *joy*. **Amen!**

Now, after my short-lived bathroom *celebration,* and while still high in the *Spirit,* I stepped out of my bathroom, immediately facing the wall of my hallway — and there all around me, embedded in the wall, were the most hideously demonic faces that could ever be imagined. And when they looked at me, they *squirmed* in a maddening frenzy as they suddenly realized that they were no longer invisible, '**and they knew instantly that their time was up.**' And without any hesitation on my part, I knew, as if I were an old pro, exactly what to do. With complete author-ity, I preceded to cast them out while simultaneously realizing with an acute awareness that I had been baptized in the **Holy Ghost** and was now operating in the *power* that was described in *(Acts 1:8 - But ye shall receive power, after that the Holy Ghost is come upon you)*. And just like that, my house was made clean. — Thus, on that **night,** my training in **Spiritual Warfare** and walking in the *authority of faith* began [***Those with ears to hear let them hear what the Spirit is saying to the Churches: to him that over comes will I give to eat of the tree of Life*** – Rev 2:7,(11),(17),(29) — Rev 3:6,(13),(22)]

INTERMISSION PART II —

The Battle is not Yours

As Sons of God, as Children of God, — as *Daughters* of the Highest God — even before the battle is brought to us. If we are walking by faith, as *(Habakkuk 2:4)*, and discerning the word of God. We would know for sure how to prepare for a *battle* that's not ours. And get out of the way of our own victory, as we stand still to see our salvation unfold by the hands of our Lord. We must become wise in this matter as we allow revelation to come forth in the development of *spiritual* growth. So that the *father* can have *his* way, sending forth the Holy Ghost as our defender. So that we will stop delaying our blessings and no longer be spent trying to help God fight for us. Why do I say this? It's very simple. Because our job is to *'fight the good fight of faith'* and to *trust* God. To put on by faith the **whole armor of God.** And when we do this, then our victory is assured in its proper season and time. —Scripture Reference: *(1Ti 6:12)* – *(Ep 6:11)*

– *(2 Chr 20:15)* – *(Deut 20:1)* – *(1Sam 17:45-47)* – *(Ps 20:1-9)*

POETRY PRAISE # 1

No Mo Rain – *(April 1991)*

I woke up this morning, finding the *rain* in my life had gone with it went my teardrops —no mo *crying* in my soul. Only *Son*-light through my window shone, and before my feet could touch the floor, I heard the *Angels* shout with glee —Oh, what thrill it was to know that the *Angels* thanked God for *me,* another soul brought to God by the **Blood** that set us Free. And so, I thank you Jesus, *my Lord,* and *my Redeemer* — For the <u>storms</u> you've brought us through. Amen! **(Now, if you're able to by reason of spiritual sanity, then maybe, just maybe, you should thank Him** *too. So, just praise Him where you find yourself. For all the blessings he's blessed you with —and for His word that's forever True. Selah, Amen, and Amen).*

THE SOUND OF FAITH

Revelational Insight Part 2: *(The After - Effect)*

— *(Revelation on - 2 Kings 7:1 thru 16 — *— Date: Feb 17, 2007)* —

*This revealed secret was delivered to me by the Holy Ghost while I was in the middle of studying this great Chapter of demonstrated faith. He began to speak to me very clearly. And so, I will deliver it to you as it was given to me. (**Those with ears to hear let them hear**). So, I pray that you will be able to discern what the **Spirit** of God will reveal to you, what you need for the benefit of your **faith walk**. And I pray that it will offer you the same kind of faith that the Lepers in this true story received and instinctively acted upon, though they never actually heard the command from the Prophet's lips verbally (**seeing that they were nowhere near him when he spoke out loud the prophecy by faith**). But their desire to live was on such a heightened level of hearing, that I believe they caught it from out of the **Spirit** realm, the place where faith Lives. — And so, as Elisha spoke prophetically into the atmosphere (**where faith cometh by hearing Rom 10:16,17**), like a radio wave transmitting, the Lepers caught it. Not only did they catch it, but they were moved by faith in response to it and saved not only their lives but the lives of many, which is the <u>evidence</u> as far as I'm concerned, that it happened exactly when the Holy Ghost revealed it to me, Amen!* And so, I do know by this, and am fully persuaded that just like those Lepers, our *spirit* does hear from heaven, *as many of you well know*. Yet, we do know that hearing is just one part of the equation, but the other part is the most revealing, in location to where we are in our *faith* journey. It's the part of the equation where we act upon what we've heard, and of course, this is often-time where we stumble — but we must *'come up'* in this area of our *spiritual* Maturity, and of course we will!

The scriptures to be studied in their proper order, in reference to this awesome *revelational insight,* are as follows: [**2Kings 7:1** *thru* **16**]

The Clarion Call of *Faith* — ACT - I *(2Kings 7:1-16)*

Verse 1 -Then Elisha said, hear the *voice of the Lord:* Thus says the Lord; *Tomorrow* about this same time — a <u>Seah</u> of fine flour shall be sold for a shekel, and two measures of barley for a shekel, in the Gate of *Samaria.*

— *(The Prophetic Word Declared)* —

The Response of *Faith* —

Verses 3,4 - Now there were four *Leprous* men at the entering in of the *Gate,* and they said one to another —*why* sit we here until we *die? [Now at this moment I believe that the words Elisha sent by prophecy into the Spirit realm, was captured by the faith of those 4-Lepers, as they were moved by the Spirit of life in them, Pushing them forth to Live. — How? Simple:* **Faith comes by <u>hearing</u>, and hearing by the <u>Word</u> (Spirit) — of God** *(Rom 10:17).* — <u>**Spirit**</u>-Word - **It is the Spirit that quickens; the flesh profits nothing: the**<u> </u>**Words that I speak unto you, they are Spirit, and they are Life** *(John 6:63). So now we see, that by the action of the Lepers, the* **Prophetic Word is received.]** — **The Lepers:** If we say, we will enter into the City, then the famine is in the City; and we shall die there: if we sit still here, we shall die also. Now therefore come let us fall unto the host of the *Syrians:* if they save us alive, we shall **live;** and if they kill us, we shall but *die.* — *[***What** *are they saying here? Well, I believe that what they're saying by faith is, that they have no other option than that of self-preservation, but they were willing to speed up their demise. And so either way, what differ-ence does it make, we have nothing to lose. But of course, like all* *of us who live by faith, we must be willing to lose our lives if it means we will save it. Yet we're not always privy to what God's ultimate intentions are concerning, what we hope for, and how it might be delivered to us, we just simply move by the Spirit of his Word. Now of course the Lepers didn't have the Holy Ghost to guide them the way that we do. But because we have the Holy Ghost, we have an unction to know what it is that we hunger for. Which for me has to be God and knowing that my hunger for him will produce for me all things pertaining to Godliness, therefore having all things pertaining to Life.* —(The Prophetic Word <u>*Acted upon*</u>)

Scripture Reference on our quest for Righteousness: *(Mt 5:6 / Mt 6:33 / 2Cor 5:21 / 1Ti 6:11 / 2Ti 2:22 / 1Jn 2:29 / 1Jn 3:7 /)*

THE FOUR LEPERS

The Clarion Call of *Faith* — ACT - II

So, we see in this witness of *faith* — the Leprous *four*; become the Lord's impulsive action, as they respond with a sense of urgency to the invisible sound of *faith*... a sound that one can only hear with the ear of the **Spirit**. And even though they may not have realized at that moment that it was their collective act of *faith* that motivated them to take action. — I do believe in retrospect *(after their fame had been broadcasted throughout Israel)*, that they continued to live moving forward, by the history or experience of their then unwitting response to a *Prophetic **word*** of *faith*

Because of the Obedience of a Prophet

And so, when *Elisha* **prophesied**, proclaiming the **word** of the Lord, he had no idea how the Lord would perform it nor who God would use to bring it to pass. But to an obedient servant, that should be of no concern. The only concern should be obedience.

And so, because Elisha knew the *Voice* of God, he knew as well that he was the *voice* of God. Therefore, speaking out by *his faith* — he sent his *faith* out; declaring: ***"Hear ye the word of the* Lord: *Thus saith the Lord* (2Kg 7:1).** And just as he spoke, so it became reality by the action of the *four-Leprous* men, even though they were not in the same place as the **man** of God. Still, *faith in* them amid their life and death situation. Hence, with their desire to live, God was able to attach to them those *Spirit-filled* words sounded out by the Prophet. — So here, at this juncture, a question was posed to me, and it is this: **Will faith always find faith?** Well, let's look at how the Bible poses that same question before we answer. — *(Lk 18:8 - Nevertheless, when the Son of man cometh, shall he find faith on the earth?).* (ANSWER: *Rev 2:13 - I know thy works, and where thou dwell, even where Satan's seat is and thou hold firm to my name, and hast not denied My faith* (the *God kind of faith*). And again, read **Rev 13:7,10, -(7. *And it was given unto him to make war with the Saints, and to overcome them: — 10.: etc. Here is the patience and the faith of the saints....***

So, we see in this **witness** that God had already chosen the Lepers, before they ever acted out, as we see firsthand the act of **His** predestinated will in *action.* **(Eph 1:10 - 12** [The Book of *Ephesians* is a great study on who we are in God's predestinated will for our lives, in and as the *Church)*

The Predestinated Plan for *Israel* —

As we watch God's plan for Israel unfold, we see that it's <u>his perfect will</u> that all of Israel be saved, not just the so-called clean. Hence, God chose for those four Lepers *(on behalf of the host of Israel)*— to receive from Elisha a *sudden* — A divine and *spiritual* intervention brought forth by the action of those who hungered outside of the Gate, on behalf of those who were hungry within. The Father had predestined Israel's survival for a witness unto us, *'for indeed His mercy endures from predestination to Predestination, from glory to Glory' — Amen*!

Meditation Rewind: [A] - **2 Kings, *Chapter 7: 1 - 6***

Elisha - An Administrator of God's **word** and *His Will...*

The Four Lepers - The Receivers of God's **word**, by way of hearing, speaking, and acting upon, by *faith* those things pertaining to *Life*...........

Those outside of the Blessings of God - The Syrians *(Who are not of the Household of Faith)*, **verse 6 - For the Lord had made the host of the Syrians to hear a noise of chariots and a noise of horses, – verse 7 - Wherefore they arose and fled in the twilight, and left the camp as it was)*. For us, the fleeing Syrians are no more different than that disease, sickness, devil, or demon that we have to attack in order to achieve the outcome we desire. When we become desperate in our stance for a *victorious Life*, as a sure testimony on behalf of the Kingdom, to the *Glory* of the Father — then there's no limit to what sent forth *faith* will accomplish.

Verse 5 - And they rose up in the twilight, to go unto the camp of the Syrians: and when they were come to the uttermost part of the camp of Syria, behold no man was there. [Refer to *v. 6*]

Notes: Meditation Rewind Wrap-up for (A) - [Pay special attention to **verse 16]** [Read **Chapter 7:5 thru 16**, then read **Hebrews 11:1 thru 40]**

— In this **study**, my hope is that you will come to know (*if you don't already*) how **faith** demands a manifested result, and without a doubt, the result can't be anything else but a manifested hope to an answered **prayer. *Selah*!**

Elisha's Confirmation: *It is Finished —*

Verse 16 - And the people went out and spoiled the tents of the Syrians. So, a measure of fine flour was sold for a shekel, and two measures of barley for a shekel, according to the words of the Word of the Lord ...

<u>Meditation Rewind: (B)</u> - **2 Kings, *Chapter 7:1*** [*Financial Depression*].

At this *place* in our study, let's take a glimpse into the financial condition of the Nation of Israel. Here we find that because of the deterioration of Israel's relationship with their God, their economy had collapsed, far beyond the condition of a people who actually served a real God, one who'd chosen them amongst all the people *he* could've chosen, but like all disobedient *children*, they tried to plot their own course and failed.

Shekel Value; based on today's est. value, both (Gold & Silver)

Gold @ 1 Shekel value - $1,920 — Silver @ 1 Shekel value - $128.00

Dry Goods Value; based on Measurement ....

One Seah - *equals* -7 quartz, or a <u>1/3 Ephah</u>

One Epha - *equals* - .65 bushel, or <u>20.8 quartz</u>

*[So, let's take **(verse 1)**. Here the **revelation** is given to me in the form of a colloquialism, so I will paraphrase]* — Now, the verse doesn't clarify whether the shekel was *gold* or *silver*. But either value was a lot to pay for a <u>*seah* (**7 quarts)**</u> of fine flour. So, think about it for a moment, and be honest with your *faithful* evaluation of the following example, and consider how you might receive the same word if it was spoken to you in the lingo we might use in today's society.

Example: *Hey Bob, the Lord told me to tell you, by this time tomorrow, when you go to the store to stock up on your flour, be prepared to pay an* *exorbitant amount of* $\underline{\$1,920}$ *for your seven quarts of fine flour —* **(that's equivalent to 3-bags of flour at approximately 4.7 pounds for each bag)** *And if you need your regular supply of barley you better have enough cash to pay for it, cause it's gonna cost you* $\underline{\$3,840,}$ *for the* **14-quarts** *you normally purchase. —* **(That's an equivalent to 4 bags of barley at 7 pounds each) —**

So, Bob, just be prepared for the sticker shock cause for both the flour and barley, your cost minus tax will total a mere $\underline{\$5,760,}$ *and that's of course, your cost at gold's current currency value. But you can get off a lot cheaper if you're paying with* **silver shekels;** *but of course, that's based on where you purchase what you need in these cursed times. Now, of course I'm being sarcastic, because unless the Lord intervenes, we're all going to starve the death. God help us all. Selah, and Selah!*

Okay, I see; right now, you might be scratching your head at all I just described, and I hope it grabs your attention. And while you're maybe meditating on your response *(if you have one)*. Let's take a *meditation break*. So that you won't get too preoccupied with what your reaction, or of course, inaction might be. But you can always '*mark this spot*' and come back to it, but remember, in case you don't return to this *Rewind Section* anytime soon. That; we get **revelational knowledge:** 'here a little there a little' — *but never all at once.* As the *scripture says:* **'For we know in part, and we prophesy in part** *(1 Cor 13:9)***'** So, let's take a break from this interesting place and move to a different location of insight and study. **Amen**!

Knowing and Understanding, What the *Word* of God Is

Now, the **word** of God, for those of us who are **born-again,** — is the sole source of our existence. Without it living on the inside of us, springing up out of us *(as we thirst in prayer and supplication)* as living water: we'd never seek God's will for our lives. But because we are completely filled with a well of *his* overflowing love, we are consumed by the washing of *his* **word**, thus becoming true worshipers and righteous representatives of *his* poured out love, which is an expression in us of *his* dear Son — *who* is the author and finisher of our *faith (Heb 12:2)*. In whom the Father has made known to us *(by the Holy Ghost)*, the mysteries of the ages. —

(Col - 1:25 - 27). Yes, Christ is indeed in us that **word and** is written up- on the *table* of our surrendered hearts — as we bear witness, by *his* to us, in the manifested person of the *Holy Ghost* — who is the Third one in the *threefold cord* of the Trinity. A *Trinity*, which is the oneness of the **God!**

Yes, Christ in us; is the *living logos* — that powerful **word** springs forth in us unto everlasting Life. The **word** that has witnessed our surrender and now moves in us, and by *us*; as a *faithful* witness on course, to deliver its witness of the **Kingdom** to those who **now**, by the authority of God's dear *son* —have access to the very **throne** of God, by way of the *Holy Ghost!* And by him (the *Holy Ghost)*, who is the only mechanism by which the **logos** of God in us is disseminated. So that we might be true disciples of God's will and purpose on the earth. We disseminate, by our testimony, the free *gift* of **Salvation.** —

Demonstrating to the world the power of God as only living *epistles* can do. Oh yes, the revealed *word* in its glory and splendor is in us a constant *fire* of refreshing. It restores and rejuvenates our **souls** so that we may boldly declare the *glory* of the *Father* amongst those who are searching. Letting them know Christ is the way and *he* will be for them that **word** softly speaking into the darkness of their soul's despair. A *word* spoken to them in the changing seasons of their lives.

Yes, that same **word** of life that was demonstrated in the halls of History in reference to the *giants* of **faith** in the Bible is for us, unchangeable. And the power of their use in our lives today is just as potent as then, and they are more than able to set the captive free.

The Whole Armor *of* God:

The ***word*** of God is for us, the ***whole-armor*** *(Ep 6:10-17)*. — Henceforth, we're without excuse. In other words, how can we so boldly declare God as our helper and not be discerning enough to utilize the ***weapons*** of our warfare? Weapons *he* has gifted to us for the benefit of our own defense and for the *battle* we engage the enemy in, for the sake of our loved ones and for the others *He* has so gracefully allowed us to intercede on behalf of. And, of course, we, as learned men and women, do know that Christ in us is the hope and instrumentality of our voice, the weaponry of the spoken ***word.*** Therefore, greater is **Christ** that is in *us (1 Jn 4:4)*: *'Then all that is in the world, the lust of the flesh — the lust of the eyes — and the pride of life (1 Jn 2:16)'*. **Amen and Amen**!

the word made flesh

(LITTLE CHILDREN — LIVING EPISTLES)

PART I THE WORD MADE FLESH FOR OUR REDEMPTION:

The *word* made flesh *(Important Highlights from — Jn 1:2,3) - [14]*

1. In the beginning was the *word,* and the *word* was with God, and the *word* was God......
2. The same *(I Am, that I Am - Ex 3:14 and Jn 8:58)* was in the beginning with God....
3. All things were made by *him* *(Let there be. Gen 1:3)*, and without *him* was not anything made....
4. And the *word* was made flesh, and dwelt among us *(And we beheld his Glory, the Glory as of the only begotten of the Father, full of Grace and Truth)*

So, we see and do understand that Christ was that *word-made* flesh, so that *he* could in the flesh identify with us in our wretched condition. He also appeared to many in his flesh *(body)* before *his ascension.* Even unto Thomas, whom we know, did not believe that *Christ* had risen. And after seeing *him* in the flesh, he finally believed unto repentance, as Christ delivered him from his unbelief. But rebuking him strongly, declared to Thomas saying: — *'Blessed are they that have not seen, and yet have believed (Jn 20:29)'*. And of course, Jesus is speaking to Thomas of us now, and all those who followed *him* long after *his* ascension. Oh yeah, we are blessed. How? Because we have *him* in a greater measure than Thomas, we have *him* if we believe completely by *faith*. For *he* is that *word*, which is transferred in us, unto the transformation of our hearts as we walk in *him* — through the corridors of our lives. Why? So that others may witness the goodness of *his* glory being demonstrated through us, outside the sometimes-sedimentary confines of the traditional *Church*. We must have a spiritual realization that in fact we are the ambassadors of Christ, as we conform into the image and demonstration of *his* **word**, whose *word* we are, as long as we allow *him* <u>**free rein**</u> in and over our individual *lives,* so that the Christ in us (the *hope* of **glory**); will always get the Glory, as we *glorify him,* even as mortal beings.

And we do *glorify him* when we allow ourselves to be used by *him* — as instruments of change in the lives of others, to the **glory** of the *Father,* for **his** good pleasure. *(Lk 12:32)*. So, we know that as we continue striving to move forward and upward on behalf of the *kingdom,* we are always living in bearing witness, by *word* and deed; as living **epistles**. Hence, we're forever gazed upon by the *Father* as *he* sees us *(hidden in Christ),* watching with the *admiration* of a *Father* as *his children* give testimony to what *his* great sacrifice has accomplished for the **Kingdom** on behalf of us all — because of the obedience of *his dear* **Son.** The Son who by *his* action transformed those who believe, from darkness to light, and from glory to glory, becoming daily in us; the only *begotten* **word** of the Father. ***Hallelujah, Hallelujah, Amen***! *(Heb 2:9, 10 —* ***But*** *we see Jesus, who was made a little lower than the Angels — for the suffering of death — crowned with* **glory** *and honor; that he by the grace* *of God should taste death for every man. — **For** it became him, for whom are all things, and by whom are all things, in bringing many sons unto* **glory**, *to make the* **captain** *of their salvation perfect through sufferings. —*

(1Jn 1:12 – Rm 8:14 – Rm 8:19 – Gal 4:6 – Heb 2:10 – 1Jn 3:1,2)

Commentary on Sons (*Spiritually Speaking*) – Sons of God are also called the Children of God... Now, I believe that the Children of God, who are called the Sons of God, are so called because of their conversion by *faith* into the *Kingdom* of God. And are thus *new creatures (Spiritually Speaking)*, being recreated in the image and likeness of God and *his* Angels, who are totally Spiritual in nature and are Sons of God because they are Spirits. But, unlike the Angels, we are made Sons by our *faith*. A first-fruits of our kind, made so by the power of our *surrender* to Christ. **(Read More on the Sons of God — Genesis 6:1-4 and Job 1:6 /2:1).**

THE SACRIFICE OF THE WORD FOR OUR REDEMPTION

Foundational Scriptures, on the **Word's** *Sacrifice: (Mt 24:35 - Mt 26:5 - Mt 26:53 - Mt 28:18 - Mk 13:31 - Lk 21:33 - Is 53:7 - Ac 8:32)*

So, what was the sacrifice that the **Word** made on our behalf? That's a very deep question. And my answer to that question might be just a tad different than what has been given before. And I don't believe I've ever heard anyone answer it before. But to be frank with you, up until the compilation of this '*varied*' study guide, entitled *"A Sheep's Faith Journal"* I'd personally never heard any other revelational compilations like the ones in this book. And so, just for your spiritual ears, here's another one for your delight!

And so, as it was given to me, here goes: *(please adjust your Spiritual antenna):* Until Christ, *The Word of God was never successfully plundered, even though the attempt to waste it has been tried through the centuries, always failing. Hence, the Word has never been diminished. Yes, wicked men have tried and still do. And it's always tried by some earthly decree, influenced by demonic minds. Though many people, nations and other doctrinal creeds have fallen by the wayside in their attempt to put silent the Word, the Word keeps advancing onward and upward, always ceaseless in its purpose, and goal to destroy the works of the Devil.* (Read: Mk 13:31 and Lk 21:33). *And so, as God declares in the Book of Matthew, chapter 24:35, saying* (Heaven and earth shall pass away, but my words shall not pass away). *So, it is evident that the Word can't possibly pass away, nor be stopped, for the blood of the martyrs has proven that. Therefore, you and I once again can claim heritage to the 'Tree of Life' which Tree we now have in the Son of God. So really, the Word not passing away is not the issue for us, but Sacrifice is. Now you may ask: what sacrifice? Since Christ has so eloquently done so, on our behalf. Well, since you asked, let me explain: —*

Sacrifice, Example # 1 — When Christ surrendered *his* right to himself in the garden, it was as a witness to *his disciples* then and now. And the sacrifice of *his* flesh was for me a record, showing what great sacrifice in following Christ's example, we too must make. And as *he* was able to confront the appetite of *his* will, so must we. So, as we deny our self-willed flesh, we expose *Satan's* desire to do to us what he failed to accomplish against Christ at the cross. He didn't know that Christ could not be murdered but indeed *sacrificed.* As we learn in the scriptures, Satan himself was no different from any other non-believer when it came to understanding and discerning *'parables.'* Why do I say that with such confidence? It's very simple to *me (now)*! Based on three *scriptures,* I'm convinced that he can't know anything pertaining to the saints' care and wellbeing, except for what the saint divulges to him: **Scripture #1** - *John 8:32 And you shall know the Truth, and the Truth shall make you free:* —

Scripture #2 -*1 Corinthians 2:7,8 But we speak the wisdom of God in a mystery, even the hidden* **wisdom,** *which God ordained before the world unto our glory: Which none of the princes of this world knew: for had they known it, they would not have crucified the Lord of Glory.* — And finally, **Scripture #3** - *John 10:17,18 Therefore doth my Father love me, because I lay down my Life, that I might take it again.*

No man taketh it from me, but I lay it down of myself. I have power to lay it down, and I have power to take it again. — *This commandment have I received of my Father.* —

And so, we see it confirmed just in these three Scriptures, and they are much more for our spiritual understanding. No, he did not know that the sacrifice of the innocent blood of Christ would be his demise. He couldn't know that his blind act of diabolical evil would release us by our *faith* from his reign of tyranny against us since Christ was made a *living sacrifice* on behalf of our undeserved redemption and toward the eventuality of the literal and final destruction of *death, hell,* and *the grave.*

Once more, "just to be clear, what sacrifice?" —

Sacrifice Example #2 -

- When *Christ* remained silent at the hands of *his* executioners by proxy. Not uttering one sound of *power* **(power he declared he had - Mt 26:53 when simply asking the Father to defend him).** He remained dumb. Thus, *he sacrificed* obedience to the immutable **Word**. The **Word**, who *he* is, and is of *himself* the very authority that *he* has arrested himself with. Even as *he* Showed and revealed to us in, — *Matthew 28:18 (**declaring**)*

All power is given unto me, in Heaven and in Earth. — And so, we see by his witness of *sacrifice,* according to *(Isaiah 53:7 and Acts 8:32).* That we now have as an ***example of*** the price that was paid for our redemption and the cost that we too, must incur as we fight the good fight of *faith* in our battle to overcome, through the obedience of our sacrifice, **'working out our own salvation'** by way of our Covenant in Christ, on behalf of the **Kingdom. Amen!** Hence, I believe that we must receive every true revelation that points us to the surrendered act of Obedience — And this is a powerful one to me: ***"Obedience is the Master over sacrifice, and without it, our sacrifice has no consequential effect in the affairs of our walk of faith."*** But ***Sacrifice offered up through the Obedience of our surrender is attributable only to the Love of our Father, and his will carried out by us is pertinent to the advancement of the Kingdom!*** —

So, you see, for me to understand fully what sacrifice is, I must search and listen in order to receive revelation on the use of it in my upward call to perfection. In my conclusion here I see *two* verses on sacrifice, in ***(Psalms 51:16, 17),*** that at first glance seem to oppose one another, but in actuality, they show balance in the differing *perimeters* of the two. — Let's read them and see. ***Verse 16 - For thou desire not sacrifice; else would I give it:*** — ***verse 17 - The sacrifices of God are a broken spirit*** *(surrendered spirit, or will)*: ***a broken and contrite heart*** *(a repented heart)* —

THE DUAL PURPOSE OF THE WORD —

Scripture Reference: *(1Jn 3:8 / 2Th 2:3,4 / Jn 1:29 / Jn 16:8 -11—*

Rev 12:7 - 13 / Ezek 28:13,14 / Lk 10:18 / Rom 9:20,21 / Gen 3 (all) 1s 14:3 - 15 —

To **Destroy** the *works* of the Devil.......................

To **Take away** our *Sins*...

The History of the Reason: *Destroy the works*—

Now, before we delve into the purpose and reason for our *Gift* (*our* **Lord and Savior.the only begotten Son of the Father**). Let's first begin to examine the *history* that warranted us needing a *Savior*. A *Savior* planned even before the foundation of the world. Before pride was ever found in the heart of Lucifer, or even before the desire of Adam to chart his own path by disobedience was ever born. The need for a *Redeeming Savior* and *Champion* of Righteousness was already prepared [*For more needed reference, you can search for yourself in the Book of Revelation and in other Biblical record, describing the war, and turmoil in the Heavens, the <u>Book of 'Matthews, chapter 11'</u> is a good record of the violence, spoken of by Christ. You will see, the first recorded battle ever fought was begun by Lucifer and finished by* **Archangel Michael and his Band** *when they kicked him out of the presence of God, and with majestic force of rebuke, hailed him and his horde of reprobates into the middle earth.*

Which lead to the eventual fall of the first Adam]. And so began the storied history of *Satan's* perpetual fall. Perpetual because he ain't stopped falling yet, even though we might not quite under-stand how nevertheless, that is his reality until his final Destruction. What a great fall from grace for a **Being** who once held one of the highest positions of any created *being* before him. And was also held to be one of God's most beautiful Angels, according to the _Book of Ezekiel, chapter 28:13-15,_ _'till iniquity was found in him'._ — He was also known as the anointed _cherub_ _(28:14)._ One who covered the **Throne of God**. And yet, with all of his ordained splendor and high position, he could not be content. He lusted after the "All _and the_ Awe of who God is, was, and has always been." Yes, he wanted to transpose _himself_ from who he was into the very "**I AM**" that created him. In other words, and in simple layman terms: He simply wanted to be his own God. — Amen!

But as _Apostle Paul_ so eloquently stated by revelation in the _Book of Romans, chapter 9:20 - 21,_ _Nay but, O man, who art thou that replies against God? Shall the thing formed say to him that formed it, why hast thou made me thus_ **(this way)**_? Hath not the potter power over the clay_ **(created thing)**. No, he wouldn't be satisfied, just like many of us who inherited that self-same evil nature before coming to Christ. And even after coming, that nature of pride still plagues us in our effort to fight the good fight. And if we're not careful, like Satan, we will be deceived as he was **(but I pray to God we want)**. Yes, what a fool he was, and vain was his imagination when he thought to overthrow the **Kingdom**. And being deceived by the wisdom of his own folly, he could never have fathomed in his prideful heart his own calculated defeat. — And just as quick as he imagined in his heart, his _victory_, the war was over, as he and his cohorts were spoiled by **Archangel Michael and his Band of Brothers.** And the Lord _exclaimed_ in the _Book of Luke, chapter 10:18_ **(saying)** _I beheld Satan as lightning fall from Heaven._ — And again, as _John_ declares in the _Book of Revelation, chapter 12:9, And the great dragon was cast out, that old serpent, called the Devil, and Satan, which deceived the whole world: He was cast out into the earth, and his angels were cast out with him._ — Now, as we read _Revelation 12:12._ We see the perpetual fall of Lucifer _(just as I mentioned on the previous page)_. It is revealed to _John_ in quite a different way **(chapter 12 vs 12 — Saying)**. _Woe_ *unto the inhabitants of the earth and of the sea! For the Devil has come down unto you, having great wrath, because **"He knows that he hath but a short Time"**.* A short time indeed. (Note: My observation. The amount of time the Devil has is expressly defined in numbers *7 & 8* of the, — *Oxford University Press, online Dictionary (as quoted). Time - (7). n. the length of time taken to complete an activity. — 8. n. time as allotted, available, or use:* —

In other words, his time to be used against God's people as a *'fiery trial'* and *'sifter'* will soon come to an end. And though he's reigned in this earth domains, *heaven*; as *'lord of the flies,* and *prince of the air'.* Anything less than eternity, for a *creature* such as he, what a frivolous waste of immortality. Especially since there's no redemption for *Satan*, but thanks be to God, Jesus won it for **us**. So let us <u>not</u> also be frivolous; with so great a time as we have, seeing it's not on our side either. And after all, <u>*time waits for no one*</u>. And with that conclusion, let us now move beyond the *'History of the Reason'* for our deliverance onto the obedience of the **One** who was manifested. For the **dual purpose** of destroying the works of the Devil and... *(To Take away our sins, which for us, was imperative to our only salvation)* Hallelujah! **Glory to His Name ...In Him we overcome).**

*(Note: I will list a few of the **evil** works that were authored by **Satan** [but not in any particular order] and was thus condemned with him.)*

1 John, *Chapter 3 vs 8 - For this purpose the Son of God was manifested that he might destroy the works of the Devil* — **What Works?**

Murder —

John 8:44 - You're of your father the Devil — and the lust of your father you will do. He was a **murderer** from the beginning, — and abode not in the **truth**, because there is no truth in him. When he lies, he speaks of his own. *(his self, his demons, and his* *human agents)*; for he is a liar and the father of lies. *(For reference, also study verses 30 thru 47)*

Murderer —

John 3:15 - Whosoever hates his brother is a **murderer**; and you know that no murderer hath eternal *life* abiding in him *(remember, Satan was a murderer from the beginning)*, since he hates the creation of man. And when Satan was expelled from Heaven to Earth's Eden, he went straightaway, out to destroy God's *perfection*, who was the first man; Adam. Yes indeed, perfect because of his inalienable right to *choose*. Though, unlike the *devil*, who after his rebellion against God, by his choice; could find no place to file his petition of repentance. Hence, no forgiveness was found for him. But man through the great mystery of God, in Christ —*was* given away out, even before the *foundation* of the *world*, and before any sin of man was recorded. So, according to the **Book of Revelation, chapter 13:8 - the lamb who was slain before the foundation of the world.** —Gave us a way out! So, now we see the mystery unfurl, being hidden from the eyes of the prudent, and given unto babes *(you and I)* as a light of witness in the darkness, showing that no weapon it can form against us shall prosper. And we, having been engrafted into the plan and mystery of God, to establish the **kingdom.** Are made to be those foolish things, *confounding* the wise, doing our part toward the continual and *perpetual* fall of **Lucifer, son of the morning**!

Accuser —

Revelation 12:10 - And I heard a loud voice, saying in **heaven,** *"Now is come Salvation and strength — and the Kingdom for our God, and the Power of His Christ: for the accuser of our brethren is cast down, which accused them before our God Day and night.* —

Lust —

Timothy 4:1 -(3),4 - For the time will come when they will not endure sound doctrine — but after their own **lust** shall they heap to themselves teachers Jude *(gen. Epistle)* **vs** 18, 19 - How that they told you there should be *mockers,* in the last times *(days),* who would walk after their own ungodly **lust.** These be they who separate **(wickedly sanctify),** themselves, sensual, having not the **Spirit** of God **(The Holy Ghost)** —

Liar —

John 8:44 - He was a murderer from the beginning and abode not in the <u>truth,</u> because there is no <u>truth</u> in him. When he speaks a *lie,* he speaks of his own **(the original liar):** for he is a **liar,** and the father of it **(he is an evil living entity, and once his lie is received, it begins to create diabolical consequences: so we see in this verse, that a lie is an invisible living entity, created to obey it's father. It develops its own deceptively subtle character. And once it has been released by the teller, the lie teller becomes its servant, until repentance is found).**

Liars —

John 2:18 *(and vs21,22)* - I have not written unto you because you know not the *truth,* but because you know it, and that no *lie* is of the *truth* — Who is a **liar,** but he that denies*(does not live for the truth, and rejects),* that Jesus is the Christ, that denies the *Father* and the *Son* —

Romans 3:4 - God forbid: yea, let God be *true* and every man a **liar (the children of the devil).** [You can study *chapter 3:1-31,* to get a first-hand view of sin at work in our mortal being, as it constantly, without ceasing, seeks to overthrow the *Truth of God* in us] —

Father & Offspring of both Good and Evil:

John 8:30 -(44) - You are of your *father* the *devil*, and the *lust* of your *father* you will do *(as you pace yourself with this study, read vs. 30 thru 59)* 1 John 3:10 - In this the *children* of God is manifest *(all who are born of the Spirit of God)*— and *(also)*the children of the devil are manifested *(all who are not born of the Spirit of God)* —

Note — on the next page, I've jotted down a few definitions of what I've labeled as **_keywords_** pertaining to the *devil*. Words that warrant a closer examination, helping us to recognize the subtle and the overt schemes that *Satan* uses in his arsenal _to destroy us_. And as a *father*, his job is to make sure that each one of his *children* has access to his arsenal.

Evil seeds. Now, each one of these **_keywords_** are used in some form or fashion by the *children* of disobedience. But, as **Children** and **servants** of God, we should never allow *evil seeds* to grow unto manifestation in our lives. **Repent, Repent, Repent** —

Key-Word Definitions:

"Webster's New World Dictionary (WNWD) & Oxford University Press (OUP)"

Father -(*n*). 4. creator ... (*v*). 3. to bring into being; create; invent

Lust - (*n*). 1. a strong desire...(*v*). To feel a strong desire (*WNWD*)

Lust -(*n*). 1. Strong sexual desire. 2. a passionate desire for something. 3. *Theology* a sensuous appetite regarded as sinful — (*v*). *lust for/after* - feel lust for someone or something —(*OUP*)

Liar -(*n*). a person who tells lies

Murderer -*(n)*. a person who is guilty of murder *(WNWD)*

Murderer -*(v)*. kill unlawfully and with premeditation

Accuser *(n)*. 1. to charge someone with doing wrong, are breaking the *law* — 2. to find fault with; blame —

The Purpose of Christ - *Our Salvation, the Finished work of God:*

To Take *away* Our Sins:

John, *chapter* 1 *vs* 29 - Behold the **Lamb** of God, who takes away the sin of the world. — And so we see the second part of this **dual purpose** that our *Savior* was sent to accomplish, as *he* makes a way for us to escape so great a damnation. His death, burial, and resurrection were the payment for our *redemption*. Therefore, we now have an avenue for *repentance*, where we are now able to become *children* of God once more, never to lose our rightful position again. And having obtained <u>*salvation*</u>, we now have access always to the **Father!** —

*(**Salvation** n. 1. saving or being saved from danger, evil, etc. **2.** a person or thing that saves. **3.** in Christian belief — the saving of a soul from sin and death. [WNWD]* —

The Day of *Salvation:* 2 Corinthians, *chapter* 6 *vs* 1,2 - We then, as workers together with *him (Christ)*, also plead with you not to receive the *Grace* of God in vain. For *he* says:

"In an acceptable time, I have heard you. And in the day of Salvation, I have helped (saved) you." Behold now is the acceptable time; behold, now is the day of **Salvation.**

Salvation:

Now, just as Christ confirms *himself* in men, of the **new dispensation** on the revelational knowledge of *salvation*, as the Apostles and teachers dispersed it among the newly baptized converts. *He (the Holy Spirit)*, on behalf of the Christ to come, likewise bear witness in the days of the *law,* and the *Prophets,* to them the revelations of a new and living way. As *He* revealed mysteries, He did show them in part, God's blueprint, through type and shadow of the **Salvation** in Christ that was to come. And even though they did not fully comprehend it. The showing of it urged them on in hope, to believe and wait patiently for the conclusion of the mysteries of **salvation** to be visited upon in their children and the offspring of their children's children. And this was the patience of their hope, as they lived in the presence of their children's future, anticipating the awesomeness of that day, when in the *Spirit* of Unity, the **"Last and the First"** shall merge as ONE **Body;** and the **Body** shall be made **complete** with its Head: who is our Lord forever and ever, Amen. And just as the **Author of our Faith** so eloquently declared on the cross over 2000 years ago; **"It is Finished."** So shall it be said by us: **Hallelujah, Hallelujah, it is Finished** in Christ for us all. Selah, and Amen again....

Okay, let us now look at: Genesis, *chapter* 26 *vs* 3,4 - And I will perform the **Oat**h which I swear unto Abraham thy *father.* And in thy *seed* shall all the nations of the earth be *blessed!* — So, here we see and do understand that Christ was that *seed* that was sown in **faithful** Abraham for a sure remedy too the healing and deliverance of our **soul**s, and as a ransom for all our trespasses against God. Yes, **Christ is** that divine **Seed** sent to us as the *True* Vine. The *vine,* in whom we as gentiles were engrafted, and made partakers of the *heavenly* call. *Therefore,* thanks be to God, who has freely given of **himself** —to us an obedient *Son.* A *Son* made not like the first man, *Adam,* whose disobedience confirmed the will of the **Father** and plunged us all into a *cessation* from our proposed relationship with God. A relationship that was all but aborted. But thanks be to God, even our Lord, who counted the innocent blood of Abel as a down payment toward our redemption, which was to come by the obedience of the Son of Man who is our *Savior* forever, Jesus Christ, to the Glory of the Father. So let us continue to be found worthy to be the *'Fruit of His Labor"* as we too, **sow seeds** produced by the *salvation* that was so freely delivered unto us.

Sacrifice unto Salvation:

Hebrews, **Chapter** 10 *Verses* 5 - 12 — Wherefore when he cometh into the world, *He* said: — *Sacrifice and offering thou wouldest not, but a body hast thou prepared me. In burnt offerings and* sacrifices *for sin thou hast had no pleasure.* *** *Then said I, Lo; I come (in the volume of the book it is written of me), to do thy <u>will</u>, O God.* Now what is the volume of the Book? — It is the <u>**Whole**</u> and complete Epistle of God. It is the *Holy Bible* and no other Book. In this Book, is the full record of the *parabolical similitudes* pertaining to the coming of Christ, and also many *Prophetic-type, shadows, and models* of *him* before his coming. And *his* arrival was confirmation to us, That God's **word** will never return void *(1s 55:11)*. And by the authority of our *faith* in Christ, it will always accomplish the will of the **Father.**] —

And so, as was stated in the previous paragraph, referring to *(Heb 10:5,6 - Sacrifice and offerings* (and) *In burnt offerings and Sacrifice for sin thou hast had no pleasure.* [which were offered according to the Law*.)* Then *he* spoke in <u>*vs 7,*</u> *saying: (Behold, I come to do your will; O God).* And so, in this, we see that *he* takes away the *first* (Law), that *he* may then establish the *second* —. And in the *second (Law),* which is, rather called *"His Blood of New Testament" (Mk 14:24),* we have been Sanctified by the *Offering* of the *Body & Blood,* once and for all.......

No more Priest and their *sacrifices* — *(Heb 10:11,12 - And every priest stands daily ministering and offering many-times the same sacrifices, which can never take away sins:* — * — *But this MAN, after he had offered <u>One Sacrifice for Sins</u>* — *forever:* (then) *sat down on the Right Hand of God,* And so, I thank God that there is no more place for Priest of the old *dispensation,* nor of the new, since Christ is the fulfilling of them *both. Amen!* Now, my hope for you while you're consuming what you've read is that you will meditate on all that is beneficial for you. And of course, my hope is that it will begin to inspire you to earnestly search out the scriptures for yourself. So that you too, will begin to understand in depth; how the **Word** of God has been laid down and established by Christ as the only Truth by which *we* shall live. It is the single *Key,* that unlocks the door of our daily salvation, enabling us to **'Work out by faith, our hopes for Tomorrow'**

The **Word** of God *(proclaimed by those called to declare it)* is the only prophetically time released seed ever sown to produce not only life here but more abundantly so, in the *Paradise* of our longing, namely **Heaven.** And by faith, it is sown into the life of all the *saints* who stood on it. — Those of the past and of the present, who presently we are. Those of the past looked off into the distant future by faith and seeing in a figure the hope of their faith. Producing for them; the fruits of their labor, which is that of — the promised **Salvation.** A salvation that we now have as *Spirit filled,* born-again children of the highest God. Though, often-times we who are the so-called modern Christians never fully grasp nor understand the awesomeness of what they envisioned and believed salvation for all men really meant, when truly; they were looking at things far-off, through the *lens* of Jewish hope, not really for all men in the broader sense, but for their *children,* who would one day receive a salvation that could only be achieved by the sacrificial death of the only begotten **Son** of the **Father.**

And even as many of them gave up their own lives for *righteousness* and all things pertaining to *holiness,* never being able to physically experience the spiritual reality of salvation, they still somehow lived in the hope of the vision and of what *so great a salvation* would accomplish. *(Yet so many of us who have what they longed for, just don't pursue the full measure of its benefit. — Benefits delivered to us, by the sacrifice and obedience of One at the cross)* And they looked forward to a hope that was given to them by a promise given to *Father* Abraham. Because all they had in their types and shadows was a salvation that had the propensity to change from season to season, based solely on the righteousness of their *King* or *Priest, and* what they yearned for was the kind that we have. A kind based on the righteousness of God, in Christ Jesus, in us. And being newly born of that fruit bearing tree, which is Christ, in us the hope of Glory, we indeed have the fulness of *His* **Salvation.** Therefore, we are now in their lineage, which is of a **Royal Priesthood (1Pet 2:9),** and of a Holy Nation, in Christ Jesus, the *children* of Abraham. Now we do have record that in another time — *King David* did speak in <u>*provincial authority,*</u> declaring with all boldness *(Ps 116:13* (saying) — *"I will take the cup of Salvation"*). He continually sought, with great zeal, to know how he could repay the **Lord** for all of **His** goodness. And through his thanksgiving, he discerned that all he had *(in substantive Glory)* already belonged to God. So, he decided to repay **Him,** by doing good unto others; rendering *Justice (in place of vengeance),* and allowing His righteousness to glorify His **God.**

Salvation Experienced: The Manifested Fruit

Glory - The Stuff of Salvation; David's Evidence —

And with all His Glory (the stuff of salvation): He did bring glory to the name of the Lord. We see it evidenced by the riches of his Storehouse he left to his son Solomon, who was obedient to the heavenly vision, and plan of God. And because of David's reverence and love for the Father. Solomon was able to fulfill the desire of his father's heart. By building the House of God from the continual overflow of his father's "Cup of Salvation" —for truly it did run over (Ps 23:5 & Ps 116:13) — Amen!

The New fulfills the Old - The Seed of Prophesy Bearing Fruit Meditation Time - Please take your time to reflect on what you've been able to glean from all that you've read up until this point, whether it's by the randomness of what, or how you consume what you've read, or will read, by selective prowess in the circumference of what I call, 'the Arena of Salvation.' My desire for you, as well as for myself, is that we might be able to grasp by immeasurable faith for our own lives what is: the depth, height, width and length of the measure of Salvation that it takes for each one of us to work-out, in the success of our <u>everyday walk of faith</u>!

Manifested Fruit:

1. Prophetic Salvation Revealed —

The Plan of Salvation before the *fall* - 1 Peter, *chapter* 1 *vs* 19,20 - But with the precious blood of Christ, as a lamb without a blemish and without a spot: Who verily was fore-ordained before the foundation of the world. But was manifested in these last times for you ***Manifested in Rome: in the days of strong persecution, of the Jews first, and then others. But none were as brutally persecuted as the Church. They were not only persecuted to death by Rome but also by the religious zealots from the hierarchy of the Jews. And yet many were made martyrs, even though they had never known Christ in the flesh, yet because of hope burning brightly within them, their faith was undaunted. And that same fire of faith still burns bright, being manifested in us, who are rightly called by Paul's epistle — of the Household of Faith (Gal 6:10).*** ---And, even as I write these words of *commentary* on the verses of scripture here *(and throughout this Journal)*, that have revealed their *truths* to me in this my **"book of continuance"**. —

I can almost hear my *Lord* admonishing Thomas *(as he looks out into the future of where we are today)* with words of Love, *saying:* ***O Thomas, because thou hast seen me, thou believed: but blessed*** *even more is my servant: John and Sheila, Frinnie and Mary, and all those who believe, yet have not seen —their faith is sure. —*

Revelation 13 *vs* **7 - 9** *(The Hell we were In)* - And it was given to him *(Satan)* to make war with the *Saints,* and to overcome them: And power was given to **him (by the will of God, because of the sin of Adam #1, with epilogue, to the final conclusion)** over all kindred's and tongues, and nations *(1Cor 15:22 - for in Adam all die).* And all that dwell upon the earth shall worship Satan, whose names are not written in the *(Lambs)* Book of Life. If any man has an ear, let him hear. *(Many haven't spiritually come to understand how brilliantly orchestrated the plan of God was to our salvation; even before the foundation of the world. Even before Lucifer fell. And even before Adam succumbed to his own lust. God's plan of redemption for the saving of His Image (**Man**) was already established.*

And so, as you already know by now, Jesus was that Plan of God. For *He* is that Lamb, crucified before the foundation of the world. Now, as we regress back to our earlier understanding of sins nature, we see by the disobedience of the *first* Adam, condemnation was our lifelong position. But in the **second Adam**, obedience is found. And by our acceptance of **Christ's** righteous response to the Father's *love* on our behalf, there is therefore no more condemnation, – '**for those who walk not after the flesh, but after the Spirit' (Rom 8:1)**. So, for me the Book of Revelation simply proves to me, and maybe to others who've laid claim to their rightful place or position in the Kingdom of our God, that even from the *foundation* of creation, we were *purposed* for God's glory. We had already been purchased by the *blood of the Lamb,* and our names were written in the *Lambs Book of Life* (**Rev 21:27**). And seeing this through the lens of a *relationship* with our Lord and *Savior* Jesus Christ, we're better able to understand, the Godly sorrow that brought us to repentance. And seeing that God cannot lie *(Tit 1:1- [2], **In hope of eternal life, which God who cannot lie, promised before the world began**).*

Revelation 5 *vs* 6 - And I beheld, and *Lo in the midst of* the Throne and of the four beasts, and in the midst of the elders, stood a *Lamb* as it had been *slain.* Here we see clearly that Jesus is the Lamb, though we could never fully *fathom,* or comprehend, the magnitude of our *Saviors Sacrifice* for us. We can, by the Spirit, discern how we, too, can be examples of sacrifice, not only to one another in the Body Church, but also to those *we* must witness our salvation to. Sacrifice must become a *realized* part of our new nature as we seek to fulfill the *"Great Commission".* Therefore, it is by our own revelation of *sacrifice* that gives us the Power to press through our own self-interest, to become sacrificial lambs in our own calling, as we win the lost, having the power to **remit** the sins of others, based on *(John 20:23).* [Remit - *v.* **3.** to forgive or pardon – **4. to free someone** *(to remit a prison sentence; to remit a debt)* Also, included in our sacrifice is the anointing to retain even unto absolution. Just as Christ was able to free us from the prison of sin, we too, through *him,* are made able to do the same. Even as *John* the Baptist declared at the river Jordan: (saying) — *'Behold the Lamb of God, which taketh away the sins of the world' (John 1:29 and 1:36).* So, as we examine the Power of these two words, we see them both on display in *Mark, chapter 2 verses 5 thru 10* - (so, Jesus speaking to the man with the palsy, when *he* saw the faith of his friends), *5 - Son, thy sins be forgiven thee...*(and discerning the wicked hearts of the scribes, then began to rebuke them, saying), *8 - Why reason ye these things in your heart? 9 - Which is easier to say to the sick of the palsy. Thy sins be forgiven thee: or to say, arise, take up your bed, and walk?*

10 - But that ye may know that the Son of man (including us) *also hath power on earth to forgive sins. 11 - I say unto you* (speaking to the palsy man, while admonishing the scribes), *arise, and take up your bed, and go your way unto your house.* And so, we see in this example; how Christ *retained* the sins of the palsy man, and by doing so, shows us that for us to do both *(remit & retain)* sins, we must have compassion operating at a high level, for healing and salvation to take place. But for these things we are made witnesses of, so that we may become fruitful workers of **His** *Vineyard*.

the benefits of the cup of salvation — part 1

THE BENEFITS OF THE CUP: AFTER ACTS 2:1 - 4 —

So here we are, with: 'The Cup of **Salvation,**' and for me, this is an intense study, but a very exciting and rewarding topic of discovery, in reference to our '**Kingdom Benefits.**' I hope you'll agree. But, before we delve into this great **Benefits composite** that I was inspired to compile since I desired to know and understand what my **Salvation** really meant, and for me to find out as much about our guaranteed **Benefits**, as I could possibly retain or better yet, *comprehend*. And of course, the search was not only for me but for the greater *Body* of the Household of **Faith**, now, and for all those who would come later, as they would, in their season: *began,* to follow after the **Son** of **Righteousness**, who is for us all; a constant and *Benevolent* release of *Good*, meted out to us on behalf of the **Kingdom.** So yes indeed, before we begin to grapple unto comprehension, let's take a look at *Agape Love: 1 John 3:1 -* **Behold what manner of love the Father hath bestowed upon us, that we should be called sons of God** (like unto Angelic beings, totally Spirit, the Heavenly Sons, Children of God -**read Job 1:6/2:1 /**

Jn 1:12 / Ph 2:15 / Jn 3:2 / Rm 8:14 / Rm 8:19) — It is amazing to know that God has chosen us, to demonstrate, the kind of illustrious Love that only *He* can deliver. So let us look at a few '*naturally discerned* words' that help our natural mind understand more aptly how to apply spiritual wisdom to how we need to govern our lives, using appropriate words that help us to live in victory, being always aware of the power of their uses, for either good or evil purposes in this natural world. And so, to better equip us in the function of our daily *faith walk*, I believe that we should be able to define the purpose and frugality of important words that we speak into our world. So, we will look at some definitions of a few words that are crucial to our success and ability to infiltrate this world on behalf of the *Kingdom*. These words will be a great resource in tying down our thought progression in relation to what's familiar to us in our exhaustive study of *word* usage. As *2ⁿᵈ Timothy, chapter 2:15 (so studiously presses us to do)*. So, as you read and study these *words* and their definitions, my hope for you is that you'll be further encouraged to *press on* even deeper — Amen!

So, when I began my journey into this matter of concern, referencing the *Benefits* of our *Salvation.* I began to contemplate the workings of a human **Will** and how it is that the Benefits of Salvation, upon further discovery, are fundamentally set up on the same premises as our own – 'Last Will and Testament'. And just like the legal documents concerning our inheritance. Our *Salvation Benefits* are also instruments of *Righteous Legalities* based on the Righteous Law of God. Hence, our *Salvation* in Christ is the *unit* by which our unearned *inheritance* and blessings are released. It is the '***Last Will and Testament of Christ.*** So, while on this *faith journey*, I started to view and see natural words and their definitions open more clearly my *spiritual comprehension* as I sought to learn more about my Benefits relative to who I am now, as a Child of God and Servant to my Lord and Savior Jesus *Christ*. Now, the layout of this Word study starts with "Will" and every other Word defined will follow in their proper order, relative to how they were impressed upon me. *(Please Enjoy)* —

Will (*n.*) **5.** *a legal paper (document) in which a person tells what he wants done with his money and property after he dies.* (*v.*) **3.** *to leave to someone by a will, as property.*

Benefactor (*n.*) *a person who has given money or other help to someone in need.*

Benefit (*n.*) **1.** *help or advantage; also, anything that helps.* **2.** *often* **benefits,** (*pl.*) *money paid by an insurance company, the gov., etc., as during old age or sickness, or death.* (*v.*) **2.** *to get good from; be helped by; profit* [the children **benefitted** from the fresh air and exercise at camp]

Heir (*n.*) *a person who gets or has the right by law to get property or a title when the person holding it dies.*

(a) **Inherit** (*v.*) **1.** *to get from another when he dies; receive as an heir.* **2.** *to have or get certain characteristics because ones parents or ancestors had them:* (**Study Note Area for Reader: Find certain characteristics or traits that identify us as Believers and Citizens of the Kingdom of God and jot them down on the next two Pages set aside for your participation, in understanding what Benefits you have already received, and those you've not yet retrieved.** — [*you will find some of mine listed as you read this Study Journal, and as well, those I seek to apprehend along my journey*] — **Since this Book is yours, you're free to write your thoughts wherever**).

E. (b) **Inheritance** (*n.*) *the act or <u>right</u> of inheriting.* **2.** *something inherited.* —

Inheritance Commentary:

Now, because obedience was the mechanism by which Christ was led to the Cross and the measured Unit that brought us our New Birth, in Him and by which we accept *(by Grace)*, so **great** a **Salvation**. And so, we do accept by His righteous act of *obedience*, an **Inheritance** that gives us the right to come *boldly* to the Throne of Grace, with petition to the Father, for what **now** rightfully belongs to us. So without hesitation or any trepidation, we, by the *assurance* of our **faith**, call those things that be not*(that is to say, the invisible stuff of our inheritance)* to be realized completely *(nothing missing)* into the manifested reality whatever *Benefit* we might need in the now, of our future. And since we have this Right as true **Heirs**, we can no longer sit back on our laurels and be lazily satisfied, '*daydreaming*' with a "Pie in the Sky" mentality. O yes, I've been guilty of that sort of laziness, which '*I believe*' has caused many of my beneficial blessings to be held up. We must be relentlessly proactive in our daily pursuit to please the Father. So that we can better live in the fullness of all that Christ has suffered for, on our behalf — Bringing many sons and Daughters into the fellowship of His *glory*. That is to say, with more clarity: 'To bring us all into the full substance; of what has been allotted to us as a Group, as a Family; and as Individuals, in this our **'Benefits Package'** called *Salvation*. —

Structural Support

So, now that we've touched on some of the Keys to the <u>**structural support**</u> and makeup of the **Will**, and who its Benefactors are, and who gets what the Benefactor has *willed* —let us now investigate and understand in some depth what the *word* **Benefit** means to us, regarding our **Kingdom** Salvation Fund, and how pertinent it is to the release of our individual glory, which is not only the prospering of our *soul*, but also our health and material wealth. *(Please look at the two scripture witnesses: One in*

Deuteronomy 8:18, the other in 3 John 2). Now of course, these *two scriptures* really reference our Earthly needs, pertaining to being fit for the *Master's* use, as we glorify Him with all that we've been blessed with, for the sake of *His Covenant*; as *He* swore to our *Spiritual fathers* of antiquity. So, we see here that truly God is the originator and *Benefactor* of the first Benefits offered to mankind, not only from the perspective of Adam and Eve, being the first ones to receive the full *Benefit Plan*, but also of Abraham, the Nation of Israel, and now us.

And so now, when I look at the *Benefits of Kingdom*, I see it in relation to an Employment Compensation plan package, which includes Wages and a Health plan, as well as other *compensation benefits*. Now of course, we do understand clearly, with these plans, that you have to be actively employed, and in the majority of *cases*, you have to be a Full-time Employee in order to receive the full benefit of your Package. Now, the number one benefit we all desire from any job is our paycheck; then if we stay there for a while, we will usually enroll in some type of Retirement Plan. There is also a list of other entities from where we might collect some type of benefits, such as a Social Security Check after we retire. And if we're unemployed, we might also collect an Unemployment Check. Now of course, more than likely, we've all fallen into one or more of those *benefit categories*, needing and relying on one or two of these types of benefits, and we understand our necessity and rights to many of these awesome benefits *(benefits we need and must have, in order to survive in this dog eat dog world)*. But, for some reason, as the people of *faith* that many of us label ourselves to be, we do oftentimes miss out on receiving the full *Benefit* of our *Salvation,* mainly because we don't receive revelation on how to access the full measure of Benefits allotted to us. *Benefits* that we so often pray to receive in our season of need; for whatever reason we deem. And so often, we'll seemingly have more faith in what we want from the faultily flawed *system of this world*. We'll have almost complete confidence in the kind of happiness we believe the world can afford us, and when the system doesn't seem to produce what we want, we will begin to say things like: "Well, if I just had a little more of what I already have, I'd be a lot happier" or "If I could at least earn 50% **more** of what I already make, we'd be on easy street" — So you might ask, okay John what's your point here. It's simple. We wrangle and argue about how we wish the system would give us more. We know all the benefits that the *World System* offers, and how we hope, and dream of ways to benefit from it. Yet, we don't put forth much effort in pursuing what's *Spiritually* necessary for us to access the *Benefits* of the *Kingdom* that's presented to us as '*Children of the Most High* **God**'. Now, don't get me wrong, I ain't got it all together either, but as I tarry in the *faith*, growing stronger and hopefully wiser in my *relationship* with Christ. I'm coming to the realization that if I'm not content with receiving the limited benefits of what my superficial little unemployment check might bring *(now I started this Faith-Journal while drawing unemployment)*. Then, I'll never be content with what the *riches* of the Lottery <u>might or might not bring.</u>

I say **might bring** (speaking parenthetically), in the sense of much despair and misery, allowing for a greater chance of mismanaging the abundance of your newfound wealth if you've not learned how to manage the little that you've been blessed with. O, I'm not putting a finger in your eye, I'm guilty of this sin and haven't been a good steward in the wellness arena area of financial health, but I'm on the road to recovery. O yes, we must learn to be thankful for the benefits that we have now, both natural or spiritual. And begin to understand, with greater sensitivity, the importance as Christians of getting to know our Benefactor, who is Christ; the Lord of our Harvest. He is the source of all our **Benefits**, whether natural or spiritual. So, let's *remember* the words King **David** rehearsed in his spirit before outwardly declaring, in the record of his *Prayers—Psalms, chapter 116:12,13 - What shall I render unto the Lord for all His Benefits towards me? I will take the 'Cup of Salvation' and call upon the name of the Lord.* — So, let's enlighten ourselves and engross even more in the meaning and full thrust of these two *powerful Words:* **"Benefit & Beneficiary."** So, let us define and examine a few of their derivatives that I've made reference to in this Limited Benefit's Concordance.

E. (c) **Beneficiary** *(n)* **1.** *a person who gets benefits.* **2.** *a person who gets money or property from a* **<u>Will</u>** *or insurance policy.* — *(Beneficiary Commentary: an individual who gets certain rights and benefits, according to their faith; such as houses and land with properties built and previously owned by someone else — kingdom beneficiaries (The Body of Christ) —*

Benefits Scripture Summary *and* Limited Concordance:

As I write this section on the Benefits of Salvation, a question entered my *spirit*, one which had never entered my conscious before, nor had I ever heard it, pondered it, seen it written, or asked before. And it's this. John, have you ever read or seen any book since you've been born-again that covers the Benefits of Salvation? —The answer to that question is a resounding **NO.** — No! I've never come across any Christian book that specifically outlines or describes the Benefits of our *Salvation...* though I have read about the Benefits and Blessings that were upon the Jews when they walked in obedience. But I've never read a book written to show and describe to me in layman's terms and categorize the beneficial aspects of my understanding. And with those questions posed to me, my quest to learn more about the *Benefits* of our *Salvation* grew into this limited study on this *important subject matter.*

Henceforth, this Limited Concordance of our Benefits became for me and my *spiritual* need, a must-have. I had to see for myself what the **Sacrifice** of Calvary, in Christ Jesus, the Son of the Living God, had won, not only for me, but for His Body Church. Being made the only testator of an oath; able to guarantee for us the Rights of True Heirs to all the Blessings of *Father Abraham*, through the *righteous* act of obedience, by One so much greater than *righteous* **Abraham**, the *father* of our **faith.** And so, we, as **Heirs** to the Promise, now have access to those Benefits. And in this <u>Benefits Summary</u>, I've tried to outline specific **Scriptures** and **Faith Summaries** to hopefully whet the appetite of the Reader, as to spur you along with me, on this *faith-filled* journey into a deeper relationship with the Lord, and to increase more in the knowledge of what being an **Heir** of the **Kingdom** is all about. Now I know me *(and my attention span),* and so I must honestly tell you and hope you don't take it the wrong way — But I do believe that, in this Section of Study, you will find a more studious and attentive *spirit* is required in order to absorb what is intended and purposed for you, myself included. I hope you won't find it too boring, but it might remind you of the great chore you may encounter when studying 1ST Chronicles, with all those names and all those genealogies *(you know, when you're not spiritually up to the task or the challenge). [Man, all those NAMES.....(LoL).]*

STUDY TO SHOW THY SELF-APPROVED UNTO GOD, A WORKMAN THAT NEEDS NOT TO BE ASHAMED, RIGHTLY DIVIDING THE WORD OF TRUTH. (2ND TIMOTHY 2:15)

BENEFITS CONCORDANCE

A *thru* **G**

Access

Rm 5:2 - By whom also we have **_access_** by faith

Eph 2:18 - For through Him we both have **_access_** by one Spirit

Eph 3:12 - In whom we have boldness and **_access_** with confidence

Adoption

Rm 8:15 - But you have received the Spirit of **_adoption:_**

Gal 4:5 - That we might receive the **_adoption_** of Sons.

Eph 1:5 - Having predestined us unto the **_adoption_** of Children by Jesus.

Angels *Now here, my conversation about Angels is limited since we're all instructed not to worship the Angels, as the* **Book of Colossians** *teaches us in* **Chapter 2 vs 16 thru 18 - Let no man therefore judge you in meat, or in drink, or in respect to a Holy day, or of the new moon,— or of the Sabbath Days — Which are a shadow of things to come; but the Body is of Christ — Let no man beguile you**(trick or deceive) **of your Reward in a voluntary humility**(by enticing you into)**worshiping of Angels** *— Also we must be careful who we entertain*(For Godly Reasons), *seeing that it is possible for us to entertain Angels unaware, as they do sometimes appear in physical form, as a human, while obviously on some type of assignment for God. Look at what the* (**Book of Hebrews, Chapter 13 vs 2**). *There, we see the Holy Spirit instructing us to be hospitable towards strangers since one just* *might be an Angel. Sent there to test your 'Love Discerning Skills', I say it that way because Godly Love is Spiritual, and you must be able to discern between good and evil while at the same time being spiritually mature enough to by faith, still show love without fear. Now, you may ask, why should you even attempt to entertain strangers in this wicked world since you don't know whether or not they mean you any good? Well, it's simple, but not easy... don't walk in fear, but have faith in love. Because perfect love, which is Spiritual, has the power to disarm the enemy, you just have to know where you are in your* **Faith Walk** *in regard to being Spiritually mature; just be careful and know who you are. — So, to sum it all up, Angels are sent by God as helpers on our behalf — but you're not to try and conjure them up for your benefit; you're not God). —*

Ps 34:7 - The <u>**Angel**</u> of the Lord encamps round about them that fear **him and** delivers them.

Ps 91:11 - For **he** shall give **his** <u>**Angels**</u> charge over you to keep you in all your ways.

Ps 104:4 - Who make **his** <u>**Angels**</u> spirits; **his** ministers a flaming fire

Dan 6:22 - My God has sent **his** <u>**Angel**</u> and has shut the lion's mouth

Acts 5:19 - But the <u>**Angel**</u> of the Lord by night opened the prison doors and brought them forth:

Acts 10:22 - And they said, Cornelius the centurion, a just man, and one that fears God, and of good report among all the nation of the Jews, was warned from God by a holy <u>**Angel**</u>, to send for you into his house, and to hear **words** of you.

Anointed

Acts 10:38 - How God <u>**anointed**</u> Jesus of Nazareth with the Holy Ghost and with power: who went about doing good and healing all that were oppressed of the devil; for God was with **him.**

2Cor 1:21 - Now he which established us with you in Christ, and hath **_anointed_** us, is God

Heb 1:9 - Thou hast loved righteousness and hated iniquity: therefore God, even God, hath **_anointed_** you with the oil of gladness above thy fellows.

Anointing

Is 10:27 -, and the yoke shall be destroyed because of the **_anointing_**

Jm 5:14 - Is any sick among you? Let him call for the elders of the Church; and let them pray over him, **_anointing_** him with oil in the name of the Lord

1Jn 2:27 - But the **_anointing_** which you have received of **him** abides in you, and you need not that any man teach you: — but as the same **_anointing_** teaches you of all things, and is truth, and is no lie, and even as it hath taught you, you shall abide in **him**.

Apostle(s) *(Apostle — is the first of the five Gifts that God has given to us in Christ —for guiding us into a new order of Holiness, moving us closer to a more Perfect Man/Woman in the Plan of God) —*

1st Gift to the Church - _Apostles_ (Jesus, who is the 'author and finisher of our faith' [**Heb 12:2**]. The Alpha Omega of all that is [**Rev 1:8**] is also the leader and **_Apostle_** of a new and better Covenant, whose mark we wear as **his** disciples ...And as **his** disciples, not only do we have great blessings of all kind bestowed upon us as the Body of Christ, but to have such a **G**ift as the **_Apostles_** is extraordinary, seeing that by them God turned the world of their antiquity upside down, causing a spiritual snow-balling effect; that till this day, is still upsetting; and vanquishing the wicked plan of our enemy. And the miraculous thing about the **gifting** of the **_Apostle_** to the Church is that any one of us has the potential in Christ to be called in the *anointing* of the **_Apostle_**: yes, even now...**Amen!**

Heb 3:1 - Wherefore, Holy Brethren, partakers of the Heavenly call, consider the **_Apostle_** and High Priest of our Profession, Christ Jesus.

1Cor 12:28 - And God hath set some in the Church, *first* **_Apostles_**.

Eph 2:19,20 - Now, therefore, you're no more strangers & foreigners, but *fellow-citizens* with the saints, and of the *household* of God; and are built upon the **foundation** of the **_Apostles_** —

Eph 3:5 - Which in other ages was not made known unto the sons of men, as it is now *revealed;* unto his <u>Holy **_Apostles_** &</u> by the *Spirit.*

Eph 4:11 - And *He* gave some **_Apostles,_** *(For the Perfecting of the Saints)*

The **_Apostle_** Paul, a Jew, called to be an **_Apostle_** – To former Dogs like Me and to all other People Groups:

Minus the Jews!

(Mt 7:6 / Mt 15:26,27 / Phil 3:2 / Rev 22:15)

Armor

Rom 13:12 - Let us therefore cast off the works of darkness and let us put on the **_Armor_** of Light.

2 Cor 6:7 - The *Word* of Truth, by the Power of God, by the **_Armor_** of Righteousness on the *right* hand and on the *left*...

Eph 6:11 - Put on the <u>*whole **Armor***</u> of God:

Eph 6:13 - Wherefore take unto you the <u>*whole **Armor***</u> of God:

Assurance (Cast not away your confidence, hold fast to your *F*aith, for our *G*uarantor has given us access to our *reward* by way of *H*is obedience)

Acts 17:31 - Because *H*e has appointed a day, in which *H*e will judge the <u>*world*</u> in **Righteousness** (Please read entire *S*cripture): wherefore *H*e has given <u>***Assurance***</u> unto all men, in that *H*e has raised *H*im up (Who is Christ), from the dead.

Col 2:2 - That their hearts might be *C*omforted, being knit together in **love**, and unto all riches of the full <u>***Assurance***</u> of understanding... to the acknowledgment of the *M*ystery of **God**, and of the **Father**, and of *C*hrist. (*While copying this scripture verse, my* **spirit** *was suddenly alerted to something I'd never seen before in this* W*ord... the writer very keenly speaks of only two members of the* **Godhead**, *and he's clearly speaking of them as if the* **Holy-Spirit** *wasn't there, yet it's evident that Paul still Speaks of them as a* T*riumvirate force. So while I was pondering this openly in my mind... my* **spiritual** *mind was enlightened —and with simplicity, in explanation; a short story line was formed in reference to the writer's skillful description of Order in the unity of the* **Triad**, *and so it appeared like this in my* **spirits-mind** *—* (1). **God,** the ultimate authority over all creation, the *Alpha:* **"before matter existed" and** the *Omega:* **"end of all things as we know them"** (2). **Father-God,** the creator of Man, the Lover of our **souls** (3). **Christ Jesus,** the ultimate expression of *sacrificial Love*...the kind of Love that only an *emotional* **Being** can produce, toward *His Offspring* **(born-again children)**, the love of a **Father** — the kind of Love that separates by nature, a Man from a *beast*. A **God** sovereign over all other Gods, made up or real...**Amen!**)

1 Th 1:5 - For our *G*ospel came not unto you in *W*ord on, but also in *P*ower, and in the Holy Ghost, and in much <u>***Assurance:***</u>

Heb 6:11 - And we desire that every one of you, do show the same diligence to the full <u>***Assurance***</u> of *hope* unto the end

Heb 10:22 - Let us draw near with a True heart, in full _Assurance_.

authority

Authority (**This word** *"Authority"* is an awesome *word* of Power, though for some reason, many of the <u>Household</u> of Faith are simply uneducated about its great importance in their lives ***it's one of the Keys to our Victory***.) We can, of course, consume all How-to Manuals or books that our intellect tells us we need as we try to figure out within ourselves just how to *wield* such a weapon. Yet we forget that it's no different from other things we must learn. It must be absorbed with patience and experience, which allows us to endure all Seasons in order that we might become seasoned in the areas of our lives where we include Christ because it's by Him, in the person of the Holy Ghost, that we learn by obedience to walk in the Spirit of *Authority*, as we prayerfully, with humility, walk in the grace of our Lord. Now, we have many examples of this type of *Authority* being used in the lives of God's people. And one of those examples is of a young *shepherd boy* who lived in that kind of Power. He was anointed to be King over Israel when he was very young and before he was ever ready. But one day, he was called upon by God to subdue Israel's enemies, and he did because he knew who he was as a covenanted child of God. But shortly after the display of his *Authority* —he was put to flight because that jealousy made the King want him dead. But after successfully escaping the King's wrath and restraining himself in the Lord to keep from laying hands-on God's anointed King, even though he had many occasions to kill him. He still waited patiently on the Lord for his turn to walk in the full Assurance of his *Authority*. And while he waited, he learned valuable lessons; on how he would use his *Authority* to advance the cause of the Kingdom. And so, by the guiding hand of the Holy Spirit, he patiently endured the wilderness with all of its bad actors. And when his time came, his life became a living testimony to how we too must operate in that same *Authority*. So, before we continue with our **Word** Study, I'd like to share a testimony on one of the Lessons we learned as we walked in the **<u>Authority</u>** of Faith as a Babe. Please receive it in *strength*.

*Walk in the Light [**of His Authority**] and You will not Fulfill The desires of the Flesh [**of death Hell and the grave**]*

(1 John 1:7)

<u>Authority</u> *by* **Faith** *equals our* **Victory**

Another Testimony:

The simple act of shopping for groceries when you're financially challenged must also demand and command the simplicity of walking in the active **Authority** of Faith. Because this Faith Walk (to a new babe in Christ) is not yet established in them as an unshakeable fact. Until it begins to transform itself into the manifested reality of **their** need or hope, and once they're able to see what their invisible act of adolescent Faith has produced in plain sight, then the learning begins. And every time you step out into the realm of your new-found confidence in your Faith **(knowingly or unknowingly).**

The boldness of your **Authority** will begin to slowly accomplish the thing you send it to accomplish, according to the will of the Father. And then you can watch from within how much your confidence ignites the outward flow of what you believe. For such was the case for me. In this story of my early beginnings to the introduction of Spiritual **Authority**, as a Babe....

It was somewhere after April of 1991, early May and well after I was set free from the filthy habit of nicotine. And before, I'd been filled with the in-filling of the Holy Ghost. At that time, I was unemployed and solely dependent on my wife Sheila's income even though we'd been blessed to have found an unlikely ally in our landlord, my former foreman for the City of Charleston Parks Division, Mr. Thomas Raynor, a worldly man at the time. Who, by the outstretched Hand of God, was instrumental in our survival. Hence, I always said to myself (**God had an Angel waiting on us in Charleston; in advance of our arrival, and not just for our Natural deliverance: but more profitable, for our Spiritual needs as well**). *And of course, I'd never known Mr. Raynor prior to moving to Charleston* (**Tom as he preferred**). *— But since God never does anything out of character. He brought to us a man who'd grown up in the City of Moore Head, NC, approximately four hours away from my hometown* (**Shelby, NC**). *And only by the providential hand of God was this reality not a coincidence. You see, as a child; Tom's family was neighbors to a family that I'd known almost all of my life as my neighbors. At least since I was around eight years old, they were "the Secret family". And here, some 23 years later I met a past neighbor of my childhood neighbor. Now, I could've convinced myself that this was just luck or a chance encounter. But I say to you: there's no way you, or an angel, could ever convince me that this was just some freakish coincidence; not in a million years could you ever get me to evolve into that worldly way of thinking. Nevertheless: to make this life event into a short testimony and not a novel, I'll just tell you emphatically as LOUD AS I CAN, it was a Miracle.*

*So (**with just a little more back story**). I met Mr. Raynor when I was hired by the City of Charleston, Parks and Recreation Division. Mr. Raynor was my Foreman. And at that time Sheila and I had rented a room from a lady named 'Ms. Pearl'. She needed the extra income, and we a promotion from the Shelters. Hence, our own semi-private room. Now, after about a month of rooming with Ms. Pearl. I started working with Mr. Raynor after we'd gotten off work. He was a brick-mason for the City of Charleston, SC. And so, one day, on our way to a job, he began to tell me more about himself, and in his brief synopsis of his life in North Carolina and then learned that we shared a common past. And that common past, as previously stated, was of course the Secrets family.*

*And with that reality, and the fact that I was working with him after work, he quickly disclosed to me that he owned Real Estate. And that he owned a house in North Charleston that had come available, but that it had a little damage, with some manor wear and tear. But, if you want to rent it, you can do some of the repairs, and I'll rent it to you for $212.50. And with that said I was speechless and overwhelmed with numbness. After I gathered myself, I exclaimed with delight. We'll take it. (**Now, I'm telling you that the sovereign God of the universe — through the faithful prayers of my mother; worked out our deliverance, even before the foundation of the world. And I say that because, I don't believe that God does anything except that it has already been done in Christ Jesus, and the future manifestation of it, I believe, is simply based on the faith prayer of the believer — whether by another or by you**). —*

Can you believe it: $212.50, for a 2-bedroom house, and even with all its minor problems which were a few —the house, because of where it was, could've still fetched anywhere from $575 to $700.00 per month, at that time (1990) —

"God never does Anything Out of Character"

Now, back to 1991: So, with this obvious miracle, we were able to move out within two weeks. We would be paying Tom exactly $12.50, more *than what we paid Ms. Pearl (**A God-fearing woman**). And thanks be to God, we were able to pay rent, by food, pay our electric bill, and take care of a few other small necessities (**now that was all great**) until one of my unregenerated habits crept back into view (**of course I was a backslider at that point**). But there was nothing there to prevent me from being who I was. So, I quit my job because of an 'extenuating event' that's for another time. Not now!*

*And so, without a momentary thought, I quit my job. Never thinking once how disrespectful it was to my wife. Being such a self-centered individual at that time, that kind of thinking just wasn't a part of my reasoning (**no wonder my wife called me a casual bomb when we first met, and you know what, I laughed at it, though I'd never classified myself that way, she was right**). And to be honest, at that time, I just didn't consider her as a factor (**and if I had I'm pretty sure I wouldn't have quit my job**). I know now, that if I had discussed it with her then, 'in no uncertain terms' she would've told me not to quit my job. But I was strictly reacting with my emotions when I responded to the remarks my supervisor made about me not being a hero, in regard to my Military service... My response to him was swift. — It was a very self-exuberant, and high-minded description of what type of hero I deemed myself to be to my wife. But little did I know that my words, like an arrow, found its mark. — A mark that I had no idea existed. But over the next few weeks, I noticed a change in my supervisor's disposition toward me. He'd become very cold towards me. And began to give me some of the harder work assignments. — Well, one day, after he left us with our Foreman to go pick up supplies, I asked Tom what the supervisor's problem was. Tom laughed. Well, John, he has it in for you. Why? (**I naively asked.**) It's simple, Tom replied*

*(**I will paraphrase here with the gist of Tom's remarks**) Back when he was around 27 years old, his wife left him for an older man, a man in his 50's. When you told him that you were a 'hero' to your wife, you pissed him off. And now he's become your enemy. That blew my mind. — Now this was on a Friday, when Tom informed me (**chuckling**) about my*

*supervisors' childishness. —It bothered me the whole weekend, but of course, I didn't mention it to Sheila (**I should have**). On Monday, she packed my delicious lunch, I left the house as usual on my way to catch my ride... But instead of walking to meet him, I caught the bus down to the HR Department and resigned. (**But ain't God good even in our spiritual adolescence**), cause, before leaving downtown I found another Job but wouldn't be starting until the next Monday. So, after corralling that bit of good news, I hopped a bus and headed home. Once settled in my seat, I began to reflect on all that transpired from Friday to now (**Monday**). And suddenly, like a rock falling from the sky, it pommeled me. What had I done, 'quitting my job? Had I lost my freaking mind'. I became petrified. How would I explain this to Sheila? (**Now let me be perfectly clear, when I wrote this book, hindsight was not 20/20 — regarding this bad decision. I was selfishly immature as a babe in Christ**). I knew then that I was being selfish. Yet, even in the selfishness of my immaturity, somehow, I still believed God would work it out. (**But of course, I now know that to be a copout on my part, selfish or not**).*

*Nevertheless, 'I quit my job' without my Wife being involved in any part of this equation; and now, unwisely, I'd created an unnecessary problem. What a boneheaded decision; we'd only been married a little over a year. And even though I was blessed with a job, starting in just over a week from today (**on Monday**), that was my least concern, right now was my dilemma. And I was embarrassed at my stupidity. —After a rough week, with Sheila really upset with me, though she never argued with me, I felt her sting of indignation and believe me I deserved it. — Thank God, the next Monday was finally here, I was starting my new job, very proud of how quickly the God I was newly serving had moved on our behalf. — But approximately two weeks later I was out of a Job again... They weren't paying people, though I got mine (**in a personal check that was not only late, but also hard for me to get cashed**). Now comes the cold, harsh reality and the cost of me quitting my job at the City of Charleston. Because of it, I'd really put us on the verge of being homeless again.*

*Carelessly placing us in the middle of a self-inflicted pressure cooker. But most importantly, the pressure I put on Sheila to be the main income bearer while working part-time. Making her have to stretch an already stretched budget (**if we had one at all**). And how in the world could she stretch any more of that which could not be stretched. —*

Here Is Now the Place We Find Ourselves —

It is now the middle of summer. Money is very tight, beyond that faithful day of inextricable difficulty, quitting my job with the City has cost us. We were now basically broke. I was still unemployed, and we now depended heavily on my wife's part-time paycheck, we were down to bare necessities. On top of that, we also had a dog to feed, and we all needed some food. Now, our faith must take a giant leap forward. —

*So, '**here is now the place we find ourselves.**' Somewhere on our way to this place, we purchased a $35.00 Money Order from Food Lion. I believe it was for a bill, but at the moment, the urgency was food. But little did we know that this Money Order would be the catalyst that would open our spiritual minds to knowing how to walk in the **<u>Authority</u>** of our Faith. Causing the hidden man of the heart to begin to move to the forefront of our relationship with Christ and being led by the Holy-Spirit, even when it's not obvious to us that we were being led because of your adolescence, an inexperience to the leading of the Spirit of God. (**Please read 1 Peter, chapter 3:4**) Now, at this time, I do believe that Sheila was more Spiritually sensitive to God than I was.*

But like many men in this male dominated culture ignorant naivete, who weren't really raised in a sensitivity regarding women in society at large. Such was my own hidden attitude. Hence it really became evident in some of the earlier decisions I'd made. Now as I was saying before my philosophical rant. There we were, for lack of better terminology, constantly stealing from Peter to pay Paul, and whomever else we owed. Seemingly always behind the eightball. So, on this particular day we were just about out of food, our cabinets were just about empty. With that reality I needed to go to the store. It was approximately 2 miles away, I would have to *walk there because of how the bus route ran and then catch one home. The grocery store was Food Land, we had bought a $35 money order from them for another purpose, but it would now serve our immediate need. Since we bought it there, I felt as though they would be able to cash it there. After about an hour walk, i arrived and immediately began my shopping, had to time it with the round trip of the next bus.*

It took me around 35 minutes to finish my shopping, really trying to be as frugal as I could with just $35 dollars to spend, but I think I calculated close to what I had to spend, plus leave change for bus fare. Knowing that there was no wiggle room at all, seeing that I did not won't to be embarrassed by having to put items back, 'please God spare me the embarrassment.' So, while standing in line at the checkout, I quietly went back over my grocery estimate, and still feeling pretty comfortable with my estimate, I was next. I placed all my items on the counter. As I watched the cashier efficiently add each item, I was feeling pretty confident. After finally ringing up the last item the total left me around $2 and some change, the bus ride was only $1.50... Amen. Then I handed the cashier my money order, and without batting an eye, the cashier said: "Sir we don't take Money Orders for grocery" and with that I was floored, and all the vigor of my frugality melted away.

*But Mam; I exclaimed: I bought it here; it's got your Store name on it. I understand (**she said**), but it's against our policy. (**I stood there for about 30 seconds or more, speechless, in quiet humility. Finally, I snapped out of my despair, politely surrendering to my present dilemma**). Then, just as I was about to put everything back in the cart, an elderly gentleman walked up to the counter as if drawn by some unseen force. As though being in a rush, he calmly startled the Cashier, as her attention was fixed on me. And turning towards him in a smooth- abruptness, said: Can I help you, Sir?*

Angels Unawares —

*Yes, (**he responded**), I would like to buy a Money Order (**cashier**). Yes Sir, what's the amount of your Money Order? (**His answer: I'd like a***

$35.00 Money Order). Sure thing, let me void his grocery order, then I'll be glad to help you. (**Now I stood there in total disbelief, frozen for just a second or two, I couldn't believe it. And after quickly shaking off the freeze, I butted in before the Cashier could finish).** *Excuse me Sir, did I hear you right, you need a $35.00 Money Order, he looked at me with a slightly peculiar stare and responded: yes, that's correct. Well I said, glancing back and forth in a subtle way to both Cashier and to the Heaven-sent <u>Stranger</u>.— (**my ram in the bush**) (**Hebrews 13:2 -Be not forgetful to entertain Strangers: for thereby some have entertained Angels unawares**) Then in the momentary refrain, I quickly apologized to the Cashier; while at the same time, repeating my former question to my Ram in the bush. And standing there with uncommon patience, when at first entrance he seemed rushed, he cautiously responded (**again: that's correct**).* [Now, as I take a moment to reflect backwards into this rearview mirror called experience, with many years behind me, as I still endeavor to run with **patience** my own **walk** of faith. I, now perceive more clearly that this ever-increasing faith moment was indeed orchestrated by God –as a Stranger with 'Uncommon Patience' showed restraint to another stranger, just a babe in the **patience** arena.] *As soon as he affirmed his reason for coming into the store, which was to purchase a $35.00 Money Order. Without hesitation, I showed him my Blank Money Order. While briefly explaining my dilemma. He listened, and then he said: "If it's alright with Cashier, sure; I'll buy yours." (**She nodded yes, and then a verbal: 'of course that will be fine'**). And just like that, my Grocery problem was solved. I reached him the (**M.O.**), and he handed me $35.00, thanking me, as I simultaneously and humbly showed my enthusiastic appreciation, and with a God bless you or two, he received it with a smile, and out the door he went. I turned back to the cashier, who responded (**That was nice of him**), and I agreed as I happily replaced the items that I had taken off the counter, with my spirit re-inflated back to its previous state of frugality pride. My very courteous cashier and I were once again on the same page: with her doing her job, she delightfully carried out her duty, as I packed my own grocery*

bags, which was not unusual for me. I told her how much I appreciated her patience and kindness towards me, I paid her and grabbed my bags, and with that done, I blessed her with a "God Bless You" while headed out the door, my bus would be coming soon.

Testimony Conclusion:

*No sooner had I arrived at the bus stop, I glanced to the left, and the bus had turned the corner, just seconds away from the stop: 'And I thought to myself, – boy, just in the nick of time.' With the brakes squeaking to a stop, I jumped upon the Bus, paid my fare, found my way to the back of the Bus, and took a great big sigh of relief. Once I settled into my seat, the magnitude and the pressure of all that had transpired in those few moments in the store made me break out in silent praise, inwardly shouting, with joy —to the top of my spiritual voice, the name of the Lord. As I continued to rejoice with thanksgiving in the closet of my heart (**still a babe to spiritual expressions, both inwardly and outwardly. Still, I knew I had to praise the Lord**)*

*With a full heart overflowing with Hallelujahs, I knew I had to release all that would come out, and for me, there were two primary release valves for whatever I needed to say. One of them, since I was 6 years old, was Art, and the other was Writing, predominantly Poetry (**thanks to my High School Art Instructor: "Ms. Myra Ware" who discovered within me, my writing potential**). And right then, on that bus, with my shopping list pad; I knew I had to pen my joy. I had to release that which had been newly born, deep within my Soul of gratitude for all that He's done, will do, and is doing for me now. Therefore, I was moved by the Holy-Spirit to write this Poetry of Praise, after receiving a mighty revelation on the basic <u>tenets of Faith</u> and the **Authority** it wields. As was evidenced by my assumption: "That I was going to buy groceries for the house and catch the Bus back home." And with that simple assumption, I was moved by a child-like faith to accomplish my goals, and with that kind of innocent faith, everything else that would follow was setup in advance. Henceforth, from the time*

*I left the house to the moment I returned, I was walking in **Victory, by the Authority of my Faith**— it was all ordained in Christ by the Father. With that said, I hope you can hear what the Spirit is saying to you. Cause for me, it was simply this: John, when you wield your Authority, whether as a babe in Christ or a giant in the Faith, your Victory is always the result. Now, with that said, let me share my poetry of praise!*

Victory Praise:

I see our Victory, coming to mine and me. Shot like an Arrow from the rainbow of **Heaven**. I see our Victory. All **hail** to Thee — who by grace set my captive soul free...I shout Victory...***Hallelujah, Hallelujah*** — In the Spirit, I see all my enemies as they scatter, hide and flee. ***All glory to thee, I shout Victory*** Amen!

2Cor 10:8 - For though I should boast somewhat of our <u>**Authority**</u>, which the Lord hath given us for edification:

Titus 2:*(11)* - 15 - These things speak, and exhort, and rebuke with all <u>***Authority***</u>. Let no man despise you.

Blessed *(Definition -* **adj. 1.** holy; sacred. **2.** full of bliss; fortunate*)- [Word of Knowledge As we walk the walk, and talk the talk, while living daily in the order of righteousness we then have access to all that God has prepared for us and has* <u>***Blessed***</u> *us with. According to our daily provisions freely given to us in Christ.* **Amen.***]*

Eph 1:3 - <u>***Blessed***</u> be the God and Father of our Lord Jesus Christ,

who has <u>***Blessed***</u> us with all spiritual blessings in heavenly places in Christ:

Rom 4:7 - <u>***Blessed***</u> are they whose iniquities are forgiven.

Rom 4:8 - <u>***Blessed***</u> is the man or *(woman)* into whom the Lord will not impute sin. (*Definition* - Impute *v.* to be considered guilty of; blame; charge)

Jam 1:12 - **_Blessed_** is the man or*(woman)* that endures temptation:

Jam 1:25 - But whoso looks into the perfect law of liberty, and *will* continue therein, he being not a forgetful hearer, but a doer of the work, this man or *(woman)* shall be **_Blessed_** in his or *(her)* deeds....

Seven Sacred Promises to the _Blessed,_ from the Book of Revelations:

Rev 1:3 - **_Blessed_** is he/*she* that read, and they that hear the *words* of this Prophesy: and *keep* those things that are written therein: for the time is at *hand.*

Rev 22:14 - **_Blessed_** are they that do *His* Commandments, that they may have a *right* to the **Tree** of Life:

Rev 22:7 - *Behold,* I come quickly: **_Blessed_** is he/*she* that keep the sayings of the Prophesy of this Book.

Rev 16:15 - *Behold,* I come as a **thief, _Blessed_** is he/*she* that watch, and keep his/*her* Garment:

Rev 14:13 - **_Blessed_** are the *dead,* which die in the Lord from hence-

-forth:

Rev 19:9 - **_Blessed_** are they which are called — unto the *Marriage Supper* of the Lamb.

Rev 20:6 - **_Blessed_** and *Holy* is he/*she* — that has *part* in the First–**Resurrection:** on such the Second *death* has no **P**ower, but they shall be **P**riests of God and of Christ, and shall reign with **Him** —

Blessing – (*Question:* What is this **Cup** of **Blessing**? *Answer:* So, I believe that the answer to the foundational question can be found in the book of 'Matthew, *Chapter 26:27–28* (it reads) - *And He took the Cup, and gave thanks, and gave it to them; saying —* **"Drink ye all of it: for this is My Blood of the New-Testament**(will, covenant), **which is shed for many for the remission**(forgiveness) **of sins"**)— Now, I personally believe from a spiritual perspective, that this act by Christ; sealed forever the release of the **Blessing**. And you will find this confirmed by revelation to Apostle Paul in 1 Corinthians, *Chapter 10:15–16*(and it reads) *I speak as to wise men, judge ye what I say. The* **Cup** *of* **Blessing** *which we bless: is it not the communion of the* **Blood of Christ?** So as you can see, this *Glory* that has been freely given to us, has been so given; that we might not suffer lack. —Seeing that where lack exists in our lives, the Kingdom cannot be properly assisted by us toward the timely completion and furtherance of the Gospel's reach to the uttermost parts of the Globe. Just like God declared to Queen Esther by the mouth of *His* Servant, Mordecai **'the Book of Esther,** *Chapter5:13–14'* *saying: Think not with thy self that thou shalt escape in the King's house* (to hide, or shirk from her duty), *more than all the Jews. For if thou altogether hold thy peace at this time, then shall their enlargement, and deliverance arise to* **(Them)** *the Jews, from another* **(source) Place,** *— but you and your Fathers house will be destroyed.* Therefore, I do believe that it's vitally important to God how we handle this **'Cup of Blessing** because when we partake of the **Cup**, we must realize, with great *spiritual audacity,* that the **Cup** is the Foundation from which all the Benefits of the Kingdom, are to us Given, and not just because of us —but because of who is identified in *us*, that is to say: 'Christ in us, the Hope of Glory.' He who, for the Joy that was set before Him, in a voluntary display of sacrifice, endured the *Cross* on behalf of *'we, the beneficiaries.'* Delivering to us once and for all this *indelible* and unremovable **Cup of Blessing**. Therefore, for us, there is no more need for a **death** sacrifice of any kind, except for the *"Living*

Kind.") (Roman, Chapter 12:1 - I beseech ye therefore brethren, by the mercies of God, that you present your bodies "A Living Sacrifice" Holy, acceptable unto God, which is your reasonable Service.) —

And in conclusion to this 'Commentary,' we must make sure that when we partake of this, our very own **Cup of _Blessing_**, it does not ever become a stumbling block by our immaturity—wherein we began to *worship* the **Cup**, instead of the One from whom all **Blessings Flow. —Amen!**

Rom 15:29 - And I am sure that, when I come unto you, I shall come in the fulness of the **_Blessing_** of the Gospel of Christ.

1Cor 10:16 - The Cup of **_Blessing_** that we *bless,* — is it not the *Communion* of the Blood of Christ?

Gal 3:14 - That the **_Blessing_**_of Abraham might come on the gentiles(*us*) through Jesus Christ.

Heb 6:14 - Saying, surely **_Blessing_** I will bless thee, and multiplying I will multiply thee.

1Pet 3:9 - Not rendering **evil** for evil, or **railing** for railing: but contrariwise **_Blessing_** knowing that you are thereto called, that you should **_inherit_** a **_Blessing_**

***Ezek 44:30 - And the **first** of all the First fruits, of all things, and every oblation [offering] of all, of every sort of your oblations, shall be the priest's: you shall also give unto the priest the **first** of your dough [*old meaning bread. Revelational meaning substance. Slang and modern term for money*], that he [*the priest, Jesus*] may cause the **_Blessing_** to rest in your house (**_Example_:** *first apple on the tree, first apple tree—first wages earned or a tenth of your dollar, first 24-min's. of 2-hrs & 40-min's, or first 2-hrs & 40-min's of a 24-hour day, etc. any scenario will work, you choose: Now this is all in regards to sowing and reaping, tithing, and offerings, according to*

Abraham, who did not tithe or sow under the Law, and as an example by Paul, in reference to him raising money for the Gospel's sake, and also, for the need of the people: **1 Corinthians, chapter 16:2 - Upon the first day of the week let everyone of you lay by him in store** [*bank it or save it*] **as God has prospered him, that there be no collecting when I come**)****

Boldness - *(You shall receive Power after that the Holy Ghost has come, etc.* **Acts 1:8**)

Acts 4:13 - Now when they saw the **_Boldness_** of Peter and John, and perceived that they were unlearned and ignorant men, they marveled; and they took knowledge of them, that they had been with Jesus.

Acts 4:29 - And now, Lord behold their threatening and grant unto thy servants, that with all **_Boldness_** they may speak thy **word**.

Eph 3:12 - In whom we have **_Boldness_**, and access with *Confidence* by the faith of ***Him...***

Phil 1:20,21 - According to my earnest expectation and my hope, that in nothing I shall be ashamed, but that with all **_Boldness_**, as always, *so* now also Christ shall be magnified in my body, whether it be by life or by death. For to me, Christ is Life, dying is Gain...

Heb 10:19 - Having therefore, brethren, **_Boldness_** to enter the Holiest, by the ***blood*** of Jesus...

Charity - (*Charity,* for me, is a proactive demonstration of Love, Loving, and Caring for all in need, but especially for the least of us, even for the so-called unlovable or unredeemable of us. But without any kind of reservation whatsoever, I truly believe that the word Charity is the full outward expression of God's Love and is therefore very important in how we approach the delivery of the Gospel of Christ, "the *Good News*" to the lost, and to the poor, so I will not skimp here. I will try to be very concise with this word, *Charity*, in the space allotted to me here. *So,* as you study this **word,** just let its power begin to soak into your spirit. And while you do so, there are a few scriptures in the *book* of Matthew (*Chapter* 25:34 - 40) that Jesus uses to describe the proactive Saint. The Saint, who, because of **Christ's** Love-Nature in them, shows forth the tenderness of **Christ's** love by the comfort that <u>*Charity*</u> delivers to so many in need. Now, without further ado, here are the Scripture verses in *sequence*. — *(Then shall the King say to them on his right hand. Come, ye blessed of my Father,* **(and)** *inherit the Kingdom prepared for you before the foundation of the world —For I was hungry, and you gave Me meat—I was thirsty, and you gave Me drink—I was a Stranger and you took Me in—I was naked, and you clothe Me— I was sick and you visited Me—I was in prison and you came to Me: Then shall the righteous answer Him, saying: Lord, when did we see You hungry and feed You? Or thirsty, and gave You drink? —When did we see You as a stranger, and take You in? Or naked, and clothe You? Or when did we see You sick, or in prison and come to You? —*** And the King shall answer and say unto them *** Verily I say unto you — "In as much as you have done it to the least of these My Brethren, you have done it unto Me)* ***

1Cor13:1-13 - Though I speak with the tongues of men (*different languages*) and Angels (*tongues, gifts of tongues, unknown tongues*), and have not <u>*Charity,*</u> I am become as sounding brass, or a tinkling cymbal: —

And though I have the gift of prophecy, understanding all mysteries, and all knowledge: And though I have all faith, so that I am*(able)* to remove mountains, and have not <u>*Charity*</u>. I am nothing. And though I bestow all my goods to feed the poor— and though I give my body to be burned, and *(still)* have not <u>*Charity*</u>: it profits me nothing. — <u>*Charity*</u> suffers long and is kind; <u>*Charity*</u> envies not; <u>*Charity*</u> boasts not of itself, is not puffed up, *(and)* does not behave itself unseemly, *(does not seek* its own *glory)*, is not easily provoked *(and)*thinks no evil. *(It)*does not rejoice in iniquity, but rejoices in the Truth bears all things, believeth all things, hope*(in)*all things, endures all things. <u>*Charity*</u> never fails, but whether there be **prophecies**, they shall fail. Whether there be **tongues**, they shall cease: whether there's **know – ledge,** it shall vanish away: for we know in part, and we **prophesy** in part. *** But when that which is perfect has come, then that which is in part, shall be done away. — * — When I was a child *(unlearned and ignorant)*, I spake as a child *(immature, like an immature and young child, a babe in Christ not yet mature in Spiritual matters – **1King 3:7 - And now, O Lord my God thou hast made thy servant King instead of David my father; and I am but a little child: — I know not how to go out or come in)*,** I understood as a child, I*(also)* thought as a child: But when I became a man *(Spiritually Mature, Spiritually responsible for my own Faith Walk)*, I put away childish things. For now, we see through a glass darkly, but then face to face: Now, I know in part, but then shall I know even as also I am known. And now abided **faith, hope, <u>Charity</u>,** these *three*: but the **greatest** of these is <u>*Charity*</u> —

1 Cor 16:14 - Let all your things be done with <u>**Charity**</u>.

2 Th 1:3 - We are bound to thank God always for you, brethren, as is proper. Because your *faith* grows exceedingly, and the <u>*Charity*</u> of you towards each other abounds...

1 Tim 1:5 - Now the end of the *Commandment* is <u>**Charity**</u>: Out of a pure heart, and of a good conscience, and of*faith* unfeigned.

2 Tim 2:22 - Flee also youthful lust: but follow righteousness, *faith,* <u>*Charity*</u>, peace; with them that call on the Lord out of a pure heart.

1 Pet 4:7,8 - But the end of all things is at hand:*(so)* be you therefore sober, and watch *(as you)* pray. And above all things;

have(*intensely*) fervent **_Charity_** among yourselves. For **_Charity_** shall cover a multitude of sins.

2 Pet 1:7 - And to Godliness, brotherly kindness; and to brotherly kindness, **_Charity_**.\

Rev 2:19 - *I know thy works, and **Charity**, and service, and **faith** —*

CHILDREN

Rom 8:16,17 - The *Spirit* itself bears witness with our *spirit*, that we are the **_Children_** of God. And if **_Children_**, then heirs. Heirs of God, and joint-heirs with Christ: if so be that we *Suffer* with Him — That we *might* be also Glorified together.

Rom 9:8 - That is, they which are the _children_ of the flesh, these are not the _children_ of God: but the **_Children_** of the Promise (*those who are Born-again*) are counted for the Seed.

Gal 3:7 - Know you therefore that they which are of *faith*, the same are the **_Children_** of Abraham.

Gal 3:26 - For you are all the **_Children_** of God—by *faith* in Christ*

Eph 1:5 - Having predestined us unto the *adoption* of **_Children_** by Jesus Christ to *Himself*, according to the good pleasure of His will.

Eph 5:1 - Be you therefore followers of God as dear **_Children_**: —

1 Th 5:5 - Ye are all **_Children_** of *Light*, and the **_Children_** of the *Day*, we are not of the night, nor of *darkness*..

Children: Simply, Love One-Another

1 Jn 3:10 - In this the **_Children_** of God are Manifest —and (*also*) the _children_ of the devil: Whosoever does no Righteousness, is not of God, neither he that **loves** not his *brother*.

1 Jn 4:4 - Ye are of God, little **_Children_**; and have Overcome them *(the evil one, and his demonic cohorts)*. Because **G**reater is *He* that is in you, than *he* that is in the *world.*

Discern – (To be able to **Discern** for a Christian is like a blind man who is able, by way of a sixth sense sensitivity, to maneuver himself around town as if he had sight. But just like the blind man who is not trained in his extra sensory capabilities, we too *(without spiritual discernment and a sensitivity toward the Light of God)*, would have a hard time surviving, thriving, and living a successful life in Christ.

Likewise, we too cannot escape the fiery trials and tests that come to make us strong. Causing us to dig deeper into the hidden places of the word of God. As we fight with great effort to reach the heights in Him, that will keep us sharp to the devices of the enemy. And just as the blind man, through the eyes of his hands, takes hold of braille to his own glory. And by his mastery of ordering his steps by his guide dog, he masters the ability, as much as he needs, to discern and navigate his world. Likewise, a saint must become his own student, to the mastery of spiritual discernment, as much as he is able to receive, towards the prosecuting and carrying out of his *new-life* agenda, which is the Life that he or she must live by **faith** in the Son of God, who is their purpose. — **A**men!

Heb 5:14 - But strong meat belongs to them that are— of *fullage*: even those who by reason of use, have their *senses* exercised — to **_Discern_** both good and bad. —

Discerned (Please *Refer* back to the previous paragraph and commentary on the significance and the importance of why we must learn to **_Discern_**)

1 Cor 2:14 - But the natural man receives not the things of the *Spirit*

of God, for they are foolishness unto him: neither can he know them because they are *spiritually **Discerned***. —

Discerning (Hereto, please *Refer* back to the previous commentary on the word discern.) *

1 Cor 11:27-30 - Wherefore whomever shall eat this **bread** and *drink* this **Cup** of the Lord unworthily, shall be guilty of the **Body** & **blood** of the Lord. But let a man examine himself, and so let him eat of that **bread** and *drink* of that **Cup** (*finding himself worthy by spiritual discernment of the Cross*). But he that *eats* and *drinks* unworthy, *eats* and *drinks* damnation to himself, not **Discerning** the Lord's **Body**.

For this reason, many are weak and sickly among you, and many **die**.

1 Cor 12:10 - To *one* the working of **miracles**; to another **prophecy**; to another ***Discerning*** of Spirits: —

Evangelist (*The* dominant purpose of this call is predominantly used for the furtherance of the *Good News*, as it calls out into the highways and the hedges for men, women, boys and girls who haven't yet heard the saving **grace** of the Good News. This strategically called position is the main outreach by which *Evangelists* who are gifted in this ministry, and to those who have the evangelistic responsibility, as parents, friends, and all those who reach out in witness to the *goodness* of God, to the winning of a soul. Out of all the Gifts of the Spirit, I believe that it has contributed to making more disciples (*in my opinion, if I could be so bold*) than any of the other **Four-Gifts**. Hence, we read in the New Testament [Mark, *Chapter* 16:15] on how the *Foundation* was laid, following the direction of Christ, as He **commanded**, saying: **"Go ye into all the World, preaching the Good News to every creature"**) —

Definition of: **Evangelist *n.* 1.** Anyone who preaches the Gospel*(proclaim)* especially a preacher who travels from place to place holding religious meetings. **2.** Any of the *four* writers of the Gospels; *Matthew, Mark, Luke or John.)* —

2 Tim 4:5 - But watch thou in all things, endure afflictions — *do* the work of an <u>*Evangelist*</u>, make full proof of <u>*your*</u> Ministry.

(*The 3rd Gift—The most Versatile and Interchangeable of the Five*)

Eph 4:11 - And *He* gave some: Apostles, and some Prophets, and some <u>*Evangelists*</u> — *[Please Refer back to the <u>Evangelist - Commentary</u>]*

Faith (*Faith:* is to a Saint, as oxygen is to all Life. Without it, all creatures great and small would cease to exist. And of alike importance —<u>*Faith*</u> for the Child of God is the single force that not only sustains us in our press toward the *Target*, which is our Goal and Prize in Christ, but without it, we would never be able to please the Father. Or let's put it another way: Your <u>*Faith*</u> is the only Power that will move God through Christ on your behalf. It caused God to move on behalf of a Lost-Creation, — sending his stealthy weapon prepared before the Foundation of the *world*. And by this weapon called Christ, *the Anointed One.* – The Father reaches into the emptiness of our souls and creates in us a *new heart* and by our <u>*Faith,*</u> gives us a better Covenant. One that gives us the Authority, to daily experience for ourselves the ***Plentifulness of the Kingdom.*** Giving us access to gifts like joy, peace, and the Security of Heaven. Not to mention your own Home, with a crown of *Righteousness* as your reward *[According to Apostle Paul: 2 Tim 4:8]*

Foundational Scriptures & Definitions for this Benefit:

Webster's New World Dictionary — DEFINITIONS:

Faith *n.* **1.** belief or trust that does not question or ask for Proof. **2.** belief in God and religion [Job kept his *faith* in spite of his **troubles**]— **4.** being loyal; allegiance [the **Knights** *pledge* their *faith* to the King] —

Kings James Version — SCRIPTURES:

Faith - 1. Hab **2:4**-Behold: his soul which is **lifted-up**, is not **upright** in him: "But the Just shall *live* by his *faith*"- **2.** Mk **4:34**-And *He* said unto her: *"Daughter, your faith hast made you whole."*

Acts 6:8 - And Stephen, full of <u>**Faith**</u> and power, did great wonders and miracles.

Acts 11:24 - For he was a good man, and full of the Holy Ghost and of <u>**Faith**</u> *(and by his faith)*: many people were added unto the Lord.

Acts 26:18 - To open their eyes, and to turn them from darkness to Light, and from the power of Satan unto God. That they may receive forgiveness of sins, and *(to)* gain inheritance amongst them who are sanctified by <u>**Faith**</u> that is in <u>**Me**</u> *(Christ)*

Rom 1:17 - For therein is the **R**ighteousness of God revealed, from

<u>***Faith***</u> to <u>***Faith***</u>: as it is written, 'The just shall live by <u>**Faith**</u>'.

Rom 3:20-22 - Therefore by the deeds of the Law shall no flesh be justified in *His* sight: for by the Law is the knowledge of sin. But now the Righteousness of God without the Law is manifested, being witnessed by the **Law** and the **Prophets**— *even* the Righteousness of God, which is by <u>**Faith**</u> of Jesus Christ unto all*** *(that believe)*. —

Rom 3:28 - Therefore, we conclude that a man is justified by _Faith_, without the **_"hard labor"_** of the Law.

Rom 5:1 - Therefore being justified by _Faith_: we have peace with God, through our Lord Jesus Christ...

Rom 10:8, 9 - But what saith it? The **word** is near you, even in your mouth, and in your heart: that is, the **word** of _Faith_ that we preach: That, if you confess with your mouth the Lord Jesus, _and believe_ in

your heart that God has raised **Him** from the dead, you'll be saved.

Rom 12:3 - "God dealt to every man _(woman, boy, and girl)_ the measure of _**Faith"**_.

1 Cor 16:13 - Watch ye, stand fast in the _Faith_: _(Be still. Be strong)_!

2 Cor 5:7 - ("For **we _Walk by Faith — and not by Sight_** ")

Gal 2:16 - : _Even_ we have believed in Jesus Christ, that we might be justified by the _Faith_ of Christ, and not by the works of the Law.

Gal 3:9 - So then, they which be of _Faith_, are blessed with _faithful_ Abraham.

Gal 3:11 - But that —no man is justified by the Law in the sight of God, it is evident: **_'For_**, the just shall live by _**Faith'**_.

Eph 2:8 - For by grace are you saved through _Faith_; and that not of yourselves: it is the **G**ift of God.

Eph 6:16 - Above all; taking the _Shield_ of _Faith_ —

1 Th 5:8 - But let us who are of the **Day**, be sober; —putting on the **breastplate** of _Faith_ and Love:

2 Tim 2:22 - Flee also youthful lust: —Follow Righteousness, *Faith*,

Charity, Peace, with them that call on the Lord out of a pure Heart.

2 Tim 4:7 - I have **fought** a **G**ood *fight*, I have finished my course, I have kept the *Faith.*

Heb 11:1 - Now *Faith* is the substance of things hoped for, (*and*) the evidence of things not seen.

Jam 1:3 - Know this, that the trying of your *Faith*— works patience.

2 Th 3:1, 2 - **Finally** Brethren pray for us. That the **word** of the Lord will have *free* course, and be **G**lorified, even as it is with you. And that we be delivered from unreasonable men(*who*)don't have *Faith*.

Father (**W**e now have open access to the Father, by way of Christ: this is the single and most rudimentary benefit that we must simply not take for granted at any place or time in our '*born-again*' walk. It is a critical issue of the utmost importance and demands a keen, and constant awareness on this *faith-walked* journey. A walk that encompasses all types of levels, causing us to confront many issues of life. Many issues that can only be confronted by us since we now have access '*by faith*' to the *Father*. And I truly believe that we must seek to become more intimately enthralled in our new and *living* access to the *Father*. An access that is in us. That is to say: *"Christ in us, the hope of Glory"*, who is: our one-way *Ticket* to the *Father)*. — Amen!

Acts 1:4 [*Jesus last in person meeting with His disciples before His Ascension*]-

And, being assembled together with them, commanded them that they should not depart from Jerusalem. But wait for the *Promise* of the **_Father_**, which*** you have heard of me.

Rom 8:15 - For you have not received the spirit of bondage again to fear, but you have received the **S**pirit of **adoption**, whereby we cry; *Abba,* **_Father_** —

Rom 15:6 - That you may with one mind —*and* one mouth **G**lorify God, *even* the **_Father_**

2 Cor 1:3 - Blessed be God***the **_Father_** of our Lord Jesus Christ, the **_Father_** of *mercies*, and the God of all **C**omfort......

2 Cor 6:17, 18 - **W**herefore come out from among them, and be you separated **saith** the Lord, and touch not the unclean thing: and I will receive **you**. And I will be a **_Father_** unto you, and you shall be my *sons* and *daughters* — **saith** the Lord **A**lmighty.

Gal 4:6 - And because you are *sons*, God has sent forth the **S**pirit of **His** Son into your hearts crying —**A**bba, **_Father_** Amen!

Godliness (Now, according to the Flow of the Bible regarding this **Word**, before Christ. There was no such opportunity for an individual Jew to ever choose **Godliness** for his or herself since there was no avenue in the Law that could get them there. This **Godliness**, or Holiness, was designated and appointed by God to individuals such as Prophets, Kings, and Priest. They were the only ones chosen to guide God's people through the maze of the Law that he might accomplish in it, the road map which would lead us to the cross of Calvary and into the passion of our Christ. Who for the Joy that was set before Him: for our sakes *the Last, and the First)*, He endured the agonizing consequences of His obedience. So that by it, He could bring many Sons and Daughters to Glory — as He watches His word accomplish what it was purposed in us to do: producing in us, once again, the image of a *Triumvirate* God, which is the image of **Godliness**: and is for us, our one *Perfectible Vision*.) [*Please read: Mt 19:30/Mk 10:31/Lk 13:30*] — Selah!

1Tim 2:1, 2 - I exhort therefore, that; first, supplications, prayers, intercessions, and giving of thanks; be made for all *men:* For Kings, and for all that are in Authority. That we may lead a quiet and peaceable Life in all **_Godliness_** — *and* Honesty.

1Tim - 3:16 - And without controversy, — great is the Mystery of **_Godliness_**: God was manifest in the flesh, justified in the Spirit, seen of Angels, preached unto Gentiles, *(and)* believed on in the world: Received up into Glory. Amen!

1 Tim 4:7, 8 - But refuse profane, and *old* wives fables, and exercise thyself rather unto **_Godliness_** — *for* bodily exercise profits little: but **_Godliness_** is profitable unto all things:

1 Tim 6:11 - But you, **O** man of God, *flee* these things; and follow after Righteousness, **_Godliness_**; *faith, love, patience, meekness.*

2 Pet 1:3 - According as **His** **D**ivine **P**ower —hath given unto us all things that pertain unto Life and **_Godliness_**...

2 Pet 3:10, 11 — *And the elements shall melt with a fervent heat, the earth also, and the works that are therein, shall be burned up.*

Seeing then that all these things shall be dissolved: What manner of **Person** ought you to be, in all Holy *Conversation*; and **_Godliness_**:

Godly (*No* excuses. - We can now live a **Godly Life**)

2 Tim 3:12 - Yes, and All that live **_Godly_** in Christ Jesus shall suffer:

2 Tit 2:12 Teaching us that by denying **ungodliness** and worldly lusts, we should live soberly, righteously, and **_Godly_**: in this

present world **Good** (*Good* news folks: we are now able to do *good* daily, as much as we desire to: or shall I rather say. We are now able, by revelation and discernment, to do as much **Good** as we want to. Doing **Good** is all up to you, based on where you are Spiritually in your *faith -walk*, and your Love-Affair with Christ) —

Acts 4:9, 10 - If we this day be examined of the **good** *deed* done to this impotent man, by what means he is made whole. — Be it known unto you all that by the name of Jesus Christ of Nazareth: whom you **crucified**, whom God raised from the dead: even by Him doth this man stand here *W*hole...

Gal 6:10 - As we have therefore opportunity, let us do **Good** unto all *men*...especially unto them who are of the *H*ousehold of Faith.

Eph 2:10 - For we are **His** *W*orkmanship —, Created in Christ Jesus unto **Good**-works, which God has before ordained:

1 Th 5:15 - See that none render evil for evil unto any **man**. But ever follow that which is **Good**, both among yourselves and to all *men*...

2 Th 2:17 - Comfort your hearts, and establish you; in every **Good**

word, and work.

1 Tim 6:12 - *F*ight the **Good** fight of Faith, lay hold on *Eternal Life.*

2 Tim 2:3 - Thou, therefore, endure hardness as a **Good** *S*oldier
***

1 Pet 3:10 For he that *L*ove Life, and see **good** days—, let him *hold back* his tongue from evil, and his lips from speaking *crafti-*

ness. Let him *shun, stay away from* evil, and do **Good**: let him seek Peace, and *follow - after* it.

Grace (*Foundational* Scripture - *St John* 1:17 - *For the Law was given by Moses —, but Grace and Truth came by Jesus Christ.* Amen!)

Acts 13:43 - Now, when the congregation was broken up, many of the Jews and *religious* proselytes followed Paul and Barnabas, who speaking to them, persuaded them to continue in the **Grace** of God.

Rom 1:5 - By whom we have received **Grace**, and Apostleship; *for Obedience* to the Faith (*the Body of Christ and the Plan of God*) ...

Rom 12:6 - Having then *gifts* differing according to the **Grace** —;

1 Cor 1:3 - **Grace** be unto you, and Peace from God our Father, and from the Lord Jesus Christ...

2 Cor 9:14 - And by their Prayer for you, which **long- after** you for the Exceeding **Grace** of God in you...

2 Cor 12:9 - And He said unto me: *My* **Grace** is sufficient for you—

Eph 2:4,5 - But God: (–) when we were dead in sins, has quickened us together with Christ (*by* **Grace** *you are saved*) ...

Eph 2:8 - For by **Grace** are you Saved through Faith: (it is The **Gift**)

Heb 4:16 - Let Us therefore come *boldly* unto the Throne of **Grace**, that we may obtain *mercy* —and find **Grace** to help in time of need.

For You Know the **GRACE** *Of Our LORD, JESUS CHRIST: That Though HE Was RICH*

*Yet for YOUR Sakes HE Became POOR That YOU Through HIS POVERTY (Might be) MADE RICH****[**2Corinthians 8:9**]

HOPE

Rom 8:20 -25 - For the creature was made subject to vanity, not willingly, but *(because)*of Him who has subjected the same in <u>*Hope*</u>. Because the creature itself **(will)** also shall be delivered from the Bondage of **corruption** into the glorious liberty **of** the Children of God [**Now I do believe that the creature, in this verse, is the very life-force of the Earth, for it to was corrupted by the fall of Man**]– For we know that the whole creation groans, together until now. And not only*(do)* they; but ourselves also who have the <u>*first fruits of the Spirit*</u>: even we ourselves groan within ourselves, waiting for the Adoption *(that is to say, namely)* the Redemption of our *Body* —. For we are saved by <u>*Hope*</u>: but <u>*Hope*</u> that is seen, is not <u>*Hope:*</u> —*for* what a man sees, why would he yet <u>*Hope?*</u> But if we <u>*Hope*</u> for that, we see not: then do we with Patience wait for it...

1 Cor 9:10 - Or saith *He* it together for our sakes? *(Of course) for* our sakes, no doubt; this is written:*(so)* that he that plow, should plow in <u>*Hope*</u>. And he that *"separate the seed"* in <u>*Hope*</u>, shall be partaker of **His***(Christ)* <u>*Hope*</u>.

Col 1:27 - To whom God would make known, what is the Riches of the Glory of *this* Mystery among the **gentiles** — which is Christ in you the <u>*Hope*</u> of Glory:

1Th 5:8 - But let us, who are of the *day*; be Sober: — putting on the *Breastplate* of *Faith* and *Love*; and for a *Helmet:* — the <u>*Hope*</u> of Salvation....

Heb 6:11 - And we desire — that every one of you do show the same

Diligence to the *full* Assurance of <u>Hope</u> until the end:

Heb 6:19 - Which <u>Hope</u>, we have as an Anchor of the *Soul*...

Holy Ghost *(There are* two ***terminologies*** that exist for this Third Person of the *Trinity*. The one here is more widely spoken of and used in the New Dispensation, which is the Church, but the other, the *Holy Spirit*, is not as widely used in the New Dispensation, as prominently as it was in the Old. But you might want to broaden your own research on the Era and Time of use of both ***terminologies*** for your own increase. And for me, I will do the same, but for ***now***, this is where I desire that we can join together to seek out for ourselves the *Deep* Things of God. So, let's enjoy the ride in either form we choose: the ***Holy Ghost*** or ***Holy-Spirit***, your Choice.)

Rom 14:17 - For the Kingdom of God is not *meat* and *drink*, but Righteousness and Peace, and Joy in —the <u>*Holy-Ghost*</u>...

Rom 15:13 - Now the God of ***hope*** fill you with all Joy and Peace in believing: That you may ***abound*** in ***hope***, through the Power of the <u>*Holy-Ghost*</u>...

1Cor 6:18, 19 - "Flee Fornication" What? Know you not, that your Body is the Temple of the <u>*Holy-Ghost*</u>; which is in you— which you have of God, and you are not your *own*!

2 Cor 6:6 - By *pureness–knowledge–longsuffering–kindness*, by the <u>*Holy-Ghost*</u>, and by Love Unfeigned *(by Genuine Love)* —

1 Th 1:5 - For our Gospel came to you not in *word* only, but also in Power, and in the <u>*Holy-Ghost*</u>:

1 Th 1:6 - And you became *followers* of Us, and of the Lord, having received the ***Word*** in much affliction – with Joy of the <u>*Holy-Ghost*</u> .

Tit 3:5 - Not by *works* of **R**ighteousness which we have done, but according to His *Mercy*, ***He saved*** Us; —by the washing of **R**egeneration: and*(by)* **R**enewing of the <u>***Holy-Ghost***</u>....

Heb 2:4 - God also bearing them *witness*, both with **S**igns and*(with)*

Wonders, and with *Divers-miracles*, and **G**ifts of the <u>***Holy-Ghost***</u>:

1 Jn 5:7 - For there are **T**hree that bear <u>record</u> in Heaven, the Father, the ***Word***, and the <u>***Holy Ghost***</u> — and these <u>***Three***</u> are One!

Jude *vs* 20, 21 - But you Beloved, building up yourselves on **Y**our most Holy ***faith***, Praying in the <u>***Holy-Ghost: —***</u>

2 Cor 13;12 - 14 – **G**reet one another with a *Holy-kiss*: all the Saints salute you. The Grace of the Lord Jesus Christ, and the Love of God and the ***Communion*** of the <u>***Holy Ghost***</u>: be with you **A**ll. —Amen!

Holy Spirit *(Primarily* used in the Old Dispensation *[Law]:* —For me, the ***foundational*** **S**cripture is found in the Book of Psalms. There, King David describes the desperation and poverty of his soul without the ***Holy-Spirit*** in his life: listen to how he describes it in Psalms 51:11, 12 - " *Cast me not away from thy Presence, and take not thy **Holy Spirit** from me, restore unto me the Joy of thy Salvation"* *** And of course, even before King David; that same ***Holy Spirit*** was called the ***Spirit*** of God. And by demonstration and Power, we see Him involved in Creation:— Genesis 1:2 - *"the **Spirit** of God was hovering over the face of the deep"**** Later in the Books of the Law, and the Prophets; and as well, also, in the New Testament, we see the ***Holy-Spirit*** being received by revelation, and later, by demonstration as the ***Holy - Ghost***, in the individual lives of God's People, in Christ. ***Selah***!)

Ps 51:11 - Take not thy _**Holy-Spirit**_ from me....

Is 63:10, 11 - but they rebelled, and vexed His _**Holy Spirit:**_ —***
Then He remembered the days of 'Old'— Moses, *and* his people, *saying.* Where is He that brought them up out of the sea with the **Shepherd** of His Flock? Where is He that Put His _**Holy-Spirit**_ within *him*?

Lk 11:13 - If ye then, being *evil*; know how to **G**ive **G**ood **Gifts** unto your *children*: how much more shall *your* **H**eavenly Father **G**ive the _**Holy-Spirit**_ to them that ask Him....

Eph 1:13 - In whom ye also **T**rusted, after that you heard the **W**ord of **T**ruth, the **G**ospel of your **S**alvation: in whom also *(afterwards)* ye **B**elieved *(and was then)* **S**ealed with the _**Holy Spirit**_ of Promise....

Eph 4:29, 30 - Let no *corrupt communication* **P**roceed out of your mouth, but that which is **G**ood to the use of **E**difying –. That it may **M**inister Grace to the *hearers.* — And **G**rieve not the _**Holy Spirit**_ of God, whereby you are **S**ealed unto the **D**ay of **Redemption: Amen!**

1 Th 4:7, 8 - For God has not called us unto **U**ncleanness, but unto **Holiness.** – *He* therefore that despises– **D**espises not *man*: but God who has also given unto us His _**Holy-Spirit**_!

Same Purpose — Same Name

Here's a List of a few names attributed to The *Holy Spirit*: — The Spirit of God, The Holy One of Israel, and The Holy Ghost, from Both the Old and New Covenants. Just wanted to show the Nature and Personality of God with His Creation. He is the Expressive *Will, and Spirit* of God, who has always desired to Communicate with his own Express Image *(Man)*. And no matter which **Period** or time, before Christ, that you see or hear those other names used, they're all representative of One Spirit, with the same Nature and Purpose: that is, to carry out the plan of God in His Creation, starting first with Mankind*(who because of his sin, caused all of Creation to suffer, with every breath of the Life of God in them, crying out for Change, let's look at few Scriptures, starting with:* **Rom 8:22, 23 - For we know that the whole Creation groans, and travails in pain together until now. —And not only they: even we ourselves groan within ourselves, waiting for the adoption; that is to say, to the redemption of our Body)** And because of the fall of Man through his blatant disobedience, the **Holy Spirit** in all of His Splendor has been the guiding hand to the orchestrated Plan of all Mighty God. And now we see *Him* because of Christ, in a more intimate position regarding us, His Creation *(His greatest treasure)*.

OUR CONSUMMATION

Unlike all the other attributable "Punctuation Marks" that he became in God's effort to spare man *(**The Holy Ghost by God, and through His All Knowing Wisdom, regarding His Plan of Salvation for Us, before the foundation of the World – 1 Pet 1:20 and Rev 13:8**)*: Set in motion: all things working for our Benefit, and for the Good of Kingdom, as He had already Purposed *(**Rom 8:28**)*. Hence, we now see the same **Holy Spirit,** but acting on our behalf under a New Mandate. A Mandate issued directly from the God of Love, who by the obedience of Love, which is Christ in us our Hope, Commanded His Love toward us to be delivered by that Holy-Spirit of Promise and Comfort: The Holy Ghost. And now, we see fully the True Purpose and will of the Holy Ghost, which is to develop for the need of the Kingdom in each individual soul; a new directive which is identified and confirmed in *(**1 Peter 2:9**)*, which proclaims in us as *New* Creatures; our Born Again Status: ***"a Chosen Generation – a***

Royal Priesthood – a Holy Nation (and), a Peculiar People." And so, for the First time, beyond Adam and Eve, we once again have *Individual* Access, by the Holy Ghost into the presence of God —, and Secondly, we now can experience the Love of God unhindered, since by the peaceful act of Surrender, Christ has broken down that middle wall of *partition* that *separated* us, abolishing in **His** flesh the **hatred** of the Law. Hence Creating in **himself** a New Man: *(Eph 2:14,15)*. A *New Man* for the express Purpose of the Father's Love. And so, with the Holy Ghost in *His* New role of **Comforter** and as our Confidant we now have an avenue of *expression* by which we can openly demonstrate our Love toward the Father, for all **He** has *sacrificed*, in redeeming us back, to our original place in **Him**. Therefore, I thank God for Consummating us in Christ, through the Person of the Holy Ghost. That **Spirit** of Adoption wherein we *Cry,* **Abba, Father**! *(Rom 8:15)*

Romans 8:2 - *For the Law of the Spirit of Life —in Christ Jesus has made me Free from the Law of Sin and Death* **Me**

12-10-16 *[And that Spirit of Life in us, is the same Spirit, that now has become our free Gift, if we so Choose Him to be]*. **Luke 11:13** *how much more shall your* **Heavenly Father** *give the Holy Spirit to them that ask Him!*

Heal (We have in us, now: Christ, the **Anointed-One**, who is the source of our Power *(by the Holy Ghost)*, to **Heal,** and to be **Heal**ed. And because of that *Spiritual Reality*, we ourselves have become, to many who believe in the name of Jesus as their **balm of Gilead**. Even as we also believe and do demonstrate by the evidence of who we serve...that by His *stripes*, and His alone do we declare, by Faith; that we have Power in His Name, and in His finished work, to **Heal**, for God's Glory: Selah!

Acts 4:29 - 30 – And now, Lord — behold their threatening's, and grant your servants, that with all boldness we may speak thy *Word*, by *stretching* forth *thine **Hand*** to <u>*Heal*</u>: and that *S*igns and *W*onders may be done by the *N*ame of thy Holy-Child, ***Jesus*** —

Healed

Jam 5:16 - CONFESS YOUR FAULTS ONE TO ANOTHER... AND PRAY ONE FOR ANOTHER THAT YOU MIGHT BE <u>HEALED</u>. —

1 Pet 2:24 - Whom His own ***Self*** bare our ***sins*** in His own *B*ody on the *tree*. That we, being dead to ***sins***, should Live unto *Righteousness*: *B*y whose *S*tripes we were <u>*Healed*</u> —

Healing (The Gift of ***Healing***, I believe is not just for my own selfish need, though it may not be for selfishness' sake, that I want or need to be ***healed***. But rather, I believe that it is another expression of God's will and desire for us to be as He is, a *G*iver. Hence, we're therefore Gifted with the anointing of ***Healing*** that we may release more of the Father's Love as a *B*enefit for those who *believe* and as a witness to those who hunger and thirst after that which they know not and possibly find what they seek in their ***Healing***: thus Glorifying the Father —in ***His*** Son, when their *hunger* and *thirst* has been quenched, by the *laying* on of the **Healing-Hands** of God's Servant.)

1 Cor 12:8,9 - For to *o*ne is ***given*** by the Spirit, the word of Wisdom: to *another* faith, by the same Spirit: to *another* the Gifts of <u>*Healing*</u> by the same Spirit. —

Malachi 4:2 - But unto you that fear my *Name*, shall *The Sun* of *Righteousness* Arise, with <u>*Healing*</u> — in His Wings!

Health (This has been God's will for ***man*** from the beginning... for indeed to Prosper is not possible without ***Health*** being the main component in the stability of our Prospering, for without

Health for a believer, *prosperity* is a moot Proposition. Not debatable, I say, because from the very beginning of God's *plan*: Adam and Eve were not created with sickness, nor any other kind of **Health** issues. Just the opposite, they were Perfect in every way that the wholeness of **Health,** Prosperity and the *fruitfulness* of Multiplication can produce. Now, as you read and study about the early Patriarchal leaders of the Law, like me, you'll discover that there was never any type of illness or **health issues** that caused them to die, though the curse of death after the fall was inevitable. And afterward, it seemed that always, when man had consummated the usefulness of his Spiritual Purpose, and that often at the end of a long and *aged* run to Glory: As in *Father* Abraham, who at the age of 175 years simply gave up the Ghost. Or take Moses, the Prophet unto God, and Israel's *savior*, who at the good old age of 120, died:*(with)* his eye not dimmed, nor his natural self-diminished in any capacity of *liveliness*.

And of course, I could go on with many other examples of prolonged life and **Health** according to the **Word** of the Lord. — Yet, for us, for some reason, "our **Health** and Prosperity" has not caught up to the **prospering** of our Soul: *(and that fact has been very elusive to me, up until this point...and so; I pray "Lord help me to understand the failure of my faith in regards to the lagging behind of my prospering Health" I pray that we all might receive more revelation in this area of our 'Faith Walk', Amen!)*...But as time passes, we do begin to see the curse of sin gradually take hold of our **Health,** as some men of God became vulnerable in their old age, allowing sickness to creep in. And so as I recall the **Testament** of Jacob *(the father of Israel)*, I'm reminded of when he was *'getting up in age'*, he took sick after visiting Joseph. And after **blessing** his twelve sons and his grandsons **'He gathered up his feet into his bed, and gave up the ghost'**... Now, as history consumed time and the old covenant moved forward, the heart of man became more wicked, to the point that often, when the people of that time grew sick and diseased even unto death. It could be traced directly to the wickedness of the Priest, King, or Prophet, who was operating out of the will of God for *His* People. Hence, the curse of sin, in the form of sickness and diseases, begins to plague their lives. — Exodus **15:25, 26** - *there He made a* **S**tatute *and an* **O**rdinance... *and there He proved them*

—And said: If thou will diligently hearken to the Voice of the Lord thy God, and will do that which is right in His sight and will give ear to His **C**ommandments*, and keep all His* **S**tatutes*:*

I will put none of these diseases upon **Y**ou *—which I have brought upon the Egyptians: for I am the Lord that* <u>*Healeth*</u> **Y**ou [Also Read: Gen 1:27 / Gen 25:7,8 / Deut 34:5,6,7 / 3Jn 2 / Gen 49:33 / etc. You can also see in the rest of the Old Covenant the Pattern and downward spiral that our *Life* and *Health* took, following the *will* of the **C**urse, leading up to Christ, and once again to the **P**rospering of our **S**oul. Selah and Amen! —

3 John 2 - Beloved, I wish above all things, that thou mayest Prosper and be in *Health:* even as thy **S**oul *Prospers* —

Longsuffering *(Because* of the Obedience of Christ, and the price *He* paid for us, we now have evidence of how patient God has been with us all. And how through **R**epentance from His own desires against us *—He* has stayed *His* **hand** of Wrath. —And now, because of the unrelenting intercession for us by Christ: — Our God, now, has the *Longsuffering* **P**atience of a Father towards *His* **C**hildren. Glory to *His* **A**wesome Name, what a <u>**Benefit.**</u>*)*

Rom 2:3,4 - And thinkest thou this, O man, that judgest them who do such things, and *(you)* does the same, that thou shalt escape the *judgment* of God? Or *(do you)* despise thou the riches of God's goodness, forbearance and <u>**Longsuffering**</u>, not knowing *(yourself)* that the goodness of God leadeth **Y**ou to Repentance?

Rom 9:22 - What if God —*wanting* to show *His* Wrath, and to make *His P*ower known, endured with much <u>*Longsuffering*</u>, the Vessels *of W*rath prepared for *destruction* —

Gal 5:22 - But the *Fruit* of the *Spirit* is **(love, joy, peace)** <u>***Longsuffering***</u>

2 Tim 3:10 - But thou hast fully known my *Doctrine, Manner* of Life, *Purpose, Faith,* <u>*Longsuffering*</u>, *Charity, Patience* —

2 Pet 3:9 - The Lord is not **slack** concerning *His* Promise, as some count Slackness, but is <u>*Longsuffering*</u>: toward us —*not W*illing that any should *Perish*, but that *A*ll should come to *R*epentance....

Love (*This* kind of **Love** is no fleshy *Love*...this is the God kind of **Love** — *Without* this kind, the other kind is just a *mimic* and means nothing. You see, it's only the God kind of **Love** that's real. That's why there's really no such thing as a Marriage; that's not built from the original pattern, which is Spiritual and Purpose driven, to create in the image of God, more creatures of **Love**: which is the reason Man and Woman were Created. To be *fruitful* and duplicate, by multiplication, the very Nature of **Love**, the *product* Gods.

"TO LOVE LIKE *GOD'S*"

Now, let me take a minute to qualify my previous statement. As to perhaps prevent any misunderstanding: as to me claiming that I am, or you might be a God. But what I'm saying to you very clearly is we were meant to be. The Original plan was such. All you really have to do is read Genesis with **spiritual** simplicity, and you'll see it clearly for yourself. —That before the Treason of Adam, and before he surrendered his **Love-**Connection with his **Creator** to the Lordship of Satan, who became his god, he'd already acted in the role of a **god**. Because you see, before he named the Animals, they had no identity. It was only when he named the Lion, did the Lion know he was king of the Jungle, and likewise, for every other animal that was named, the identity of what they were to be showed up, and not one of their names, in the beginning made them Carnivores. It was only when he lost his *Love* identity, by Adams treasonous act, the lions soon after became Carnivorous. So, for me, to know that this kind of *Love* has the power to contain and restrain every kind of evil potential from springing forth unto manifestation. Makes me understand how important it is for me to walk in *Love* like my *S*avior, therefore creating a very positive and constructive atmosphere for not only my *L*ife, but for the *B*enefit and nurturing in the life of others in the *R*ealm of my *S*piritual Position of influence. This kind of *Love* is better known to the *G*reeks as *Agape*. And of course, as I've already stated previously, about the kind of *Love* that's natural, with the potential to be sensual, can never be the Godly kind. It's like the kind of *Love* the *G*reeks call *philia*, a brotherly or a friendship type of *Love*, even a fleeting or fading type of *Love*. But that of *Agape Love*, better known as the God kind, *the* *U*nconditional *kind.* It has in it no judgment nor any preconceived opinions. It doesn't willingly express itself with any kind of destructive motive that doesn't have in its purpose the rebuilding or restoration of a broken *S*oul. It must have the *A*genda of a God-minded servant. Why? Simple, because God so *Loved* us —*He S*acrificed *His* Only Begotten *Son* (*Instead of giving us our just reward of Damnation*). And He did it so that we would Glorify Him, by bypassing **Hell.** So that we might *therefore* do what He Created us to do from the *foundation* of the World. Which is to say, to *Love Him,* as Jesus Commanded us to do in— *St Matthew 22:37, 38 - "Thou shalt Love the Lord your God, with all your Heart, with all your Soul, and with all your* Mind...*This is the* F*irst* and G*reat* Commandment – Hallelujah: Amen!*)

1 Th 1:3 - Remembering without ceasing, your work of Faith: – and Labor of **_Love._** —

1 Th 3:12 - And the Lord make you to *increase* and *abound* in **_Love_**, one towards another, and towards all men...

1 Th 4:9 - But as touching Brotherly **_Love_**, you need not that I write unto you: *for* you yourselves are taught of God, to **_Love_** one another.

1 Th 5:8 - But let *Us* who are of the *day*, be sober, — putting on the *B*reastplate of *faith*, and **_Love_**—

1 Tim 6:11 - But thou O man of God, *flee* these things: and – *follow* after *R*ighteousness, *G*odliness, *faith*, —**_Love_**:

2 Tim 1:7 - *For* God has not given us a **spirit** of fear: but of Power and of **_Love_**!

2 Tim 1:13 - Hold-*fast* the Form of *S*ound *W*ords —which thou has heard of *me*, in *faith* and **_Love_**: which is in Christ *Jesus*...

Phile (5), (7) - Hearing of thy **_Love_** and *faith*, which thou has toward the Lord *Jesus*, and toward all *S*aints ...*... For we have *G*reat joy and **consolation** in thy **_Love_** —Because the *hearts* of the *S*aints are*(all)* *R*efreshed by *Y*ou, **brother** ...

Heb 6:10 - For God is not **un**righteous to forget *Y*our work, — and labor of **_Love:_**

Heb 13:1 - Let *B*rotherly **_Love_** —*C*ontinue....

Jam 1:12 - Blessed is the Man who **endures Temptation:** —*for* when he is **tried**, he shall *r*eceive the Crown of Life which the Lord has *P*romised to them that **_Love_** ***Him

James 2:8 - If ye fulfill the **Royal Law** according to the *S*cripture: thou shalt **_Love_** thy neighbor as thyself — Ye do well....

1 Pet 1:22 - *Seeing* ye have *purified* your Souls, in obeying the *Truth* through the **Spirit,** unto unfeigned <u>***Love***</u> of the **brethren** — *see* that you <u>**Love**</u> one another with a Pure Heart, *fervently*!

1 Pet 2:17 - *Honor* all Men —<u>**Love**</u> the Brotherhood*(and)* *f*ear God:

(*A Revelation of Love from: John the Revelator*)

1 Jn 2:5 - But whoso keeps (**His**)*Word* in *him* verily is the <u>**Love**</u> of God *perfected*: *(hence we know that we are in **Him**) ...*

1 Jn 3:1 - *Behold*: *What* Manner of <u>**Love**</u>, the Father hath bestowed upon **Us**, that we should be called the ***sons*** of God:

1 J 3:14 - *W*e know that we have *p*assed from death to Life, because we <u>**Love**</u> the ***brethren***

1 Jn 4:7, 8 - *Beloved,* let us <u>**Love**</u> one another: *for* <u>**Love**</u> is of God*** and everyone that <u>*Love*</u>s is Born of God, and <u>***knows***</u> God. H*e* that *Loves* not *knows* not God: *f*or God is <u>**Love**</u>

1Jn 4:10 - 12 – Herein is <u>**Love**</u>: *not* that we **loved** God, but that He **Loved** us and sent His **Son** to be the <u>Propitiation</u> *(sacrifice)* for our sins. *Beloved,* if God so **Loved** us, we ought to <u>**Love**</u> one another... No Man has seen God at any time. If we <u>**Love**</u> one another —God dwells in us: *and* **His** <u>**Love**</u> is *perfected* in *Us*....

1Jn 4:21 - ***And this*** *C*ommandment ***we have from Him*** —*that he who* *L*oves **God** *(must)* <u>**Love**</u> his *B*rother *also* —

Jude 21 - Keep ***yourselves*** in the <u>**Love**</u> of God:

Rev 2:4, 5 - ***Nevertheless I have Somewhat against You*** —***Because You have left Your First*** <u>***Love***</u>: Remember ***therefore from Whence You have Fallen, and*** *R*epent:

Rev 3:19 - ***As many as I*** <u>***Love***</u>: *I* Rebuke **and** *C*hasten, **be** *Z*ealous ***therefore and*** *R*epent.

Mercy (*Hallelujah* —*Hallelujah,* O give thanks unto the Lord *{thank you Jesus}* for your *Mercy* endures *forever.* Amen!)

Rom 9:15, 16 - For **He** said to Moses, I will have <u>*Mercy,*</u> on whom **I** will have <u>*Mercy:*</u> —*and* **I**'ll have **C**ompassion on whom **I**'ll have **C**ompassion! So then, *it*'s not of him that wills, or of him that runs, but of God that shows <u>*Mercy*</u>—

2Cor 4:1 - **T**herefore seeing we have this **M**inistry: *as we* received <u>*Mercy*</u> —we *faint* not....

Tit 3:5 - Not by *works* of **R**ighteousness we've done, *but* according to **His** <u>*Mercy, He*</u> **S**aved **U**s ***

Heb 4:16 - *Let us therefore— come* **B**oldly *to the* **T**hrone *of* **G**race,

that we **M**ight *obtain* <u>*Mercy:*</u> *and find* **G**race *to help in time of need.*

Jam 3:17 - But the **Wisdom** that's from **A**bove is *first* — **P**ure, then

Peaceable, **G**entle and easy to be **E**ntreated, *full* of <u>*Mercy:*</u>

1Pet 2:9, 10 - But *you* are a **C**hosen-<u>**Generation**</u> —a **R**oyal **P**riest -

-hood, *a* **H**oly-**Nation**, *a* **P**eculiar-**People**, that *you* should *show - forth* the **P**raises of **Him** who hath called *you* out of **darkness** into **His** **M**arvelous *Light:* **W**hich in time past*(you)* were not a **people** — but are now the **P**eople *of* God: —**W**hich had not obtained <u>**Mercy:**</u> but now have *obtained-*<u>*Mercy*</u>.......

The Sweet Mercies of God, How Durable They Are!

Money (In order to keep a proper perspective on this product of necessity, which it indeed is, we need to know what it is: and in a nutshell, *'for lack of a better term '* I will try to intelligently describe what it is, based on some of what has already been determined. So, Webster's New World Dictionary *defines* it as: **"2. anything regularly used as money 3. wealth, property, etc. (a**

man of money)". Now, when we look backwards, and see how it was portrayed in Bible *times,* the number *(2.)* definition would be a more accurate description of making use of many types of material, property, or other commodities of monetary value. And with the ownership of such currency, they were able to barter and trade with the common people, as well as with other businesses, to the point of becoming **wealthy.** Even leading up to the 19th and 20th Centuries, in this Country *(USA)*, people used bartering and the trading of goods as their main source of **Money** or income.

Now, of course, in our modern America, I believe most of us would 'flat out' starve if we had to use something else for **Money.** And *one* very good reason why we would starve or become thieves — is simply because most of us don't own anything worth trading. We're in debt up to our eyeballs with all kinds of frivolous things. *Secondly,* we don't have the land to grow our own basic bartering staples *(supply: wheat, corn, etc.).* Yes, if we had to produce our income any other way besides a Paycheck, quite a few of us would become predatory towards one another *(that day is near)*. You see, I know, I'm also amongst those that *"gotta see it in Greens$$$."* Now, let's get back to the subject of **Money** as we know it. And as we do, I will try to refocus back to the **B**iblical **N**ecessity of **Money**, and how we're not to let it become as **Mammon** *(wealth thought of as evil, that makes people selfish and greedy)*. So from this point on, let us build up our **"most holy- foundation of faith"** regarding our use and need of money, as *laid out* for our instruction, by none other than the **Wisest** Human Person, according to *(**"1Kings 4:31 - For he was wiser than all Men"),*** that ever lived. Let us look at *his* famous **B**ook of **Wisdom** on the topic of **Money:** *(**Ecl 7:12 - Wisdom is a defense, and Money is a defense.** Also, we read in the same Book, **Eccl 10:19 - but Money answers all things —** **Amen!)**

1Tim 6:10 - For the *Love* of <u>*Money*</u> is the ***root*** of all evil: *which* while some *greedily want and lust* after *what others have...* they have erred from the **Faith:** and *p*ierced themselves, with many ***sorrows.***

Mt 17:27 *(have faith that money will serve you)* - Notwithstanding, lest we should offend them *(bill collectors, tax collectors, etc.),* go thou to the sea*(an act of obedience, by faith),* and cast a hook, and take up the fish that first come up;

Mt 17:27 - and when thou hast opened his mouth, thou shalt find a piece of <u>*Money:*</u> that take, and give unto them for me and thee *(As Children of God, when we're in financial difficulty, we have to remember that Jesus is with us, right in the middle of our dilemma, whether it's our fault, or not, He is our way out).*

Acts 4:36, 37 - And Joses —, who was *surnamed* Barnabas, by the *A*postles *(which is interpreted, as the son of Consolation,)* a Levite *and* of the Country of *C*yprus—, Having land, sold it, and brought the <u>*Money,*</u> and laid it at the Apostles' feet....

5th Gift to the Body of Christ:

Pastors (Our *S*hepherd and Instructors, called to Train and *E*quip us unto *D*iscipleship.) —

Ep 4:11 - and some <u>***Pastors***</u> *****

Peace (The next 12-Benefit Words, I call: the *Powerful* "P's" — enjoy)

Acts 9:36 - The Word which God sent unto the *children* of Israel; *p*reaching <u>*Peace*</u> *by* Jesus Christ: *(He is Lord of all).*

Rom 2:10 - But *Glory, Honor,* and <u>*Peace:*</u> to every **man** that works good – to the Jew *first...*and also to the *G*entile.

Rom 5:1 - *T*herefore, being Justified by ***faith:*** we have <u>*Peace*</u> —

Rom 10:15 - As it is *Written.* How Beautiful are the *feet* of they who *preach* the Gospel of **_Peace_**...

Rom 14:17 - **For** the Kingdom of God is not *meat* and *drink:* but Righteousness, and **_Peace,_** and Joy in the Holy Ghost.

Rom 14:19 - And the God of **_Peace_** shall bruise *Satan* under your *feet* shortly. The Grace of our Lord Jesus Christ be with you, Amen.

1Cor 7:15 - *but* God has called us to **_Peace_**!

Gal 5:22 - But the *fruit* of the Spirit is —*Love, Joy,* **_Peace_**, etc.

Gal 6:16 - *"***_Peace_** and *m*ercy be upon them"—*

Eph 2:14,15 - *For He* Himself is our **_Peace:_** who has made both one and has broken down the middle wall of division *(that divided)* Us, having abolished in **His** *f*lesh the Enmity, that is the Law of Commandments **contained** in Ordinances, so as to Create in Himself, One *New* **Man** from the *Two* —thus *Making* **_Peace_**...

Col 3:15 - And let the **_Peace_** *of* God Rule in your Hearts.

1Th 5:23 - Now may the God *of* **_Peace_** Himself Sanctify You:

Heb 12:14 - Pursue **_Peace_** with all Men, and Holiness: without which, *no-one* will see the Lord.

Jam 3:18 - Now the *fruit* of Righteousness is sown in **_Peace_** *(by the* **_Peace-M_**akers*: "a foundational verse for this Scripture is found in Psalms 120:7, this was important for me to know: check it out").*

1 Pet 3:10, *(11)* -Let **him** *A*void *evil,* and do **Good** —; let **him** Seek **_Peace,_** *f*ollow *It*...

2 Pet 3:14 - Therefore **beloved:** looking forward to these Things, be diligent to be **found** by Him in **_Peace_**— *without* spot and Blameless

2Cor 13:11 - *Finally* Brethren—, farewell. Be Perfect, be of *good* Comfort, be of One Mind, *live* in **<u>Peace:</u>** and the God of Love and **<u>Peace</u>** shall be with You!

Power

Acts 1:8 - But you shall receive **<u>Power,</u> *after*** that the Holy-Spirit has come upon you:

Acts 4:33 - And with Great **<u>Power,</u>** gave the Apostles witness of the Resurrection of the Lord Jesus; and great grace was upon them all.

Acts 6:38 - And Stephen, full of *faith* and **<u>Power,</u>** did great *wonders* and *Miracles* among the people.

Rom 1:16 - For I am not ashamed of the Gospel of Christ: *for* it is the **<u>Power</u>** of God unto Salvation to everyone that Believe:

1 Cor 6:14 - And God hath both Raised up the Lord, and will also *raise* up Us by His own **<u>Power</u>** —

2 Cor 4:7 - But *we* have this Treasure in ***earthen-vessels*** — that the Excellence of the **<u>Power</u>** may be of God, and not of Us...

2 Cor 12:9 - And *He* said to me: ***"My grace if sufficient for you, for My strength is made Perfect in weakness"*** Therefore most gladly I will rather Boast in my infirmities, that the **<u>Power</u>** of Christ might rest upon me...

Ep 3:20 - Now to ***Him who*** is able to do Exceedingly—Abundantly above all that we ask or think: *according* to the **<u>Power</u>**...

Ph 3:10 - That I may know ***Him,*** and the **<u>Power</u>** of ***His*** Resurrection

Col 2:10 - And ***you*** are Complete in ***Him*** who is the Head of all — Principalities, *and* **<u>Power</u>**....

1 Th 1:5 - For our Gospel did not come to you in **word** only, but also in _Power,_ and in the _Holy-S_pirit— and in much **_assurance:_**

2 Tim 1:7 - For God hath not given us the *s*pirit of fear; but of _**Power**_

2 Tim 1:8 - Be not thou therefore **ashamed** of the Testimony of our Lord, nor of *me* **His** *P*risoner: but be thou partaker of the *A*fflictions of the *G*ospel *A*ccording to the _**Power**_ of God;

Ep 6:10, 11 - Finally my *B*rethren, *be* **strong** in the Lord, and in the_**Power**_ of **His** *M*ight. —Put on the *W*hole **Armor** *of* God —

Praise

Rom 15:11 - And *again,* _**Praise**_ the Lord all ye Gentiles: *E*xtol *Him* all ye People...

Heb 13:15 - Therefore, by **Him** let Us continually *offer* the *S*acrifice of _**Praise**_ to God: that is —*the F*ruit of our lips, giving thanks:

1 Pet1:7 -; *that* the *T*rial of your **faith,** — being much more Precious than of **gold** that perishes, though it be tried with *F*ire, *** be found unto _**Praise**_ and *H*onor and Glory at the appearing of Jesus Christ:

Rev 19:5 - Then a *V*oice came from the Throne; *S*aying: "_**Praise**_ our God all ye **His** Servants, *and* those who *fear **Him:**
—

Praises

1 Pet 2:9 - But *Y*ou are a *C*hosen **generation,** a Royal Priesthood, a Holy Nation, **His** own *S*pecial *p*eople; that *Y*ou may proclaim the_**Praises**_ of **Him** who called *Y*ou out of **darkness** into **His** Marvelous Light...

Pray

Rom 8:26 - Likewise, the Spirit also helps in our weaknesses; *for* we do not know what we should <u>*Pray*</u> for as we ought. — But the Spirit *Himself* makes Intercession for Us, with **groaning's** that cannot be Uttered!

1 Cor 14:13 - Therefore let him who Speaks in a **tongue,** <u>*Pray*</u> that he may interpret.

1 Cor 14:14 - For if I <u>*Pray*</u> in a **tongue,** *M*y spirit Prays; but my understanding is **unfruitful...**

1 Cor 14:15 - *W*hat is the result then? I will <u>*Pray*</u> with the spirit, and I will also <u>*Pray*</u> with the Understanding, I will sing with the spirit, and I will also sing with the Understanding...

1 Th 5:16 - Rejoice always, <u>*Pray*</u> without **Ceasing:** —

1 Th 5:25 - *B*rethren <u>*Pray*</u> for Us

2 Th 1:11 - Therefore we also <u>*Pray*</u> always *for* You —that our God would **count** *Y*ou Worthy of **His** **C**alling, *and f*ulfill all the **G**ood – *p*leasure of **His** **G**oodness, and the *work* of *faith* with Power...

1 Tim 2:8 - Therefore I desire *Men* <u>*Pray*</u> everywhere:

Jam 5:13 - *I*s any among *Y*ou Suffering? Let *him* <u>*Pray*</u>.

Jam 5:14 - *I*s anyone among *Y*ou **sick**? Let *him* call for the Elders *of* the **Church,** let them <u>*Pray*</u> over *him* —Anointing *him* with oil in the *N*ame of the Lord...

Jam 5:16 - *C*onfess *your* Trespasses to *one* another, and <u>*Pray*</u> *for* *O*ne another that *Y*ou may be Healed —

Prayer

Acts 12:5 - Peter was therefore kept in *Prison,* but constant <u>*Prayer*</u> was Offered to God for *him* by the Church...

Rom 12:12 - *r*ejoicing in *H*ope, Patient in ***tribulation***— *C*ontinuing *s*teadfastly in ***Prayer;***

1 Cor 7:5 *(please read in context verses 1 thru 4 for clarity, as it pertains to marriage) Do* not **deprive** one another, except with *consent* for a time —, that *y*ou may give *yourselves* to **fasting** and ***Prayer:***

Eph 6:18 - *P*raying always *with* all ***Prayer*** and *spiritual* *S*upplication

Phi 4:6 - **B***e anxious* for nothing, but in everything, by ***Prayer*** and *S*upplication, with *t*hanksgiving, let your request be made known:

Col 4:2 - *C*ontinue ***earnestly** in **Prayer**— :*

Jam 5:15 - *A*nd the ***Prayer*** of ***faith***, will *S*ave the ***sick; ...***

Jam 5:16 - The *effectual F*ervent ***Prayer*** *of* a *R*ighteous Man, avails much—

*Pray Without Ceasing — **1 Thessalonians 5:17***

The End of All Things Is At Hand: Be Ye Therefore Sober, and Watch *Unto **Prayer** —* 1 Peter 4:7

Prayers *(As* a married man, this thing called Prayer —, is wholly and completely unlike that of a single man *[generally speaking]*. Example: As a single man, my **Prayers** for security in my finances would only be centered around what I want or need for myself. Never taking into consideration what anyone else in my world needed for their comfort or necessity. But if I used that same kind of **P**rayer request for my individual need as a married man, it would only be answered based on the need as a Couple, for the benefit of the *A*ll in One, instead of for the self-willed selfishness of the singular *M*e. Now of course, that's not a put-down or a knock against being *S*ingle. It's simply the fact of how I thought when I was single, though I wasn't saved then. But there really is not much difference in that regard, except for Spirituality. And so, to be realistic in our approach to Answered *Prayers* (*since this Book is Primarily written for the Benefit of Saints, whether Single or Married.*) I believe it is necessary to point out the difference in *Prayers* between the two for the purpose of enlightenment. Let's face it: Single-Mindedness is one of the most stubborn Carnalities in our flesh of *Singleness* to let go of once we have committed to Marriage; seeing that it's no longer about *Me first*, with myself and I following. So, speaking from my now reality of being Married, I can tell you that thinking as a Single person in a Marriage is, and will be a Lifelong battle, but as I seek God in Prayer when petitioning Him with my *Prayers* for my wife and me, I always have to cast down the imagination, of what's best for *Me*. "*Cause in my flesh I find no good thing*"! But with God, *all Th*ings are Possible, in *Prayers* and *S*upplication. Amen!)

1 Pet 3:7 *(please read and study this verse of scripture in the context with 1 thru 6 for spiritual clarity)*- Likewise, you *H*usbands, dwell with *(your wife)* in understanding —*G*iving honor to the *wife*, as to the weaker *vessel (weaker in her physiology only)* and as being Heirs together of the Grace of *L*ife, that your <u>**Prayers**</u> be not Hindered —

1 Tim 2:1 - Therefore, I exhort *first* of all that Supplications, <u>*Prayers* </u>and Intercession, with giving of thanks be made for all Men....

Rev 5:8 [*Commentary: I believe that this verse confirms that when we Pray, the Prayer of faith, which is the only kind the Father will hear. Not only does He just hear them, but because of His Dear Son, He also answers them according to His will in Him for our Benefit, in concert with the Benefit of Heaven. And by His most Sovereign decree, He releases for us the thing that brings Him Glory*].

Rev 5:8 - *N*ow, when *He* had taken the *S*croll —, the *four living* *C*reatures, and the *twenty-f*our *Elders* fell down before the Lamb, each having a *Harp* —*and G*olden *B*owls *full* of incense. *W*hich are the *<u>Prayers</u> of* the *S*aints. —

Praying

Acts 12:12 - *So,* when *he* came to the *H*ouse of *M*ary, the *M*other of John whose *s*urname was *M*ark, where many were gathered *<u>Praying</u>*—

1 Cor 11:4 - *E*very *man <u>Praying</u>,* or *P*rophesying: having his head *C*overed, *dishonors* his *H*ead....

Ep 6:18 - *<u>Praying</u>* always with all *P*rayer and *S*upplication in the *Spirit* —being *W*atchful to this end, with all *P*erseverance. —

Col 1:3 - *W*e *give T*hanks to the *G*od and *F*ather of our *L*ord *J*esus

*C*hrist, *<u>Praying</u>* always for *Y*ou.

Col 4:2, (3) - *C*ontinue *earnestly* in *P*rayer: *meanwhile,* **Praying** also for *Us* – that *G*od would open unto *Us* a door of *U*tterance, to *speak* the *Mystery* of *C*hrist, *for* which I am also in *B*onds:

Jude 20, 21 - *B*ut *Y*ou, *B*eloved, *building Y*ourselves up on your most *H*oly-*faith,* *<u>Praying</u>* in the *H*oly-*G*host, *keep Y*ourselves in the *L*ove *of* *G*od: *L*ooking *for* the *M*ercy *of* our *L*ord *J*esus *C*hrist, —

Preach *(We,* as the *B*ody of *C*hrist, are all now officially under the same *C*ommand, which has been issued from the *T*hrone of *G*od. And it is *found* in our *L*ord, who is the *only* begotten *S*on *of* the *F*ather, and at no time does it ever separate, or segregate itself from the *G*reat *C*ommission given to the *B*ody: *R*ead the *B*ook of Joel, and you will find clarification on who you are in *C*hrist, and the Gifted *purpose* you are in the Earth *(Joel 2:28)*. Now as you study the Book of Joel, you will see for yourself, not all are Prophets, nor Teachers, or any other specified calling by Man's understanding. But according to Prophet Joel, all will be anointed, as the verse entails: *Saying, "I will pour out my Spirit (Holy-Ghost) on all flesh, your sons, and your daughters shall Prophesy"*. Hence, on the Day of Pentecost, the pouring out was Accomplished. It released the *gifts* from on High, as Apostle Paul so eloquently declares by *revelation* in his Letter to the Ephesians: —

(Eph 4:7,8 - But to each one of us Grace was given, according to the measure of the Gift of Christ. — Wherefore he saith: When He ascended up on High, He led captivity Captive, and gave Gifts unto men [Ps 68:18 **- Thou hast Ascended on High, thou hast led captivity Captive, thou hast received Gifts for Men, yea for the rebellious also, that the Lord God might dwell among them]***. So we see here, that in the sight of God, we're all *men*, yet not men necessarily in a good light, for where there are men, in the *plural* sense, many times there are divisions of all sorts because as men, we come with our own agenda, even for the whole.

Let's look at the Revelation King David was given, in Psalms *(Ps 82:6,7 - I have said, Ye are gods; and all of you are Children of the Most High. But ye shall die like men, [plural]; and fall like one of the princes — [the leaders of the fallen angels]*. And in this, we see the destruction of Men who have their own Agenda for how they serve God. And before we're Born-Again into the Righteous Plan of God, we're all: — as men and women, in our individuality as *spiritual-degenerates*. But as we come back into the plan of God, we do so, once again; as Mankind, that's what the Body of Christ is all about, and of course, without the Daughters of men, there is no opportunity for the seed of Mankind, in Christ to flourish. And of course, not just to flourish by the deliverance and preaching of the male seed, but also by the female offspring as well. And for me, there are two verses of scriptures that offset each other in a perfect balance, one from the '*Old*' and the other from the '*New*'. They are these: *Joel 2:28, 29* and *Romans 10:11 thru 15. (Please read them: I believe you'll see what I mean)*. So, without further ado, let me complete this Benefit Section on the Great Gift, given unto the *B*ody for its individual needs of being **Shepherded**. Since all can't be the eye, hand, ear, feet, or legs, we all must have the Shepherding of the *O*nes *G*ifted to Us. To **Preach** unto Us all, the *I*nstructions on Kingdom Living. *Amen!* — *—

Acts 10:40- 42 - **Him** God raised up the **Third Day**, and *showed* **Him Openly;** — And He *C*ommanded Us to <u>**Preach**</u> unto the *people:* —

Acts 16:6 *(**Just a Commentary Note**: This verse of scriptures reveals to us that we are not to haphazardly plan our witness or outreach to the unsaved. We must always be keenly in tune with the direction of the Holy Ghost. He must be at the Head of all our strategic planning when it comes to witnessing, or our efforts will be in vain. Now, from my place of learning, what I've found in our technological Age of modernness is that we can get <u>complacent</u> or <u>lackadaisical</u> on our misguided soul-winning tours. I say misguided for the obvious reason: "No Holy Ghost". The **anointing** and approval of the Holy Ghost must be present with our desire to please God in our outreach. We simply must seek His Guidance, and the Holy Ghost is the only Guide for the Church, hands down; no questions, it's Him, period).* **Verse 6** - Now when they'd gone throughout **Phrygia** and the region of **Galatia,** — *and* were forbidden by the **Holy Ghost** to <u>**Preach**</u> the Word in *A*sia after they came to **Mysia,** they *attempted* to go into **Bithynia:** But the *S*pirit suffered them not.

Rom 10:8 - the Word is *Near Y*ou, even in your mouth and in Your **heart** *(That is, the Word of Faith which we* <u>**Preach**</u>*)*

Rom 10:15 - And how shall they <u>**Preach,**</u> except they be sent? As it is *written* — "*H*ow *B*eautiful are the *feet* of those who <u>**Preach**</u> the *G*ospel *of P*eace"!

1 Cor 1:23 - But we <u>**Preach**</u> Christ *Crucified* —

1 Cor 9:16 - For if I <u>**Preach**</u> the *G*ospel, I have nothing to **boast** *of;* for *N*ecessity is laid upon **me:** woe is **me** if I do not <u>**Preach**</u> —

1 Cor 9:18 - What is my *reward* then? *(answer)* That when I <u>**Preach**</u> the *G*ospel, I may *P*resent the *G*ospel without **charge**—

2 Cor 4:5 - For **we do not** <u>**Preach**</u> ourselves, but Christ Jesus the Lord

Col 1:28 - **Him** we <u>**Preach**</u>: *W*arning every **man** in all *W*isdom, that **we** may *P*resent everyone *(Born Again), P*erfect in Christ Jesus......

2 Tim 4:2 - <u>**Preach**</u> the *W*ord! Be ready in *S*eason, and out of *S*eason, *C*onvince, *R*ebuke, *E*xhort: with all **longsuffering** and *T*eaching.

Preacher (Anyone who has this specific anointing and *Gift* —as their dominant *Calling* is classified as a *Preacher [Defined as - **n.** a person who Preaches; especially a Clergyman].* In Christendom, we call a *Preacher* a Pastor. Now, this is a different *Gift* from the one who *Preaches* or who *proclaims* the Gospel by *preaching.* In some Denominations, those who are led to Preach are called *"Layman [Defined as - **n.** a person who is not a Clergyman"].* So, I'll say it this way, as we would say in the Baptist *faith:* "My Pastor is our *Preacher.* Every Sunday, he *Preaches* the Word to Us, and as our *B*eloved **Clergyman,** he is invaluable to the delivery of God's Word to Us. He teaches us all as *Laymen* to go out among the *lost* and be witnesses of the *G*ood-News, that *Salvation* has come and is *free* to all. — Now, as we note here, as explicitly as we can, the *Preacher* is a most important Gift to the Body *of* **Christ.** This **anointed** function Primarily operates twofold: one, as a Deliverer of God's Word to His *P*eople, and two, as an ***instructor*** in rightly dividing the Word of *T*ruth. Showing *us* how to *live* as *R*ighteous and *H*oly witnesses, that our Lives will be the *living E*pistles, that Apostle Paul spoke so eloquently of Us *[**2 Cor 3:2**]*. Therefore, as witnesses, and examples; we indeed, by our lifestyle ***Preach*** every day the Good News of the *C*ross: ***daily** R*esurrecting Christ in *us* the Hope of *G*lory. As ***declared*** by Apostle Paul in: ***Colossians 1:27 - To them God willed to make known 'the riches of this** M*ystery ***among the** G*entiles*' which is: Christ in* Y*ou **the Hope of Glory ...Amen***)

Ecclesiastes 1:1-3 *(Truth: the doom of the Preacher, before Christ)* - The ***words*** of the <u>***Preacher***</u>, the *Son* of David, King in Jerusalem. ***Vanity** of* Vanities, saith the <u>***Preacher***</u>, —***Vanity** of* Vanities; all is *Vanity*. What *P*rofit hath a ***man** of* all his labor, which **he** taketh under the <u>*Sun*</u>?

Rom 10:14 - How then shall they call on ***Him*** in whom they have not *believed*? And how shall they *B*elieve in ***Him*** of whom they haven't *heard*? —*A*nd how shall they *hear* without a <u>*Preacher*</u> —

1 Tim 2:5,6 & 7,8 *(A message from a Preacher)*- For there's *O*ne God, and *one M*ediator between God and ***men**... the **Man** Christ Jesus: who gave *H*imself a ransom for ***all...*** to be *T*estified in due time, for which I was appointed a <u>***Preacher***</u> —an *A*postle. I am speaking the *T*ruth in Christ and not *lying*: *a T*eacher of the Gentiles in ***faith*** and *T*ruth...I wish, *t*herefore that ***men** P*ray everywhere, lifting up ***holy hands***, without wrath and ***doubting***.

Preaching (As Children of God, we're all *C*ommissioned to ***preach*** the *G*ospel. And as we step out in obedience, through our individual or group efforts, ***Evangelizing*** and ***Preaching*** the Good-*N*ews of ***Salvation*** to those searching for meaning: *W*e, by our *P*roclamation of *'the' G*ood-*N*ews Gospel, have by our obedience. Become those *sent-forth* Laborers into the ***Harvest*** of the

Lord's *Vineyard*. Whose *Harvest,* we once were our-selves. *Amen*!)

Acts 8:4 - Therefore those who were **scattered** — went Everywhere <u>*Preaching*</u> the Word.

1 Cor 2:4 - And *my S*peech, and *my* <u>*Preaching*</u> was not with enticing **words** of man's wisdom, but in Demonstration of the **Spirit** and of *Power.* —

Tit 1:1 - 3 - Paul, a **servant** *of* God, and —*an A*postle *of* Jesus Christ according to the *faith* of God's *Elect* and the Acknowledgment of the Truth which is according to **godliness**, in the hope of Eternal Life which God who *cannot* lie, Promised **before-**t*he* World began —*but* hath in due **times** Manifested His **Word** through <u>*Preaching,*</u> which *has been* committed unto **me** according to the Commandment *of* God —**Preach The Word (2Timothy 4:2)**

Press (Christ has now given us the Power through the *Holy Ghost,* not only to *Love,* which is the Greatest Commandment, but to also *Serve* out of it: and yet, not just to *Serve,* but while *serving*; to also *fight* the *G*ood Fight *of faith,* as we **Press** through this *H*ostile World, until God be **Magnified—**

Ph 3:13, 14 - **Brethren,** I count not *myself* to have Apprehended: *but* this **One** *thing* I do: *forgetting* those things which are behind —*and* Reaching forth unto those Things which are before. —*I* <u>*Press*</u> toward the Mark, *for* the Prize of the High *calling of* God in Christ *J*esus....

Priest

Rev 1:5, 6 - *(Unto Him that loved us, and washed us from our sins in His own blood), A*nd hath made Us **kings** and <u>**Priest**</u> unto God and **His** Father; to Him *be* Glory and Dominion *for* **Ever** and Ever. Amen

Rev 5:10 - *A*nd hast made Us unto our God *kings* and **_Priest_**: and *W*e shall **Reign** on the *E*arth.

Rev 20:6 - *** *B*ut *they* shall be **_Priest_** *of* God and *of* Christ, and shall **Reign** with *Him* a *T*housand *Y*ears —

Priesthood *(*You will find the Foundational Scripture *for* this Perpetually - **High C**alling, where it all began in what I believe to be — *an* "*E*verlasting **_Priesthood_** Covenant," *thus* the 'Perpetual-Calling' — *** —

perpetual - adj. 1. lasting forever, or a very long time 2. continuing; constant [a perpetual calling]— *** —*In* the *B*ook *of Numbers 25:12, 13[it reads] Wherefore say, behold, I give unto him my Covenant of Peace: —And he shall have it, and his seed after him: Even the Covenant of an Everlasting Priesthood: because he was Zealous for his God, and made an Atonement for the Children of Israel *** A*men!*)*

Heb 7:21*(Please study this Chapter, as you're being led, also look at Chapters* **8 through 10***. We can never fully get enough understanding of this "Everlasting Priesthood Covenant" and as Children of God, I really believe that not understanding is not comprehending who we really are in Christ)* 7:25 - (For those *P*riest were made without an oath: but this with an oath - *by* Him that said unto *Him*, the Lord swear and will not repent: *T*hou art a *P*riest *forever* after the order of Melchisedec:) —*B*y so much was Jesus made a *S*urety of a **Better Testament.** And they truly were many *Priests*, because they were not **tolerated** to continue to continue by reason of *d*eath: *B*ut this **Man**, because *He C*ontinued ever, hath an *U*nchangeable **_Priesthood._**

Heb 7:25 - *W*herefore, *He* is able also to *S*ave **them** to the *uttermost*, that come unto God by **Him**, seeing *He* ever *Lives*, interceding for **them** —

1 Pet 2:5 - You also, as *lively* Stones, are built up a *Spiritual* House: *A Holy* <u>*Priesthood*</u>, to *offer up* Spiritual *Sacrifices*—

1 Pet 2:9 - But *you* are a Chosen *generation*, a Royal <u>*Priesthood*</u>, A *Holy* Nation — a *peculiar* People, that *you* should show forth the Praises *of Him* who has called *you* out of Darkness — ***

2ⁿᵈ Gift to the Body: Prophets (*This* is another of those *perpetual Callings.* I'll bear witness to this with Two "Foundational *Scriptures*" of this *Gift:* But first, let me person-ally thank God for the *Prophet*. Without them and their enor-mous *Gift* to the Body *of* Christ, there would be no discerning of the *Times*. And though we're not all *Prophets*, yet, as *His* Body; we all have access to that *same* Anointing, so that we too, will be able, at times of need in our *Walk of Faith:* to Discern and see what's up ahead: —

Numbers 11:29 - And Moses said unto Joshua, "Enviest thou for my sake? (I wish to) God that all the Lord's people were <u>*Prophets*</u>*, and that the Lord would put His Spirit upon them.*

Psalms 105:14, 15 - He suffered no man to do them wrong, yea He reproved Kings for their sakes: Saying, *"Touch not mine* Anointed *and do My* <u>*Prophet*</u>*s no harm.*

Eph 4:11 - 13*(excerpt)* - And **He G**ave som*e* — Apostles, and some, <u>*Prophets*</u>* — * For the *perfecting* of the Saints, *f*or the work of the Ministry, *f*or the *Edifying* of the Body *of* Christ: — *T*ill We all come in the Unity of the *faith*......

1 Cor 14:29 - Let the <u>*Prophet*</u>s speak, *t*wo *or t*hree, and let the other *Judge....*

1 Cor 14:32 - "the *spirit* of the <u>*Prophets*</u> are Subject to the <u>*Prophets*</u>"

Eph 3:5 - Which in other *ages* was not made *known* unto the *sons* of *men*, as it is now *R*evealed unto *His H*oly *A*postles, and <u>*Prophets*</u>:

Eph 2:19, 20 - *T*herefore, *you* are no more *strangers* and *foreigners*, but *fellow C*itizens with the *Saints* —and *of* the Household *of* God: *A*nd are *B*uilt upon the *foundation of* the Apostles *and* <u>*Prophets*</u>: Jesus Christ *Himself* being the Chief Corner *Stone...*

Promises

2 Cor 1:20 - For all the <u>*Promises*</u> *of* God are *yes*, and in **Him:** *A*men!

2 Cor 7:1 - Having *t*herefore these <u>*Promises:*</u> *dearly B*eloved, let us *C*leanse ourselves *from* all filthiness of the *flesh* and *S*pirit —

Gal 3:16 - Now to *A*braham and **his** <u>seed</u> were the <u>*Promises*</u> made.

Heb 6:12 - *T*hat *Y*ou be not **slothful,** but *F*ollowers *of* them who through *Faith* and Patience inherit the <u>*Promises*</u>.

2 Pet 1:2-4 (*Grace and peace be multiplied to You thru the knowledge of God, and of Jesus our Lord*)—*A*ccording as *His* divine power hath given unto us *all T*hings that **pertain** to Life and *G*odliness, through the **knowledge** of Him that hath called us to *G*lory and *Virtue:* Whereby are given to us *exceeding* **great** and Precious <u>*Promises:*</u>

Prophecy (n. 1. *the act or power of* **Prophesying 2.** *something told about the Future as by a* **Prophet.)**

Rom 12:6 - Having then *G*ifts *differing* according to the Grace that is given to us: *w*hether <u>*Prophecy,*</u> let us *prophesy* according to (<u>*our own*</u>) —*faith.*

1 Tim 4:14 - *N*eglect not the *G*ift that is in **thee,** —*which* was **given thee** by <u>*Prophecy,*</u> with the *L*aying on of hands by the *Elders...*

2 Pet 1:20, 21 - *Knowing* this First: *that* no <u>*Prophecy*</u> of the *"Word of God"* is of any Private-*interpretation*. * For the <u>*Prophecy*</u> came not in *old-time* by the *W*ill of *man:* but Holy-Men *of* God spake as they were <u>*moved*</u> by the Holy-*Ghost*— ***

Rev 1:3 - *Blessed is he that R*eads*, and they that H*ear *the Words of this* <u>*Prophecy*</u>!

Prophesied

Acts 19:6 - And when Paul * laid hands upon them, the *Holy Ghost* came on them, and they *S*pake with **tongues**, and <u>*Prophesied*</u>.

Jude 14-15 - *A*nd Enoch also, the *S*eventh *from* Adam: <u>*Prophesied*</u> *of* These; *saying.* "Behold the Lord *c*ometh with **Ten** Thousand of **His S**aints." —*T*o *execute* **Judgement** upon all *(All in this Prophecy represents the wicked and ungodly who rejected Christ, and all that God invested in Him by way of the Cross, even for their Salvation)*

Note **of** **Reference:** The Gift of *Prophesying* in the Body of Christ is one of those *"Roll-over Benefits"* that continues to bless the People of God. It is a continuation from the Genesis of Mankind, through the Old Dispensation, unto Now. And for processing this Benefit, I'll use as a Scriptural Basis and Foundation — *the* **"Book** *of* 1ˢᵗ **Samuel"** I will make verse references from *Chapter 10:10,11* —and for me, this is truly a *Hunger Exercise,* and I hope as well for You. In it, I hope you will find for yourselves the *S*ignificant and vital importance of why we need to search out for our individual needs, the necessity of *Prophesying,* and with great enthusiasm, emphatically advance the exalting force of this Anointed *Gift* into its proper place of Prominence. And as we increase in the knowledge of this proactive force of Love, as it helps us carry out the *full measure* of its implied and expressed *P*urpose on behalf of the Kingdom, that we may be built up into the complete Purpose and plan of the Father. Always esteeming another above ourselves. As we *Prophesy* in Hope, the expediency in becoming a Church without *spot* or Wrinkle: as was *Prophesied* to us by John the Revelator, *3rdJohn* 2 *(When he shouted out to us, across that vast ocean of time; declaring in what I call the* **"Threefold Cord of a Prophetic Promise"***, saying) -* **Beloved, I wish above all things that you might prosper and be in health, even as thy Soul Prospers—.** Promises better known to me, as the Inheritance of Christ, that was Bequeathed to us in **His Estate** *(Please hear what the Spirit is saying)*.

An inheritance that King David knew as an Overflowing **Cup.** Now, please understand me, I'm writing this Book, *being* led by God, and I tell you this even while I struggle to grasp many of the **things** that I've written here on these pages; and have not fully Benefitted myself from this Food source. But still, I tell you the Truth, if at any time we would step out by *faith*, without any trepidation, and begin to utilize this Particular **Gift**, in uniformity with one another in Love and not judgment. **Hell** itself would buckle under the **Might** of our Unified Force of Goodwill toward one another, no matter the Denomination if we but received the Revelation of Edification. — Like me, Can you *even imagine* what it will be like when the Prophetic has become a reality, and the immediacy of our Posterity, as a Completed Churchwill be upon Us. "O what a grand and Glorious Day that will be. *(So let us meditate on this Prophetic Word of Hope as we listen to 1 Samuel 10:10,11)*. Selah!

*1 Samuel 10:10, 11 —*** **And when they came there to the hill, behold a company of Prophets met Saul; and the Spirit of God came upon him, and he Prophesied among them. And it came to pass, when all that knew him before saw that he Prophesied among the Prophets, then they said to each other, What has happened —** ****? Is Saul also among the Prophets?**

Prophesy *(v.* **1.** *to tell what will happen; Predict —* **2.** *to speak or write, as* Inspired by God. I personally believe this **tool** is a very <u>misunderstood</u> **Gift** and Anointing. I believe that most of us, including myself, don't fully grasp its enormous benefit in its ability to transform any group or part of the Body that's submitted to increasing *Brotherly Love amongst the Saints. And I do believe if we truly desire to be our Brothers & Sisters' Keepers, as the **Word** of God directs us to be, then we would delve deeper into a more sincere and necessary Comprehension of the importance of **Prophesying** to one another to the edifica-tion of, not just the Body: **b**ut to the edification of that indi-vidual who needs building up. You see, we as a Unit are now well able to do much more in Christ than we are presently accomplishing. Now, if we believe the **Word** *of* God like we say we do, then we're surely without excuse if we fail. We must choose to walk in the Power and authority that Grace now affords us the ability to do. After all, our Lord has **vanquished** our enemy and has now given us the **C**apacity to do in the Spirit of Love, as the Apostle Paul states in his letter to the Corinthians, saying: *1 **Cor** 13:1,2 – **Though I speak with the tongues of men and angels, and have not love, I am become as sounding brass, or a tinkling cymbal. And though I have the Gift of Prophesy, and understand Mysteries, and all Knowledge: and though I have all faith, as to remove mountains, but have not love I am nothing;*** **A**men! — So, with that declaration, let us go forward in the Spirit of Compassion **and** in Wisdom begin to apply by understanding our need to **E**dify one another in the same manner we all desire to be Edified. So let us Prophesy in Love, "for indeed, he that Prophesy's; —*Edifies*" ...

1 Cor 14:1 - * *Follow - after* Charity, and desire Spiritual **Gifts**, but *(I'd)* rather that *y*e might <u>**Prophesy:**</u>

1 Cor 14:3 - * ***But*** he that <u>**Prophes**</u>ies —**S**peaks unto **men** to*wards* *Edification,* Exhortation and *Comfort.*...

1Cor 14:5 - * *I W*ish that *ye* all **spake** with Tongues, *but (I'd)* rather that *ye* **Prophes**ied —*for G*reater is he that **Prophes**ies, than he that **speaks** with Tongues: —

Acts 2:17 - And it shall come to Pass in the **last-days** —Saith God, I will pour out of *My Spirit*, upon all flesh: *and* Your Sons, *and Your* Daughters shall **Prophesy.**....

Acts 2:18 - And on *My* **servants**, and on *My* Handmaidens, I will pour out *in* those **days** *of My Spirit:* and they shall **Prophesy.**....

1 Cor 14:31 - For *you* may all **Prophesy,** one *by* one: —that all may learn, and all may be Comforted....

1 Cor 14:24*(The Clarity and Encouragement of Prophesying amongst Brethren).* But *if* all **Prophesy,** and there come in *One* that **believes not,** or *O*ne **unlearned**. *(then once he hears in a plane tongue, he that Prophesies)*, he is Convinced of **all,** he is Judged *of all.*

Acts 21:9*(Here in **Acts 21**, we see the confirmation of **Joel 2:28** and **Acts 2:17*** *Here we see one of the Deacons, Philip, one of the **7** men that were filled with the Spirit. And he had four daughters, who were endowed with the Spirit, and anointed to* **Prophesy:** *Hence fulfilling what was* **Prophesied***. For me, I believe that this single piece of open evidence signifies the importance of Holy-Ghost filled Parents and Leaders to the Lives of not only those they lead in a group but more importantly, in the Lives of their own Children— especially their Sons and Daughters, even before they ever, experience their own freewill surrender to Salvation. Now, when you go back and experience verses **17** and **18** of Acts, Chapter 2, you'll see how God differentiates his Anointing between the Two: **17** - 'Your Children shall* **Prophesy**' *and in **18** - 'Your Servant, Workers, Handmaiden, Lay-people, shall* **Prophesy** *— Clearly there is a distinction intended here by the Father. Now, personally, I believe that His Servants are those who will become the Ox or the Donkey. But the Children are those who represent the Power of God upon the Life of a surrendered Servant who has Authority under the Anointing to produce*

Children, who are obedient to the Authority and Nourishment of their Obedient Parent, or Better said, to the Parent who is Spiritually Rooted in the 'Household of Faith' Acts 21:8, *9* - And the next day we that were of Paul's Company departed, and came unto Caesarea: and we entered into the House of Philip the *Evangelist*, which was one of the *Seven*; and *(we stayed)* with him. And *Philip* had four Daughters, ***virgins***, who did <u>***Prophesy***</u> — Hallelujah, and Amen!

For The Perfecting *of* The Saints. For The Work *of* The Ministry. For The *E*difying *of* The Body *of* Christ!
(Ephesians 4:12)

the benefits of the cup of salvation — part 2

Prosper (This Message of Prosperity, I will Prophesy it to You. The way I was led to Prophesy *it*, face to face to those I've Fellowship with in the **Body** *of* Christ. But now, by way of this Book, I'll Prophesy it to the People that I believe will read *it*. And with great Joy, I hope each Person will be able to **Prophesy** in like manner, without *trepidation*, to those whom they will encounter in their place of Worship. So, this *Word* was *Revealed* to me a few years back, but I believe that it's for us *now*. Please be assured, this **Word** was *First* **given** to me, for my own *spiritual* **B**enefit —but is also definitely for the wider Body: Thus, the Lord said *(to me)*. My **child**, one of the most important desires that I have in mind for you is simply that you **Prosper** *(be made Whole)* in every *area* of your Life. Now, as you are led by the **Spirit** *toward* the things that lead your Soul to increase. —And as you **Follow** those things revealed to you, in the **Word** that point you to *My* Purpose. You will find in them all the **Resources** you'll ever need to Glorify *My* name as you come into that Place of wholeness, which is **Prosperity**. Remember, as you seek out those things pertaining to Life and Godliness, *My* Truth will confirm in the *Word, my* desire to Give

you the Kingdom. And as you follow the Wisdom of *My Word* —
you *will* surely overflow in your **Spiritual, Physical,** and **Financial**
well, transforming you by your *faith*, as your soul is Nourished
and Benefitted *for* your Good! *"And these Three will become One"*
to the Purpose and fulfillment of God's Joy for your Life. —Just
as the **Preacher** declares in the Book *of Ecclesiastes*— Revealing
through Wisdom, the strength and focus on the Unity *of* Three:
[Eccl 4:9 -(12) -; and a threefold cord is not easily broken] —)

3 Jn 2 - Beloved, I wish above all ***things*** that You may <u>***Prosper***</u>
and be in Health, *even* as Your *Soul* <u>*Prosper*</u>s.***

Purpose *(n.* 1. *what one plans to get are do.* **2.** *the reason or use for*
*something [**a room with no purpose**]—v. to plan or intend not in*
*common use – **on Purpose**, not by accident; intentional.* **—to good**
Purpose, *with a good result."* — Now, I believe that this **word** is one
of the main *Keys* in our lives as we Pursue a complete and
fulfilling Life. Whether for happiness, peace and tranquility, or a
whole host of other *purposeful* needs and desires that help us
round out our *lives* to the full measure of *fruitfulness.*

But — without the Dynamic **power** of this one **word**, operating
as our North **Star Compass** *[pertaining to the will of God in our lives,*
by way of the Holy Ghost], we would surely be as wayward
Vessels on this **vast** sea of Living. So, **Purpose,** for me, is a
never ending moving forward **pursuit**: threading itself into the
rise and fall of our conquest to accomplish whatever Goal for
the moment that is necessary in our endeavoring to persevere.
For me, it is the **cord** that binds us in our collective efforts
through our individual and varying ways in how we seek to
please the **Father.** And though evil has its own **purpose** and
Agenda, in its desire to thwart the Plan and **Purpose** of God for
our *Lives*, it Cannot: Why? Simply put, it's not a **moral or spiri-**
tual agent of good. Therefore, its agenda to destroy us will
always work out for our good. Since the Sovereign God, and

Creator of all that is Good, still weaves and guides our steps, even when we are not *Spiritually* mature enough to know or believe it at the time—He still brings us through into our Appointed *Purpose,* for the *sake* of the Kingdom. As we carry out the **Love** *A*cts *of* the **Father.** — **(Now** *here I'll speak, by permission of the* **Father***, in the* Holy **Ghost***, my own Personal insights* on this **word Purpose:** And it's this: *"Purpose is, The Ingenious Mechanism in the Destiny of One, or Many, for the Benefit of All").* So, in conclusion to this *Spiritual Insight* and Commentary on this Powerful **Word** of Hope—*let's* look at the **Books** *of* **Proverbs, Ecclesiastes,** and *Isaiah:* —In these Three *Books,* I believe that you'll find in them revelations and new discoveries on this Powerful Word *of Destiny:* —

Proverbs 20:18 - *Every* <u>*Purpose*</u> *is established by Counsel: and with good advice make War* (attack your goal and purpose with the weapons of Wisdom) ....

Ecclesiastes 3:1*(read 1 thru 10 for greater insight)* **-** *To everything there is a Season, and a time to every* <u>*Purpose*</u> *under the Heaven:*

Isaiah 14:26, 27 - *This is the* <u>*Purpose*</u> *that is* <u>*Purpose*</u>*d upon the whole Earth: and this is the* <u>*Hand*</u> *that is stretched out upon all the Nations. For the Lord of Host has* <u>*Purpose*</u>*d, and who shall Cancel it? And His* <u>*Hand*</u> *is stretched out, and who shall turn it back?* —

Acts 11:23, 24 - Who when he came, and had seen the Grace of God, was glad, and exhorted them *all:* that with <u>**Purpose**</u> of heart they'd cleave unto the Lord. —For he was a good *man* and full of the Holy *Ghost and faith*: and many People was added to the Lord.

Rom 8:28 - And we know that, ***All things work together*** for Good to them that *love* God, to them who're called, according to His <u>***Purpose.***</u>

2 Tim 1:9 - Who hath saved us and called us with a Holy Calling not according to our works, but according to His own **_Purpose_** and **G**race: Which was given us in Christ Jesus before the *World* began.

2 Tim 3:10 - But *Y*ou have fully known *my doctrine*, manner of Life **_Purpose, faith,_** *l*ongsuffering, Charity, patience...

1 Jn 3:7, 8 - Little **children**, let no man deceive *Y*ou: — *he* that does *R*ighteousness is *righteous*, even as *He* is *Righteous*. He that commits sins is of the *d*evil; *for* the *d*evil sinned from the beginning. For this **_Purpose,_** the Son *of* God was Manifested *to destroy the devil's works.*

Renew *They that wait upon the Lord shall* **Renew** *their Strength they shall mount up wings as* **Eagles**, *they shall run and not grow weary, they shall walk and not faint* [Is 40:31]— In this Commentary, all **scripture** for this *F*oundational **word** is found in the Old Testament, but they are *eternal* and *P*erpetual.*— Now we've heard that *verse* quoted off and on, probably more then we can remember. Question: what does it mean? Well, I'm glad you asked, so let me give you the answer that was given to me when I asked that **question** of the Holy **Ghost.** And I hope that it helps you, as much as it did me. Of course, when I asked that **question**, I was spiritually **_beat-down_** and really needed some help: here's the Answer, *please* be encouraged: *We must, by our faith soar high above the situations and cares of Life, as an Eagle we must fly to whatever height is necessary, in pursuit of our sure deliverance, which is prepared for us from the Table of Heaven. We must, from a Prophetic distance, see our Promises, our Bounty, and begin to pursue it, desiring to have all that the Lord has prepared for us. The Lord said to watch an Eagle as it* <u>*pursues its prey,*</u> *— if he misses it on his initial attempt, he runs to break his momentum, gathering itself into a slow walk. Then it Angelically Ascends back to his heavenly domain, and once again, he takes* *another run in pursuit of his deliverance —Likewise, we too must become relentless in our Pursuit of God's will for our Lives. In every area of our Needs and Aspirations.* For His Glory, Amen!) —

Ps 51:10 - Create in *me* a *C*lean *Heart,* O God, and <u>*Renew*</u> a right *spirit* within *me....*

Lam 5:21 - Turn thou *us* unto thee, O Lord, and *we* shall be turned; <u>*Renew*</u> our days as *of* old...

Is 41:1 - *K*eep *silence* before *Me*, O islands; — *and* let the People <u>*Renew*</u> *their S*trength:

Renewed

2 Cor 4:16 - For which cause we *faint* not: *But* though our *outward* **man** *P*erish: Yet the Inward *man* is <u>**Renewed day**</u> by *day*!

Eph 4:22, 23 - That you *p*ut *-off* concerning the *former C*onversation the old *man* which is **corrupt** according to the deceit*ful lust*. And be <u>**Renewed**</u>, in the spirit of your *Mind*...

Col 3:9, 10 - Lie not *one* to Another, seeing that you have *put-off* the *O*ld *man* with *his* deeds. And have *put-* **on** the New *man,* which is <u>**Renewed**</u> in Knowledge, *a*fter the *Image of Him*, that *Created him—*

Renewing

Rom 12:2 - *A*nd be-not **conformed** to this *World: B*ut be-ye Trans- formed by the <u>**Renewing**</u> *of* your Mind, that *ye* may Prove what is that *Good* and *a*cceptable, and Perfect will *of* God.

Tit 3:5 - Not by **works** of R*ighteousness, *which we* have done, but *according* to **His** *m*ercy, **He** *S*aved us, *by* the Washing of Regeneration, and <u>**Renewing**</u> *of* the Holy **Ghost.......**

Repent (We now have the Power in Christ, by way of the Holy

Ghost, to not continue in **sin**. A Power we did not have before, but now we have: *'**No Mo Excuses, Period**'.)*

Acts 3:11 *thru* 19 - And as the lame **man,** which was Healed, held Peter *and* John, all the **people** ran together unto them in the Porch that is **called** Solomon's, greatly wondering. And when Peter saw it, **he** Answered unto the **people**. *"Ye men of Israel, why marvel ye at this? Or why look ye so earnestly on Us as though by our own Power or Holiness we had made this man walk? The God of Abraham, and of Isaac, and of Jacob, the God of our fathers; has Glorified His Son Jesus, whom ye delivered up,— and denied Him in the presence of Pilate: when he was determined to let Him go —But ye denied the Holy One and the Just, and desired a murderer to be granted unto you, and killed the Prince of Life — whom God has raised from the dead: whereby we are witnesses. ***And His name through faith in His name hath made this man strong, whom ye see, and know: Yes, the faith, which is by Him, has given (this man) this Perfect soundness in the presence of you All. —And now brethren, I know that through Ignorance ye did it, did also your* **rulers***: —*

*But those things, which God before, had showed by the mouth of all His Prophets, —***Christ** *should* **Suffer***: He has so fulfilled * ****Repent**** you therefore, and be Converted, that your sins may be Blotted out, when the times of Refreshing will come:*

Acts 17:30- And the *times* of this Ignorance God **winked** at: But now Command **all-men** everywhere, to **Repent** —

2 Cor 7:8,9 - Though I made you **sorry** with a Letter, I don't **Repent:** Though *(later)* I did **Repent***: for* I perceived that the same *Epistle* has made you **sorry**, though it was but for a *Season*. Now I **rejoice**— not that ye were made **sorry:** But that ye Sorrowed unto **Repentance**.

Rev 2:5 - Remember therefore, from whence thou art Fallen — and **Repent** and do the *first* Works, or else **I** will come **quickly**, and will *remove* Thy Candlestick out of *his* place, except thy <u>*Repent*</u> *(Ephesus)*

Rev 2:16 - <u>**Repent**</u> —*or* else I will come unto You *q*uickly *(Pergamos)*

Rev 2:21 - *A*nd I gave *her* space to <u>*Repent*</u>, of *her Fornication,* and *she* <u>*Repented*</u> not *(Thyatira)....*

Rev 3:3 - *R*emember therefore *how you* have received and heard, and hold-*fast* and <u>*Repent*</u> *(Sardis)....*

Rev 3:19 - *A*s many as I Love, I *rebuke* and *Chasten* —*be* zealous therefore and <u>*Repent*</u> *(Laodicea).* ***Note: there were Five Churches that were asked to repent —Why only Five? Hmmm, this will make for a Great Study —***

Personal Note: *An excerpt from my personal Notebook - 3-10-1997* ***Quote: My personal desire, Spiritually, is to openly 'at all times' walk in humility and always be able to*** <u>***Repent***</u>***. As I seek the presence of the Lord, for He is my Vision, and the Vanquisher of all my enemies: leading me in a Plain Path. For His Glory,*** Amen!

Repentance (The avenue of access for all non-Jews. An access we never had before, *Hallelujah, Thank You,* Jesus *for* our Access in *You.)*

Acts 11:18 - When they heard these things, they held their *Peace* and *glorified* God, *S*aying —*T*hen hath God also to the *G*entiles, *granted* <u>*Repentance*</u> unto Life.

Acts 20:21 - Testifying both to the Jews — *and* also to the Greeks, <u>*Repentance*</u> towards God, and *faith* toward our Lord Jesus *Christ...*

2 Cor 7:9, 10 - Now I *rejoice*: not that ye were made ***sorry***, but that ye Sorrowed to <u>**Repentance**</u> * *F*or Godly *S*orrow *produces* <u>*Repentance*</u> to *Salvation:* —

Reward

1 Cor 3:8 - Now he that *plants*, and he that *waters* are One: and every **man** shall Receive his own <u>***Reward***</u>, *according* to his own *Labor* —

1 Cor 3:14 - *If* any **man's** *W*ork abide, which he has Built-there-upon: *he* shall *receive* a <u>**Reward**</u>

1 Cor 9:16 - 18 - For though I **preach** the Gospel, I have *nothing* to **glory** of: *for Necessity* is laid upon Me if I **preach** not the Gospel! For if I do this **thing** willingly, I have a **Reward** Col - 2:18 - Let no *man* **beguile** you of your <u>**Reward**</u> —

1 Tim 5:18 - For the **Scriptures** *s*aith: *"Thou shalt not muzzle to Ox that treads out the Corn"* and a Laborer is Worthy *of* his <u>**Reward**</u> —

Col 3:24 - *K*nowing that *of* the Lord, *y*e shall receive the <u>***Reward***</u> —

Heb 10:35 - *C*ast not *away* therefore *y*our **Confidence**, —which has **great** *R*ecompense *of* <u>**Reward**</u> —

2 Jn **vs:**8 - Look to *y*ourselves, that we lose not those *things* which we have *w*rought, but that **we** Receive a *full* <u>**Reward**</u> —

Rev 11:18 - *A*nd that **Thou** should give <u>**Reward**</u> unto the Prophets, and to the **Saints**, and them that Fear **Your** Name, *S*mall and *G*reat—

Rev 22:12 - And *b*ehold, **I** come **quickly**, and *My* <u>**Reward**</u> is with *Me* to *g*ive to *Every* **man** according as *his* Work shall be —

Righteous *(Because* we have been Justified by the **Righteous** act of Christ, who was *made* Sin for Us, we are now in **Him** *made* **Righteous**...)

Rom 5:19 - For as by **one** *man's* Disobedience many were made (*to be*) **sinners**, *S*o by the *O*bedience *of **One***, shall *M*any be made (*to be*) <u>*Righteous*</u>....

Jam 5:16 - The *E*ffectual-***fervent*** *Prayer* of a <u>*Righteous*</u> *-man* *A*vails much...

1Jn 3:7 - *L*ittle *children* let no man deceive ***you:*** he that does *R*ighteousness is <u>***Righteous***</u>, even as *He* is <u>***Righteous***</u>...

Righteousness (Since we're *now* *J*ustifiably made Right in Christ, let us by the Truth of that Reality, begin to ***produce*** out our ***Righteousness*** the *fruits* of ***His Labor***, by our own Obedience.)

Rom 4:(3) - (5) - *A*braham believed God, and it was counted unto him for <u>***Righteousness***</u> *** *B*ut to him that works not, *but* *B*elieves on *Him* that Justifies the *ungodly*, his ***faith*** is added for <u>***Righteousness***</u>.

Rom 4:6 - Even as David *also d*escribed the **Blessedness**, of the *man* unto whom God *imputes* <u>***Righteousness***</u> —without Works...

1 Cor 1:30 - But *of* Him, are ***you*** in Christ Jesus, who *of* God is made unto *Wisdom* and <u>***Righteousness***</u>...

1 Cor 15:34 - *A*wake to <u>***Righteousness***</u>, and *sin* not:

Ph 3:9 - *A*nd be *found* in ***Him***, not having my *own* <u>***Righteousness***</u> — But in ***Christ***: —*—*the* <u>***Righteousness***</u> which is *of* God by *faith*...

2 Tim 2:22 - *F*lee also *youthful **lust:** but* Follow <u>***Righteousness***</u>...

2 Tim 4:8 - Henceforth, there is laid-***up*** for ***me*** a Crown *of* <u>***Righteousness***</u> which the Lord, *the Righteous* Judge shall give ***me*** at that day.

Heb 1:9 - Thou hath ***loved*** <u>***Righteousness***</u>, and *H*ated Iniquity, therefore God — even *your* God, hath *a*nointed *you* with the Oil of Gladness *A*bove *your* fellows...

Jam 3:18 - And the *fruit* of <u>*Righteousness*</u>, is sown in Peace!

1 Pet 2:24 - Who **His own-s**elf bare *o*ur *sins* in **His own-B**ody on the *tree*, that we being **dead** to sins, should *L*ive unto <u>*Righteousness*</u>, *by* whose *Stripes you* were *H*ealed —

1 Jn 2:29 - If **you** know that **He** is *R*ighteous, **you** know that *e*veryone that does <u>*Righteousness*</u> is *Born of Him...*

1 Jn 3:10 - In this, the **children** *of* God is *M*anifest, *and* the children of the **devil:** whosoever does no <u>*Righteousness*</u> is not *of* God:

Rev 19:8 - *A*nd to **Her** *(symbolically the Church)* was *G*ranted that **She** should be *a*rrayed in *fine* *L*inen, clean and *W*hite: — *for* the *fine* *L*inen is the <u>*Righteousness*</u> of the *Saints* ...

(Pause) — For Poetry Praise:

> *I woke up this* **Morning, finding** *the* **R**ain *in* **my** *Life*
>   *had* **Gone.**
> *With it went* **my teardrops,** *no more* **Crying** *in* **my**
>   **Soul.**
> *Only* **Son-light** *Through my* **W**indow Shone. —
> *Before* **my** feet *could touch the* **Floor,** *I heard the Angels*
>   *Shout with Glee.*
> **O** *what* **Thrill** *it was to Know:* —*How the Angels*
>   **Praised** *God for* **me.**
> *Another* **Soul** *Bought by Christ, and His Blood that*
>   *made* **him** Free.

Son *(Here* I want to *highlight* <u>**Jesus**</u>, the **Son,** who now dwells with us in our *spirit*: through the 3rd **Person** *of* the Godhead, who we now know Intimately as the Holy **Ghost.** And since we can now *know* **Him** *spiritually* in this way, we should then also know we have no more **excuses**. For because of **Him** and the *finished* Work of Christ, God no longer *winks*. Therefore, we must at all times choose the *Spirit* over the *flesh*, we have no choice, and indeed; we should not desire any other choice: but the *Son*. As the scriptures declare on our behalf: *"Greater is He that is in me —then he that is in the World"!*

Then, by all means, that should settle in us, once and for all; the Authority that we walk in and the Power that we wield over the enemy. Therefore, we must understand that on its own, Evil has no access to us *[except for that access we allow]*. And wherever we allow the *Son* to Reign *in our* Lives, Hell has *failed.* **Amen!)**

Rom 8:3 - For what the Law could not do, in that it was weak *in the flesh.* God sending His *own* <u>*Son*</u> in the Likeness of Sinful-flesh and for *sin...* Condemned *sin* in the Flesh...Rom 8:31, 32 - What shall we say to these *things*? *If* God be for Us, who can be against Us? He that *spared* not His *own* <u>*Son*</u>: —

1 Cor 15:28 - And when all *things* shall be Subdued unto **Him**, then shall the <u>*Son*</u> also *Himself* be subject unto God, who put *all-things* under **Him,** *t*hat God may be *A*ll in *All.*

2 Cor 1:19 - *F*or the <u>*Son*</u> *of* God, Jesus Christ— *who* was Preached among you by Us, even by *me*, Silvanus *and* Timotheus; was not *yea* and *nay.* but in *Him* was Yea—

Gal 2:20 - I *am* Crucified *with* Christ: *nevertheless,* I live, *yet* not I, but Christ Lives in *me,* and the *Life* which I now *live* in the Flesh, I *live* by the *faith* of the <u>*Son*</u> *of* God: —

Gal 4:6 - *A*nd because you are *sons,* God has sent-forth the *Spirit of* His <u>*Son*</u>, into your Hearts —*crying Abba* Father...

Gal 1:15, 16 - But when it *Pleased* God, who separated *me from* my mother's *womb* and Called *me* by His *Grace* —*to* Reveal His

__Son__ in *me*: that I *might* Preach Him among the __heathen.__ —
Immediately I Conferred not with *flesh* and *blood:*

Heb 3:6 - But Christ, as a __Son__ over *His o*wn *House*, whose *House*
are we, *if* we *hold-fast* the Confidence....

1 Jn 3:23 - And this is His Commandment: '*That* We should
believe, on the *Name of* His __Son__ Jesus Christ, *and* Love One
Another —

2 Jn 9 - *He* that Abide*s in* the Doctrine of Christ: *he* hath both
the Father and the __Son__...

1 Jn 1:7 - But if we *walk* in the Light, as *He* is in the Light, we
have *f*ellowship one with another, and the *Blood* of Jesus Christ
His __Son__ Cleanses *us* from all *S*in...

1 Jn 2:24 - *If* that which *you've h*eard *from* the Beginning, shall
live in *you. You* also shall *continue* in the __Son__, and in the
Father...

1 Jn 3:8 - *He* that Commit *sin* is of the *devil. For* the *devil sinned*
from the Beginning. *For* this *Purpose,* the __Son__ *of* God was manifest that *He* might Destroy the Works of the *devil...*

1 Jn 5:11-13 - And this is the Record, *that* God has given to us
eternal Life, and this Life is in His __Son__. *He* that has the __Son__ has
Life, and *he* that has not the __Son__ of God, does not have *life.*
These things have **I** written unto *you* that believe on the Name
of the __Son__ *of* God:

Son [as *children*] (We who are now, the Righteousness of God *by*
Christ, are in *Him,* Highly Favored. Because we are *no-longer*
Illegitimate, but now we are Counted in the Father as *sons:* And
Heirs according to the Promise.)

Gal 4:6, 7 - *And because you are sons* God has sent-*forth* the *Spirit* of His *Son* into *your* Hearts, Crying **Abba** Father. Wherefore *you* are no more a ***servant*** but a *son:*

Heb 12:5-8 - An *you* have for the *Exhortation* which speaks to *you* as unto Children: **My Son** despise not the *Chastening* of the Lord. Nor *f*aint when *you* are Rebuked *by* **Him.** *F*or whom the Lord *loves* **He Chastens and** scourges every **Son** whom **He** *R*eceives. **If** *you* endure ***chastening,*** God deals with *You* as with Sons, *f*or what **Son** is *he* whom the Father Chasten not? —

Sons (The Privileges we now *Have* as **Sons***,* is that of *Unmerited – **Favor,*** which means *we* did not earn it. It was **Bought** for *Us* at an unmeasurable **C**ost. A **P**rice that no Mortal *man* could Pay. Yet, **One** could: because of **His** Immortality as the **Son** *of* **M**an, the **Man** Christ obtained **our** *R*ighteousness by **His** Blood. So, *we* must begin *[in Authority]*, to walk in the *f*ulness of the **Price** that was **paid** for Us. *F*or how could we ***neglect*** so **G**reat an Honor, as to be *called* **Sons:** *A*nd not Live up to its **C**ost...)

Acts 2:17 - And it shall come to pass in the **last-days** *S*aith God — I *will* **P**our out **My-Spirit** on all ***flesh: your*** <u>*son*</u>s and *your* daughters shall Prophesy...

Rom 8:14 - *F*or as ***many*** as Led by the **Spirit** *of* God —They are the <u>**Sons**</u> *of* God —

Rom 8:19 - For the *E*arnest Expectation of the **Creature***,* waits for the Manifestation of the <u>**Sons**</u> *of* God....

2 Cor 6:17, 18 - Wherefore come out from among *them* and be *you* *S*eparate *s*aith the Lord, *and Touch* not the *un*clean *th*ing. And **I** *will* receive *you.* And will be a Father to *you*– and *you* *S*hall be My <u>**Sons**</u> *and* **Daughters**: *S*aith the Lord..........

Gal 4:6 - And *because you* are <u>**Sons**</u>*,* God has *sent-f*orth the **Spirit** *of* **His** *S*on, into *your* Hearts: —Crying ***Abba,*** Father!

Ph 2:14, 15 - Do *all* <u>Things</u> – without *Murmurings* and *Disputing's*– That *you* may be *Blameless*, and Harmless; the <u>*Sons*</u> *of* God —

Heb 2:10 - For it *Became* *Him* *for* who are ***all-t****hings* — in *Bringing* many <u>*Sons*</u> to Glory: *To* make the ***Captain*** of their Salvation Perfect *through* ***Sufferings*—**

Heb 12:7 - If *you* *en*dure-*C*hastening, God deals with *you* as <u>*Sons*</u>.

1 Jn 3:1, 2 - **Behold!** *W*hat manner *of Love* the Father has ***bestowed*** upon *Us* that *we* should be *called* the <u>***Sons***</u> *of* God: — ***henceforth*** the World knows *Us* not, because it knew *Him* not: *B*eloved, now are *we* the <u>*Sons*</u> *of* God, and it does not yet Appear what *we* shall *B*e: *but* *we* *K*now that when *He* shall *Appear*, *we* shall *B*e like *Him*, for *we* shall *See* *Him* as <u>*He*</u> Is.

Teach *(This* Gift must be *P*resented in *A*bsolute, there can be no *Timidity* in its delivery at all: Only in *C*omplete *Assurance of* One's *C*alling should it ever be Performed. (WARNING Please Hear from God, or Don't Do It*)*

Acts 5:42 - And *D*aily in the ***Temple***, and in every *H*ouse, ***they*** did not cease to <u>***Teach***</u> *and P*reach Jesus Christ —

1 Cor 14:19 - Yet in the ***Church***, I'd rather speak *five-W*ords with my Understanding, ***(that by my voice)***; I might <u>***Teach***</u> *others* also:

1 Tim 4:11 - These *T*hings Command and <u>***Teach***</u>!

2 Tim 2:1, 2 - Thou *t*herefore my ***Son***, be strong in the Grace that is in Christ Jesus. *A*nd the Things that *you* have heard of *me* among many ***witnesses***, the same ***you*** Commit to Faithful ***men***, who shall be able to <u>***Teach***</u> Others also...

2 Tim 2:24 - The Servant *of* the Lord must not ***fight;*** but be Gentle to all *men:* *a*pt to <u>***Teach***</u>, patient.

1 Jn 2:27 - But the Anointing which *you* have received of Him abides in *you, and you* need not that any *man* **Teach** you — But as the same Anointing **Teach**es *you* of all things, and is *Truth*, and is no *lie*, even as it has *Taught you*. *Y*ou shall *A*bide in *Him* —

Heb 8:11 - And *they* shall not **Teach** every*man* his *N*eighbor, and every*man* his *B*rother, ***saying*** *K*now the Lord: *for A*ll will know *Me*!

3ʳᵈ Gift: **Teachers** (*From* my perspective, this Gift is a Tri*fold* **instrument** of Instruction: First, after a Soul has received its Salvation, it begins its journey down the road to **Discipleship**. And for this discipline to be nurtured in the Child of God unto its fullest potential, the Soul *(he or she)* must surrender and commit to **Spiritual** Training. And so, we see here, the **First** *S*tep in the Tri*fold* calling of the **Teacher**. So, the **Teacher** must *first* be a **submissively** *T*eachable Soul, apt to receive **Teaching**, whereby creating the opportunity for the Gift in **him/her** to be exposed or revealed as their Call. Then, the **Second** *S*tep in this Potentially Trisecting and phenomenal Call is the Soul receiving the Call and advancing into the role of a *'Teacher'*. And in this Gift, they began to advance the Kingdom of God, as they nurture and **Instruct** in Righteousness, the Children of God. Instructing us in all manners pertaining to Holiness, Godliness, and other Servilities related to Servants. Giving us a solid **foundation** in "How to Walk *with* God." — And **thirdly**, the **Teacher** may as well operate in the Gift and Anointing of a Pastor: As **he** or **she**, in the capacity of a **"Teacher - Pastor"** begins the journey of Shepherding a particular part of the Body in the way it should grow and go. Making us accountable not only to one another, but to Leadership. Showing us how to Come-**forth spiritually** in an orderly-**fashion:** —Showcasing the Fruit of their Labor, whose **fruit** we are, as we demonstrate in the World, on behalf of the Kingdom; our **credibility** as Witnesses unto Christ, —**for His** *G*lory, Amen!) ***

1 Cor 12:28 - And God has Set some in the Church, — *first* Apostles* *secondarily* Prophets** *thirdly,* <u>Teachers</u> —

<u>1 Cor 12:29</u> *(Commentary: Here, for me, this verse demonstrates the Gift of a <u>Teacher</u> operating in the Apostle Paul, showing us that the Anointing of the Holy Spirit, can cause several Gifts to be divided in the Ministry and Calling of One Person, as He wills it:*

1 Cor 12:11) Are all <u>Teachers:</u> —

Tit 2:3 - The Aged women, likewise, *must* be in Behavior as becomes Holiness, not false accusers, not given to much **wine,** *(but)* <u>Teachers</u> of Good Things...

Heb 5:12 - For when, *for* the time **you** ought to be <u>Teacher</u>s: You are in need of being **Taught**— *AGAIN*...

Teaching (As we learn from our **Teachers**, bearing Witness in the **Holy Ghost**: we do receive in our Spirit the things Necessary for our **service** to God —*for* the Work of the Ministry, to the Perfecting of Christ in Us, who is the **"Hope of Glory": Col 1:27**) —

<u>Acts 18:9</u>, <u>11</u> - *(Commentary: Again, here Verse 9 shows us that we must get zoned into the Lord's voice, as He speaks in us, through the Person of the Holy Ghost. We must begin to Train ourselves with an intense urgency, as we learn our newly acquired Craft. Just as the Confession of our faith Commands us to have, in our daily pursuit, to cast out the enemy. And as we become proficient in utilizing our Gift, we will begin to enjoy many more Victories than defeats, in carrying out the Plan and strategy of God. So, we must have Ears to hear, as we await our Command. How? Simple: by fasting, praying, praising, and listening and when we prepare in whatever way God leads us, we will discern and hear whether to stand and fight this War now or save it for another time. Since today is our day of retreat, saving the fight for another day of the Lord's choosing: that the Gospel in no way be <u>hindered</u> — for this indeed is what tactical Warfare is all about (**whether spiritual or not**). You must*

wait for your orders.) - Then spake the Lord to Paul, in the night, by a Vision: *"Be not afraid but speak, and hold not thy peace—for I am with thee, and no man shall set on you to harm you: for I have many people in this City.* He continued there for a Year and six-months, *Teaching* the Word *of* God among them —

Acts 28:30, 31 - And Paul dwelt 2-whole Years in *his* own House, and received *all* that came in unto *him (Commentary: In this Verse, Paul is under House-arrest, serviced by his captors: while they wait for the final decree of his punishment to expire –(but invisible to his captors, is the fact that this is the will of God in Christ for Paul, on behalf of the souls in Rome, including his captors)–* Preaching the Kingdom *of* God and *Teaching* those things which concern the Lord Jesus Christ, with all Confidence; no man forbidding *him*.....

Col 1:28 - Whom we Preach: warning every *man*, —*Teaching* every *man* in (*all*) Wisdom. —That *we* may Present every *man* Perfect in Christ Jesus:

Col 3:16 - Let the **Word** *of* Christ dwell in **you** Richly, in **all** Wisdom *Teaching* and Admonishing *One-another*, in psalms & hymns...

Tit 2:11,12 - For the Grace *of* God that brings **Salvation**. Has *appeared* to All **men**– *Teaching* us, that Denying **ungodliness** and worldly *lusts*, that *we* should Live Soberly, Righteously, and Godly!—

Truth (*For* me, this **Word** is the Foundational Powerhouse, and it is, the Explicit and undisputable *Evidence* of the Reality *of* God. And *by* Christ, who is The **Word** *of* God in the flesh: and before becoming *flesh*, **He** was the **Word** sent *forth* by *faith* from the Mouth of God: *Saying, 'Let there Be'.* And the **Word** *by* the Power of the **Holy-Spirit**, brought into *existence;* All that is – and into Perpetuity, All that shall be. —The *Truth* is that until

Christ appeared, the World that then was one set to *doom* and *despair*, one without Hope.

Until the **Truth** *of* God was born in a Manger, created in the form of the **son** *of* Man, and who by **His** **V**irgin birth: **d**ispelled all the lies of the **devil**, and snatched away from *him [once again on our behalf]*: our **freewill C**hoice. And now, without anymore-**excuses**, we once again have the Power of self-determination. And to once and for all: settle our **D**estination, by Choosing the Freedom that **Truth** has delivered unto us— *in the Son ["For truly, who the Son sets free —is Free indeed" Jn 8:32 - 36]. —*

And so, I find in this Dynamic **Word** the Foundation on which all that we Live for in Christ **hangs** upon, as the **Truth** shows us the way to a Peaceful and Victorious Life. Showing us with great Joy not only how to *worship* the Father in **Spirit** and in **Truth**, but especially, how to Live every day in the <u>**Truth**</u>. [<u>Foundational Scriptures</u>: *St Jn 4:23,24 - But the hour comes, and now is, when the true Worshipers, shall Worship the Father in Spirit and in <u>Truth</u>: for the Father seek such to Worship Him —God is a Spirit: and they that Worship Him, must Worship Him in Spirit and in <u>Truth</u>. —**

*St Jn 8:32 - And ye shall know the <u>Truth</u>, and the <u>Truth</u> shall make you Free. —** *St Jn 15:26 - But when the Comforter is come, whom I will send unto you from the Father, even the Spirit of <u>Truth</u>, which proceeded from the Father: He shall Testify of Me. —** *St Jn 16:13 - How be it: when He, the Spirit of <u>Truth</u>, is come; He will Guide you into all <u>Truth</u>: for He shall not speak of Himself —but whatsoever He hears, that He shall Speak: and He will show you things to come. —** *St Jn 17:17 - Sanctify them through thy <u>Truth</u>: Thy Word is <u>Truth</u>. —** *St Jn 18:37 - (?) Jesus Answered: You say that I am a King...To this end was I born, and for this cause came I into the World —that I should bear Witness to the*

Truth. *(So) Everyone that is of the Truth Hears My Voice.../* Amen)! ***

I Am: The Way the Truth and the Light— *No Man Comes to the* **Father** *but by Me*—(John 14:6)

1 Cor 14:22 - 25 - *(Commentary: Here we see that the Truth is the scale that sets in proper Balance the Hierarchy of the outward and inward workings of the Church. In all of its Overseeing function, it bears Witness by the witness of those who Witness, in the Lives of others, as well as their own, the Transforming Power of the Gospel)* Scriptures: Wherefore Tongues are for a *Sign*, not to **them** that Believe, but to *them* that believe not: But Prophesying *is* not for *them* that believe not, *but* for **them** that Believe: — Therefore if the **whole** Church comes together in one Place, and **all** Speak *with* **Tongues,** and one comes in *unlearned* or *unbelievers*, will they not say that you're all Mad? – But if **all** Prophesy and one comes in that believes not, or one *unlearned,(then)* he is Convinced *of all*, He is Judged *of all:* And thus are the **secrets** of his Heart made *manifest*, and so falling down on his *face*, he will Worship God, *and* Report that God is in You *of* a *Truth*........

Eph 4:14,15 - That we henceforth be no more *children*, tossed to and fro, and carried about with every **wind** of **doctrine** by the Sleight of men, and **cunning** Craftiness, whereby *they* lie in wait to Deceive: But *Speaking* the *Truth* in Love, may Grow-**up** in **Him** in all Things, *which* is the **Head**, even Christ —

Eph 4:25 - Wherefore putting away *Lying*—, speak every **man** Truth with **his** Neighbor, *for* **we** are Members one *of* Another!

Eph 5:9 - For the *fruit of* the Spirit is in *all* goodness, and Righteousness, and *Truth* ***

Eph 6:14 - Stand therefore, having **your** Loins girt about with **Truth:**

2 Tim 2:15 - *S*tudy to show *thyself* Approved unto God—a *workman* that need not be Ashamed, *rightly* Dividing the **Word** *of* <u>*Truth*</u>...

1 Jn 4:6 - **W**e are *of* God: *he* that knows God, hears *U*s. *He* that is not *of* God, hears *U*s not: Hereby know *we* the Spirit *of* <u>*Truth*</u> — and the *spirit of* Error —

Question: *How Much* <u>*Truth*</u> *can you Know, Before the* <u>*Truth*</u> *You think You Know, Reveals to You the* <u>*Truth*</u>*: that You Really know Nothing About. And the Real* <u>*Truth*</u> *about the Nothing You don't Know is that you're Deceived into Thinking that no one Knows the Truth about You, but You. True______ or False______?*

(John 8:32 - Ye shall know the Truth, and the Truth shall make Free.)

Will *(Now,* of course, as I write about this **Word**, we all know that it is **O**ne that's used in many different ways, with different meanings and schemes, with *both* Natural and Spiritual **C**onnotations. But in the Arena of this Book, it is a significant **Benefit Word** because here I *will* disclose it as it is used in Legal Terminology: And so, for its purpose here, we *will* view it in its Legal **P**rowess, as a <u>*Will*</u>*.* This is what this **Word** is all about concerning the <u>*Will*</u> and Testament *of* Christ. A "Legal Document" established by God to Abraham, who is the *original* **H**eir to the Promises. The Power and use of this **Word** are demonstrated in the way the *Word of* God describes what the Sacrifice *of* Jesus means to us all: of course, *all* **R**eferring to those of the *'Household of faith'*. And so, as we begin our *faith* Journey into the depth of understanding our New *Benefits Package of* **P**romises laid out in what the *Testator (Christ)* has left us in <u>**His Will**</u> and Testament. Which in *Scriptural* Terminology is declared unto us; in **Hebrews 7:22** — *"A Better Testament "* or as **Hebrews 8:13**, describes it: *"A New Covenant "*, and of course there is no friction here, because they are *'one in the same'*, for they do indeed represent for us in Christ —a Complete

'*Benefits Packet* ' to the Saving of our Souls, for the sake of the Gospel, and for the Benefit of the *Kingdom.* So as we look at this **Word**, and we see it in all of its **S**plendor, pertaining to the **Will** *of* God, we have to then more clearly see it in Simple *terms*, as a Legal Document, and by revelation to us, is in full force of its intended Purpose, which is: to operate on our behalf (*according to our faith*) as a "Last Will and Testament *of* our Lord and Savior: Jesus Christ", **Amen!** Now, with that said —here's the Question: *Are we really living our* Lives *by* **faith—and do we** <u>Truly</u> **believe that we have an Inheritance?** If the answer is Yes, we do. Then why are we living beneath our **Inheritance?** And so, as I ask myself that question, I must submit to you in all Honesty, even up to this very moment, as I strike the **keys** against these Pages. I believe that it's simply a lack of **Revelation** on how to Love the Father. If you Love me, you'll keep my **C**ommandments: Well, please hear me in this because one of the Greatest **C**ommandments that we fail to seek and receive Revelation on is *found* in:*[**Commentary:** Referring back to the Previous Benefit Word -* <u>*Truth,*</u> *look at how many times it Qualifies the importance, and Presupposes that Gaius because of the* <u>*Truth*</u> *is no-doubt now fully able, and capable of obeying God's Commandment as Outlined by Apostle John, the Beloved of Jesus]* — "**3**^{*rd*} **John verse 1 thru 4 - The Elder unto the well-beloved Gaius, whom I Love in the** <u>**Truth.**</u>**—Beloved, I wish above all things that you may Prosper and be in Health, even as your Soul Prospers, for I rejoiced in a Great Way when the Brethren came and Testified of the** <u>**Truth**</u> **that is in you, even as you walk in the** <u>**Truth**</u>**. I have no greater Joy than to hear that My Children Walk in the** <u>**Truth**</u>. It's in the <u>**Will**</u> that we Prosper......

Webster's New World Dictionary:

Will - *n.* **5.** a legal paper in which a person tells what he wants done with his money and property after he dies.

Testament - *n.* **2.** in law, a <u>*Will*</u>: *used mainly in the phrase* **"Last Will** and <u>*Testament*</u> —

Matt 26:28 (<u>***Will***</u> *is the* ***Benefit Foundational Word***) - For this is ***My Blood*** *of* The New Testament, which is shed for many *for* the Pardon *of S*ins...

Heb 7:22 - By so *much* was Jesus made a ***Security:*** — *(Webster's Dictionary: surety -n.* **2.** *something that makes sure security, as for a loan.* **3.** *a person who agrees to pay the debts of another, if the other fails to pay them.)* — ***Prov 22:26*** *-27 -* ***Be not thou one of them that strike hands, or of them that are sureties for debts – If thou have something to pay, why should he take away your bed from under you*** —/ Wow, when I read ***Hebrews 7:22***, I felt a 'Tug' in my ***spirit***, for the need to elaborate on this **Word 'Surety'**. It is a Word that is not used much in this form, but we know it, and we use it every time we Co-sign for our loved ones or anyone. We are, in essence, taking on their ***Debt***. And believe me, I know that if we did a survey, **we'**d find that we either Co-signed for Someone are someone Co-signed for us, and both were foolish, and you'd more than likely find in the Survey that the Co-signer was usually the one holding the debt, and of course more than likely not a preferable out- come. Yes, this Word in all of its negative connotations, is what has caused our Nation to go overboard with debt. Since none of us are Secure enough to take on another's debt from a pure heart. The Bible *plainly* spells out for us the impending disasters behind this Word ***debt*** and its main cause—***surety***. *A*nd because of our unrestrained lust for stuff, and more of it. Our so-called Great Nation (*the United States of America*) is in Grave ***danger*** of becoming an obsolete and very volatile State. Its Greed has reached a fever pitch, and Poverty in this <u>great nation</u> is at an all-time high. Why? To me, it has become a very simple *diagnosis:* —*We* have struck hands and made pledges to many *different* Masters of ***Usury***. And we didn't all go blindly into such agreements when there's an opportunity to read the fine print *(and of course, I'm guilty and have repented from such frivolities)*. As the Book states, **"ye without sin cast the first stone,"** so I am in nowise casting any stones, just simply speaking the Truth. Because many of us knew, from the outset, that we couldn't afford that STUFF.

And many of us could **afford** whatever we wanted, according to what we Borrowed or Financed...but we just were ignorant of the wisdom of Budgeting. We were never taught it, and those in the Financial World who prey on such ignorance, and bank on our naivete. Hence, most of us *(myself also, as of this Book)* are now slaves in hiding, on the run, or just living in fear, wondering when the Masters *of Usury* will take back their stuff. Either scenario ain't good, especially for a Servant *of* God *(read Prov 6:1-5 / 11:15, and 17:18)*. And so in these Verses of Scriptures, we see the *weightiness* of **debt:** And no matter which way it is heaped upon us, it is an unwise venture. But of course, *(in reality)*, no measure or amount of man-made **debt** can compare to that of Sin since earthly Debts can be and will be resolved one way or another, whether in death or life. But the Sin **debt,** whose price is Hell, could only be paid once, and that by the **nail** Pierced Hands of God's one and only begotten Son. Who by **His** Sacrifice, **Secured** for us **A**ll, a **debt** we could've never paid. Just as the Word *of* God so **E**loquently declares in the Book *of* **Hebrews, Chapter 10 verse 5 - Wherefore when He cometh into the world, He saith: "Sacrifice and offering you would not, But a Body hast thou Prepared"**— And so here we stand, with our debt paid in full, and that because of our Master, who hast provided for us a **Surety** *of* a Better <u>**Testament**</u>. [Heb 7:22] —

Heb 9:15 - 20 - And for his cause—, **He** is the Mediator *of* the New <u>**Testament (Will)**</u>, that by means of Death, for the Redemption of the **transgressions** *that* were under the First <u>**Testament**</u> *(Read Deut 28:14, this is the First Will, obtained by the Death and Sacrifice of Animals, and the observance of the Law)* **[that]** they which are called might receive the Promise *of* Eternal Inheritance. For where a **Testament** *is*, there must also of Necessity be the **death** *of* the Testator. For a <u>**Testament (Will)**</u> *is* *in-*Force after men are dead: Otherwise, it is of no Strength at all while the Testator Lives. —Whereupon, neither the First <u>Testament</u> was dedicated without **blood**— For when *Moses* had spoken every Precept to all the People according to the Law, *he* took the **blood** of calves and of goats, with **water** and **scarlet** wool, and hyssop, and sprinkled both the Book and all the People. *S*aying: ***"this is the blood of the <u>Testament (Will)</u>, which God has Ordered unto You"***. Amen!

Wisdom

Prov 4:7 - <u>**Wisdom**</u> is the Principal Thing: *therefore,* get <u>**Wisdom:**</u> and with all thy getting, *G*et Understanding.........

Acts 6:3 - *W*herefore Brethren, seek *you* out among *you* Seven Men of Honest Report, —***full*** *of* the **Holy Ghost**, and <u>**Wisdom:**</u> whom *we* may *A*ppoint over this *B*usiness—

1 Cor 2:7 - But *we* *S*peak the <u>**Wisdom**</u> *of* God in a *M*ystery, even the *hidden* <u>**Wisdom**</u>, which God Ordained before the World unto our Glory...............

1 Cor 12:8 - For to **one** is Given *by* the **Spirit** the Word *of* <u>**Wisdom:**</u> to *A*nother the Word *of* *K*nowledge by the same **Spirit** —

Eph 1:17 - That the God *of* our Lord Jesus Christ, the Father *of* *G*lory may give unto *you* the **Spirit** *of* <u>**Wisdom**</u>, and Revelation:

Col 1:9 - For this cause *we* also, since the *Day* *we* heard it, Cease not to Pray for *you.* —And to desire that *you* might be **filled,** with the Knowledge *of* **His** **W**ill in all <u>**Wisdom**</u> and Spiritual Understanding...

Col 1:28 - Whom *we* *P*reach, warning every man and*(also)* Teaching every man in *all <u>Wisdom:</u>* —***

Col 3:16 - Let the Word *of* Christ dwell in *you* *R*ichly in all-*<u>Wisdom</u>* Teaching and *A*dmonishing one-another in *psalms* and *H*ymns and *S*piritual songs, singing with *grace* in your *H*earts to the Lord....

Col 4:5 - Walk in *<u>Wisdom</u>* towards them that are *W*ithout*(un-saved)*

Jam 1:5 - If any of *you* *L*ack *<u>Wisdom</u>* let *him* ask of God: —

Jam 3:13 - Who is a *W*ise-*man* and endued with Knowledge among *you*? Let *him* show out of a *G*ood *Conversation* — *his* *W*orks with meekness *of <u>Wisdom</u>*....

Rev 13:18 - Here *is <u>Wisdom</u>*. Let *him* that hath Understanding *C*ount the *number* of the *Beast:* —*for* it is the Number *of* a Man, and *his* *#* is 666 —***—

AND HE CAUSED ALL, BOTH SMALL AND GREAT—

— RICH & POOR — FREE & BOND, TO RECEIVE A MARK IN THEIR RIGHT HAND; OR IN THEIR FOREHEADS:

(Revelation 13:16)

Revelation (This is the last **Word** in the 'Benefits of Salvation Study.' And even though it's noticeably out of Alphabetical Order, according to the flow of all the other Words of Power, in the Benefit's Concordance Section: this is the one the *Holy Ghost* *I*mpressed upon me to place here at the End. — And I asked the *Holy Ghost:* Why? And **He** said. Because I want you to see that without the *<u>Benefit</u>* of this **Word** *[which is the single most influentially impacting one of them all concerning our faith walk].* Without it, it would be totally impractical, improbable, and defi-nitely impossible to live a Good and Successful Christian Life in this *fallen* and Distorted World. The only way we could've made it to Heaven after being Born-Again would've been by the immediacy of the Rapture, even as much as the twinkling of an eye.

Why? Because without **Revelation** and **Discernment**, which are both formed out of the same Purpose and Calling. You see, if there was no warning or discernment given to Apostle Paul and all the Others —who were Charged with the Spiritual responsibility of turning the whole World upside-down in their Ancient World, we would've never known of their valiant Conquests and defeat of Satan, not only for their World but for ours. And without the gift of **Revelation** *[Which is the revealing of a thing not yet reality]* and the sixth-sense of **Discernment** concerning our walk of faith, we could be killed at any time, but because of it, we are able to avoid many times; at the last second: catastrophic events and circumstances impeding our Progress, as we advance the cause of the Kingdom. Yes, *Revelation* is the catalyst that makes **Discernment** possible, since what I **discern** must have in it, a directional out or in answer or recourse to the present dilemma. Remember to **discern** without **Revelation** — it is like having a Secret or knowing a Mystery about something but with no way to solve it or to Assimilate it into your **masterplan.** A plan like how to win the loss or escape a mob out to Kill you. And so, we must have both operating in our lives because **Discernment** for us is to see clearly how much we need Christ and to receive **Revelation** on how to act upon what you have **discerned** about your need. —

And so, as the **Holy Ghost** revealed to me here, it's very clear: that without this awesome Gift to the Body, we would be Powerless to carry-out the **Will** *of* God on the Earth, we would all be caught off guard, and would not be able to **Watch**, as well as **Pray**. Yes, indeed, we need this essentially important and <u>**Potent Element**</u> included in our Helmet *of* Salvation. For

Righteousness Sake, we must have it. *"If any Man have an Ear, Let Him Hear."* Amen!

'*Wisdom is Principle*'

The Book *of* the Law, clearly states: *"as an indelibly Sure Force "* on behalf of our <u>*faith walk*</u> — *Deut 29:29 - The secret things belong unto the Lord our God: but those things which are <u>Revealed</u> , belong to us and to our Children forever —that we may do all the Words of this Law. —*

So, in conclusion, it is without a doubt, very simple: *if* we will receive it. *"Those with ears to hear, let them hear what the Spirit is saying"*. Just as our Lord and Savior Passionately Confirmed to us those same Words, *spoken* in *Deuteronomy 29:29*, when *He* paraphrased them, by *Revelation* in *Matthew 10:25 thru 27 (Saying) - It is enough for the Disciple that he be as His Master, and the Servant as His Lord. —If they have called the Master of the House Beelzebub, how much more shall they call them of His Household? Fear them not therefore: for there is nothing Covered, that shall not be <u>Revealed;</u> and hid that shall not be known.— what I tell you in the Darkness, that speak ye in the Light: —and what you hear in the ear, that Preach you upon the Housetops. —* And again, as making *reference* to us being able to Receive the <u>*Revelation*</u> *of* the Kingdom *of* God as *B*abes, according to the Words *of* the Master, same Book, *Chapter 11:25 (Jesus Answering, Saying) - I thank you O Father , Lord of Heaven and Earth, because thou has hidden these things from the Wise and Prudent, and has <u>Revealed</u> them unto Babes.*

And so, we see with *A*bsolute *Clarity*, that the thing <u>*Discerned*</u> is Spiritually recognized, as that which is Ordained *of* God. Just as the great Commission, which was, and is still acted upon, in *P*ursuit of Souls; by strategic Warfare: directed, and given to us by the ***Holy Ghost*** through Visions, <u>***Discernment***</u>, and other *A*rms of <u>*Revelational*</u> how- to, in our March to

Victory in the Devils *stronghold.* —*S*o now, without any further *ado,* let us move forward. And I Pray that *Ephesians, Chapter 1:18 (Come Alive in your Hearts)— So that the eyes of your understanding be Enlightened, that you may know by* <u>*Revelation*</u> *—what is the Hope of His calling, and what the Riches of the Glory of His Inheritance in the Saints, Is. Amen, and again I Say:* Amen!)

Rom 16:25 - Now to *Him* that is of Power to establish *you* *A*ccording to *my G*ospel, and the Preaching *of* Jesus Christ, *A*ccording to the <u>*Revelation*</u> *of* the Mystery—

1 Cor 14:16 - Now Brethren—, *if* I come unto *you* Speaking with *tongues,* what shall I Profit *you*? Except I shall Speak to *you* either by <u>*Revelation,*</u> or by Knowledge....

Eph 3:3,4 - How that by <u>*Revelation, He M*</u>ade known to *me* the Mystery: *(As I wrote afore in few Words: whereby when you read, ye may Understand, my knowledge in the Mystery of Christ ...*

Gal 1:11,12 - But I *C*ertify to *you, B*rethren: that the Gospel which was Preached *of me* is not after *man.* For I neither received it of *man,* neither was I *T*aught it, *but* by the <u>*Revelation*</u> *of* Jesus Christ...

Gal 2:2 - And I went up by <u>*Revelation*</u> —

1 Pet 1:13 - Wherefore *gird-up* the Loins of *your* Mind, *be S*ober, and Hope to the end *for* the Grace that is to be brought unto *you* at the <u>*Revelation*</u> *of* Jesus Christ...

Eph 1:17 - That the God *of our* Lord Jesus Christ, the Father *of G*lory may give unto *you* the *Spirit of* Wisdom, and <u>*Revelation*</u> in the *K*nowledge *of Him****

Revelation 1:1 - The Revelation of Jesus Christ, which God gave unto— John: to Show unto His Servants things that must shortly Come to— Pass!

Benefits Epilogue:

My Revelation Conclusion on the "BENEFITS CONCORDANCE" — And so I will exit this Section of the Book by giving a Warning to all who are *Spiritually Gifted:* — "Be not overzealous with the Gifts you've been given stewardship over "whether it be Prophesying, or Knowledge, or of Wisdom, or of Tongues, or of **Revelations**: or any other notable Gift. "Do not think of yourself more highly than you ought to" *(Rom 12:3).* Even as Apostle Paul was given his Cross to bear, we too must be aware of the plans that our weaknesses have so that we are better able to stop the enemy from breaking through, our defenses to stop the Plan of God in us. Because this Gospel of the Kingdom shall be preached and will not be hindered by the hands of a weak *saint.* Knowing that the Time of the End is at hand, and the Glory which shall be **Revealed** in Us, clamors with emphatic *anticipation: W*ith Bridled *passion,* prancing at the gate for the Expected Manifestation *of* the *Sons of* God... So let Us rejoice and be *exceedingly G*lad, for the Kingdom *of* God is at *H*and!*)*

2 Cor 12:1 - It is not expedient for *me* doubtless to Glory— *for* I will come to Visions and **Revelations** *of* the Lord. *A*nd lest I should be *exalted A*bove measure through the Abundance of the **Revelations***:* There was Given unto *me* a thorn in the *flesh*– the Messenger of Satan to *B*uffet *me*—, *(It's All for His Glory)*

Commentary Conclusion *on* the "BENEFITS **C**ONCORDANCE"**:**

This Section has been one of tremendous help to me since much of it is a conglomeration of notes and writings I've compiled over the years for my own walk as I was inspired and instructed by the Holy-Ghost, even by permission to *Pen* what would hopefully benefit me. Though much of what is compiled is not immediately for my consumption. *Nevertheless,* I tried with all diligence to connect all things *Scripturally* to the edifying of those who might use this Book as an instrument of instruction, guidance, and of course, encouragement. Most of what has been written to this point came from Notes of study, and revelational insight given to me over a period of nineteen years: – But with most of it written in the early years of my Faith Walk. And of course, this Section, "The BENEFITS CONCORDANCE" was inspired during the compilation period of the Book. Now, for this Section alone it has been an inspirational journey for me, and I hope as well for you. But I pray that the limited Benefits that I listed here inspire you to search out for yourself many other Benefits that were just too numerous for me to detail here, but please: have at it, and enjoy the quest. You see, I truly believe that in order for us to be about our *Father's B*usiness, we must, as Believers, stop allowing ourselves to be destroyed. Just as the Word of God so emphatically proclaims in *Hosea, Chapter 4:6 - My people are destroyed for a lack of knowledge. Because thou hast rejected knowledge, I will also reject thou.* In other words, God says: *(You will not be able to access the Benefits of Salvation) -that thou shalt be no Priest to <u>Me</u>: seeing thou hast forgotten the Law of God: (It is Commanded that we walk in the fulness of all that Christ has wrought for us at the Cross, and to do less is disobedience. Just as the Scriptures dictate to us, with no room for Error —saying, "For it had been better for them not to have known the way of Righteousness, than, after they had known it, to turn from the Holy Commandment delivered to them." (2 Pet 2:21),* and then again, as Christ Commanded us to do when *He* spoke thru Apostle Paul in: *Philippians, Chapter 2:12 (saying); Wherefore, my beloved, as ye have always obeyed, not as in my presence only, but now much more in my absence: —Work out your own Salvation with fear and Trembling.* — So, my Brothers and Sisters, if we are to obey and walk in the fulness of all that has been Gifted to *Us* by Christ, then we must, as **His** True Friends, get our Spiritual House in order. For His Glory, ***Amen!***

hallelujah

Now as we enter the Last mile of this enormous undertaking for me, giving God all the Glory. So, we will stay in the same *Spiritual Vein* regarding our *Benefits.* Here, with the help of the Holy Spirit, I will attempt to advance it a step further. As we look at and discover a few **"Building Blocks"**. On how to access what we all need and should desire. Hopefully we can achieve that goal, from consuming the final resource and Bounty, here in *my Faith Walk* Conglomeration, of all things pertaining to *my* Spiritual Need, and hope-fully *yours*. But as to what the Apostle said concerning his own walk, it also applies to mine. And it's all in a nutshell, in these Powerful Words *of R*evelation, and they are as follows in Paraphrase: *"I have not yet Arrested, that which has Apprehended Me, on behalf of Christ– Phi 3:12, and Phi 3:14 – (but) I Press toward the Mark for the Prize of Christ "*! And so, with that said, let's now Consume a little More.........

Revelational Nugget Spot - Light

Building Blocks—and Outline Keys to Accessing our Benefits Building Block #1 - The Necessity *of —*Death

One of the most important things we must learn after our **New-Birth**, and our newfound *empowerment* in and by the Holy Ghost *(once you've received Him as your Gift)*. —Is to then begin the process of learning how to <u>Die to Self</u>. And then how to allow the Holy Ghost, to resurrect you in Christ, by way of His Suffering. Hence bringing you by His Spirit into your place of Confidence. So that you may Boldly declare to the enemy, whose you are and on whose Authority you stand. And as you learn how to stand, you will find yourself no longer shaken. While your *spirit* begins to soar to New Heights, displaying the evidence of your maturity by way of your *Fruit*. —Amen. Now, before I get too much ahead of myself, let us *first* discuss Death in its natural connotation and meaning. And then for our Edification, let us receive by Revelation: Death's must Elevated status, in its necessity to the growth of *our Spirit-Man.*

Death:

Natural Degradation Without Edification: *(Webster's New World Dictionary)*—

Death *n* **1.** the act or fact of dying; end of life. **2.** any end that is like dying [*the death of our hopes*]. **3.** the condition of being dead [*as still as death*]. The cause of death [*the atomic bomb was death to thousands*] — **put to death**, to kill; execute.

Dead *n* **1.** no longer living; without life. *(Eccl 9:4 - A living dog is better than a dead lion).* **3.** without feeling, motion, or power.

7. complete [*a dead loss*]. —*adj* **1.** completely; [*I am dead tired from running*].

Die *v* **1.** to stop living, become dead. **3.** to lose force; become weak, faint, etc. [*the sound of music died away*]. —**die off**, to die one by one until all are gone. —*died*

Cessation *n.* a ceasing or stopping, either forever or for some time [*there will be a cessation of work during the holidays*]. *(Jn 9:4 (Jesus answered) - I must work the works of Him that sent Me, while it's day: the night cometh, when no man can work...*

Death:

Spiritual Edification, by Revelation *(Commentary by Me, and from the New Kings James Bible)* —

Death - When we begin the process of elimination from our own selfish will and its innate ability to only want "what's mine". We soon began to grow up. Realizing *(by the Spirit)* that as I welcome *my* choice to *Die* to my sensual Nature and all of its self-willed desires. —My Soul suddenly, and with great joy, becomes exhilarated as it surrenders to its brand-new Spirit Nature. And within a short period of time, it finds itself lining up to "*A* world that's *A*live", to the *W*ill and *Purpose of* God. And as this is all taking place, it finally hits you *(and what a revelation)*: 'You're now right *smack-dab* in the middle of' what John *the Baptist* so boldly Proclaimed, as *he R*eceived *revelation*, about his *f*uture, which was one of Decrease. Here read it for yourself: *St John 3:29,30 (John the Revelator, not John the Baptist) -: this my joy is fulfilled. He (Christ) must* Increase —*but I must* Decrease. — And just as John's personal importance in the complete plan of God had to be diminished. So, too must *ours*, as we yield to the Plan and Purpose for our Lives in bringing Glory to the Father —by way of *the Son* and of our own Cross. For by it; we must Die (*Mt 16:24* - Then said Jesus unto His disciples, *if any man come after Me, let him deny himself, and take up his Cross, and follow Me. —Mt 10:38 / Mk 8:34 / Mk 10:21 Lk 9:23 / Lk 14:27).* And after we began to learn how to die daily, living no longer after the *flesh*, with its wicked deeds. We then find ourselves, daily, looking unto Jesus, the Author and finisher of all that we <u>*Die*</u> to. So that we can Show-*forth* the Praises of **Him** who hath called us from out of the Darkness. Who has empow-ered us by the *Holy Ghost*, to put to <u>*Death*</u>, those selfish ambi-tions of self-awareness. Leading us to demonstrate in a most Illustrious and Illuminating fashion; even as Apostle Paul did in *his* Letter to the Church in *Philippi:* Listen! *Phil 1:21 - For to me, to Live is Christ, and to <u>Die</u> = <u>Gain</u>.* — And just as one of the definitions *of <u>Death</u>* is defined in *"Webster's Dictionary"* namely Cessation, in the sense *of S*topping *forever*, every Thought, and every Imagination that tries to Rise- Up above: the Knowledge, and Power *of* God. *(Paraphrase of 2 Cor 10:5)*

So, you see, once we have become the *blood bought* Born Again Children of the Most High God, *there* must be a willing necessity for the <u>*Cessation*</u> of all of those things that we know Naturally, and especially those things revealed Spiritually that are Hindrances to our walk. Being an Affront to our Savior. I can't express it enough to you *are* to my own self. We must indeed have a willingness to *stop D*oing – Being – or *saying all* that is *revealed* in us to Stop *Doing, Being,* or *Saying*. And the very enter-taining of them must Cease. Now even though I stress this, with the utmost care of importance. I do know: — like all things that come to a necessary end, there is a Process. And the Process may be longer for some, than others. Because Discernment and *revelational K*nowledge of the weaknesses in each individual need to <u>*Die*</u> sooner than later. Based on whichever one is causing the most stumbling. But, as we continue to intention-ally seek to increase in the *Will of* God through Christ, we will one day look up with great Joy, realizing that we've become mature enough in our *faith* walk to endure as a Good Soldier the challenges of our *Cross*. Even putting to <u>*Death*</u> those Secret passions and self-willed hidden emotions that always seem to pop up when we pretend *(to the audience of ourselves)* that we have *crucified* them. But in the end, because *of* Love *"they will be put to <u>Death</u>: (Refer to: Heb 12:2 / Col 2:14 / Rm 14:8 / 1 Pt 2:9)*

BUILDING BLOCK #2: WORDS *OF TRANSFORMABLE CHANGE —*

Our *first* Preference in learning about the *"Transformable Change"* in our time of *transitional Change*: from the Old Man to the *New*, should come by revelation. By understanding *the* full impact of those two Powerful <u>Words,</u> which in their own Voice, for me, speak with Clarity when defining what the *newness* of our *Change* entails regarding our *faith w*alk. —So, as you began to study in detail the indelible *significance of* these <u>Words</u> in relation to your brand-new *"life of faith"*. You must also remember *(that whatever **revelatory** information you receive, by adding this Study to the **Continuous** process of your **ever-increasing** Completeness in the Manifestation of who you're becoming in the Plan of God)*: it's not just to the Benefit of *you* but for the Necessity of Us *all.* As we, in Spiritual unison, seek daily to identify *(where applicable)*, within ourselves, those attributes *of* Christ. Who is not only our *mark*, but who is also, in Us: The *Hope of Glory* —*A*nd is for Us, our Transformable *Change*, who will find in *Himself,* whose *Self* we are, a Church without *S*pot or *Wrinkle (Eph 5:27)*. And so, for my own individual Benefit, as a Servant daily trying to sell out, my endeavor is always to persevere for the sake of the Kingdom, and to be a Completed *part* necessary for the Master's use. And I do know that as I <u>*Purge*</u> myself daily through the obedient act of Repentance, that my heart will be Conformed and *transformed* —into the Image *and* Likeness *of* Christ with a Mindset on things *A*bove. Amen!

A. Seven Foundational Words *for* **"Transformable** *Change"* <u>**(The Order Revealed)**</u>

- *Purge*
- *Born Again*
- *New*

- *Newborn*
- *Newness*
- *Pure*
- *Purged*

1. **Purge** *(our definition for this word comes from the "Oxford University Press")*

v. **1.** rid (someone or something) of people or things considered undesirable or harmful. **2.** Evacuate one's bowels, especially as a result of taking a laxative.

3. Law, atone for or wipe out (contempt of court). —*n.* **1.** an act of *purging*.

Spiritual Statement on Purge

Much like the use of a *'laxative'* this **word <u>Purge</u>** for the Born-Again child of God should be, in my opinion, one of the First Spiritual Processes taught. As we begin our journey towards the *mark* of becoming a Successful and Productive Christian, especially in the turbulent upheaval of our world and all that we hold dear. This is why it's such a Key for us to understand why we must *first* be **Spiritually Purged** from the toxic waste that we all have in us. As we emerge out of the darkness, that we were born into. Because without being **Purged,** it is hard for a Babe in Christ to fully comprehend and accept the New Creature that Christ has enabled them to be by **His finished** Work. And when they receive Revelation, they are no longer the same. And they then began to discern that their New Birth is the Key. And is the Catalyst to the **Purging** that they, we all, must endure. Since the darkness we came out of is still in Us (*even though we're Born Again*): And as we start out on our *faith* Journey, we do so as Constipated **Saints,** not yet able to reap the full Benefits *of* our Freedom in Christ, but as we go, we behold more and more of the Lamb of God, who has **taken** **A**way **(Purged)** the Sins of the World **(St Jn 1:29)**

Purge Description *and* **B**enefit:

For us to <u>**Purge**</u>, is a Key starting point for Us. And is one of the most important Processes relevant to the **finished** **W**ork *of* Christ taking place in Us. To be **Purged** is to simply allow our connections to darkness to be cast into the Depths *of* God's Love for us, which is in the Scriptural **lexicon** of accuracy, according to **Micah 7:19.** And as God also declared inside the **foundational** workings of the Old Covenant *(being He that cannot Lie)*: Speaking through the Prophet, **Jeremiah, 31:34 - For I will forgive their iniquity, and I will remember their** <u>**Sins**</u> **no more.** — So, because of God's **"Prophetic Word of Truth"**— **Psalms 103:12** Declares that by Christ, as far as the East is from the West, **He** *(God by the Obedience of Christ)* has removed **our** *sins* from Us. And so, we see, and now, begin to understand, that the Obedient act *of* Christ has removed every **curse** against Us that was in **force** in the time of King David, with the **P**enalty *of* **S**entence that would've affected Us Now. So, thanks be to God: that every **curse**, and every *sin,* was cast upon Christ, with all the other contributing factors to the cause of our despair, which did **S**pring **forth** from the Treason of <u>**Adam & Eve**</u>. Hallelujah to the Lamb, **which taketh away the sins of Us All.** And so, by the act of One who was **P**urely Innocent, and without **sin: We** are indeed without excuses. Therefore, we can no longer hold fast to any Doctrine or **error** *of* Teaching that **burdens** Us,_even <u>*now*</u>, with the <u>**Sins & Curses**</u> of our Ancestors. Supposing that the **finished** **W**ork *of* Christ was not enough. *(Please I beg you to run from this type of instruction as fast as you can).* We must Pray for **Revelation** and **Spiritual** Guidance, — concerning the <u>**Purging**</u> of ourselves from such disconcerting and destructive **R**ambling. Just take a moment and Listen to the Clarity *of* **2**nd **Corinthians, 5:17 - "Therefore if any man be in**

Christ, he is a New Creation: <u>Old Things</u> are passed away (<u>Purged</u>), (and) Behold: all things are become **New**"! —Now, of course, in our Newness as Babes. It is where the Devil seemingly has many of Us over a *"barrel of ignorance"*. Why is this, *we* ask? And what I've found out in my quest to know is really a very simple answer. And it's this: <u>One</u>, "We just don't", "we won't, or somehow can't find the time", to inquisitively seek to know how to quench our hunger and thirst for the Word that we now crave for. In other words, we don't know how to 'scratch our itch and satisfy our yearning" for all things being Newly introduced into our *spirit*. And the <u>Second</u> Reason, from the Flip side *(In many cases)*. It is, that you're not experiencing any such *Spiritual Change* at all. No desperation, no clamoring, hungering, or any immediate need to be any closer to the Father or the People *of* God. Now, if any of these examples are Representative of where you are in this <u>life-changing</u> and uncertain place of unexplainable Peace, it's okay, don't panic, and don't get over excited either way. This is why I was led to write this **<u>Book</u>**. It is not written only for those of Us who deem ourselves so-called 'Seasoned Saints'. But it is for the Increase of Us *all*. And that to the Glory *of* the One who has *called Us* out of the Darkness, into **His** **M**arvelous Light.

Note of Commentary:

Before I continue with 'The <u>Purge Description</u> and Benefit'. Let's look at the Learning Process. Now of course, we all learn *differently. As f*or me, I found that I learn better through hands-on studying and experience, even where failing exists. Since it's failing that causes me to go before the Lord for revelation on why I failed. But, regardless of how you learn, it is a Process by which you must Genuinely seek after the deep things *of* God, whether in a Church or not. And your avenue for that kind of Inquisitive *searching* is to be *filled* with the Holy Ghost, who is our Free *gift*, given to Us by *the* Father: but is only given to us, in His *fulness* by our Asking *(Luke 11:13)*. Now as for the place of your Worship, *if* not in the privacy of your own place of *abode*. *(And if you're not at this moment **privy** to Teaching that confirms your need for the Holy Ghost, whether from TV or Church, then you must Seek, by Prayer and Supplication, the Free Gift of the Holy-Spirit).* Now, jumping ahead: Now that you've Received the Gift *of* the Father. You must now begin to seek out, by the *Holy Ghost* — tools by which you're able to grasp the necessity of <u>*Purging*</u>. Tools, in this instance that are; 'Places of Worship', and of Spiritual equipping. For starters, I'd definitely seek out a Teaching Ministry. One in which the *Fulness of* the –**Godhead**– is being <u>Taught</u>. You see, *we* must not at any time Limit the Measure of our Thirst for *clarity of* Discernment, where our Perfection through *Holiness* is Concerned. Selah, and *Amen!*

Learning How to <u>*Purge*</u> Oneself:

As I've already described, although in a different connotation than here. We must, as quickly as we're able, align ourselves in the *right-P*osition of Learning. So that we're better equipped to Receive *revelation.* So that our *Ordered steps* would be a lot more Solid. Measured and *tempered* with patience so that there's no confusion in the Launch of our *'Faith Walk'*. As we steady ourselves on the True *foundation* of our *Lord* and *S*avior, Jesus Christ. For *He* did say: *"Take My yoke upon <u>you</u>, and <u>Learn</u> of Me, for My Yoke is easy, and My burden Light (Mt 11:29,30)"* ...

And no matter what the Cost. When we start our journey, we must *A*ccept all that the Finished Work *of* Christ has afforded us the Privilege of Living in. And as we <u>*Purge*</u> ourselves from dead works, we in turn, are built up in the Confidence of our Most Holy *faith.* And we receive by *revelation (because of our <u>Purging)</u>* a release of Freedom in Us because of the *sufferings* our Lord endured on our behalf: *from* the onslaught of the Forces *of* Darkness against *Him.* –Now, once we're *Spiritually* Mature enough to Comprehend, with all the *Saints* the effectiveness of the Gospel. Then it is beginning to be evident— That you are cleansing yourself as often as you become *spiritually* attuned to the prompting of the *Holy Ghost* that you're in need of a <u>*Purging*</u>.

Now I hope you believe me when I tell you that you will know ***"beyond a shadow of a doubt"*** when you've been properly taught the way you should go. Because your Old-Way of thinking begins to suddenly pass away, as your skill in <u>*Purging*</u> begins to bear fruit. As you begin to see the outward flow of the *Spirit of* God springing up from within you. Yes, you will know it. And as you increase in the Word *of* God, you will see that the Ritualistic Act of Repentance is really what <u>*Purging*</u> is (*And as often as it is Necessary, do it*). Oh, I've come to a place of realization in my own *Walk* that if I don't <u>*Purge*</u> daily or as often as the *Holy Ghost* brings it to my attention. —Then I will begin to feel the *blockage* of whatever that stuff is that I've allowed to grow and fester in me. And if the *Spirit of* God has to bring it to my attention, often it's because I haven't been studious in working out my own Salvation. But as I mature in the trues *of* God, I hope to one day be sensitive enough in my own *spirit* to hear in my *S*oul what the *Holy Spirit* is saying to my *spirit*. So that the Three of Us can become the <u>*Threefold* </u>Cord not easily *broken,* just as *Ecclesiastes 4:9* & *12* agree upon. Listen, and see if you agree with my understanding: *9 - <u>Two </u>are better than <u>one</u>; because they have a good reward for their Labor: (Now Listen Carefully to what verse 12 has to say). 12 - And if <u>One</u> prevail against <u>Him,</u> <u>Two</u> shall withstand <u>him</u>; and a Threefold Cord is not quickly Broken.* Okay, I don't know about you, but this is how I heard what was just said. (*Two in Unity as <u>One</u> has more power through agreement, than any Force of evil against them, from One to Ten Thousand*). Now, where the unity of <u>Two </u>is stuff that needs to be **purged** is made a lot easier to see since the Power of what makes you <u>One</u> in <u>Unity</u> is *your* ability to hold each other Accountable. Why Accountable? —

*S*imply put, nothing is hidden when you're in **Agreement** to be **Accountable.** But of course, that's a lot easier said than done. But with God, all things are possible. That's what the **12th Verse** is all about. For me, it is a **revelation** of the unity of Two because, for the sake of the other, you should want to be your Best. Verse 12 shows us that even against the Devil if **he** begins to prevail against <u>One</u> of <u>**you**</u> – the **Other** *of* the Two *of you* **(Namely** *the Holy Ghost)*. Because of **your** Accountability to Your Wife, Brother, or Sister, **He** *(the Holy Ghost)* will give **you** Strength, on behalf of the <u>Two</u> *of* <u>**You,**</u> to overcome the Devil.— Now I know that what I just wrote may be a Mind Binder, and I hope it is. But the way I see it, whether you're by yourself, Married, or in a Business Partnership with another Christian. It doesn't matter, you have to hold yourself and or your Business Partner accountable to the Wisdom *of* <u>**Purging**</u> in order to keep your **Faith Walk** attentive to Holiness, whether in the Business or in the House. Amen —

Now, as I close this Commentary here, on **"Building Block #2."** and its Powerful Change Word <u>**Purge**</u>. I'll end this Part with more Affirmation, and it's this: We must <u>**Espouse**</u> to Promulgate this Word to its most Prominent Place of **G**lory. So let's **see** it, the way Hebrews 1:3 Proclaims it —***Who being in the Brightness of His Glory, and the Expressed Image of His Likeness, and upholding all things by the Word of His*** <u>***Power,***</u> ***—when He had by Himself*** <u>***Purged***</u> ***our Sins: — Sat down on the*** <u>***Right-Hand***</u> ***of the Majesty on High.*** Selah! [Now, please don't take this the wrong way, it's just my own **spiritual** thought, and I say it with **unfeigned** Liberty...I believe that Jesus <u>**Purged**</u> our Sins in the Cesspool *of* Hell... **(Just** <u>**a**</u> <u>**clear-headed thought**</u>**)**. —Remember, there's no Sin in Heaven!

So, with the Commentary of this Word <u>**Purge**</u> just about exhausted, let me back up a few steps and continue studying other related Words. Related in the sense that they too, like

Purge, must become an intimate part of our **faith walk.** <u>One</u> of them holds the Relevance of them <u>all</u> and is the Key to their very reason for being necessary to our Christian Faith. So let us start in Alphabetical Order as we Journey together in apprehending their Purpose. And so, as we flow together in the same **spiritual** **V**ein of Newness. Gleaning together in increase, from the Powerful **R**esource in _these **Words.**_ So, for starters, we'll examine their **N**atural usage: **A**s they're **defined** by— "Webster's New World Dictionary". —And also, the Online Version **of** the "Oxford University Press". —Once the Natural is absorbed, we'll then top it off with the **Spiritual R**elevance of each Word, as we might appropriate them, in our **D**aily **march** to Victory. And as we eagerly do so, in the <u>**Newness**</u> of our Hearts, and in the Service **of** our Lord **and King.** Let it be accomplished in One **Voice,** as One Body, **S**houting Loudly: **"IN-C-R-E-A-S-E"**. —Go ahead, don't be ashamed: **T**ry it — (Now **Doesn't that Feel Good)**—

<u>**Definitions Section:**</u> — <u>Webster's & Oxford * Spiritual /</u> <u>Biblical _and_ (Me)</u>

Born-Again _(Oxf)_ **adj. 1.** Relating to or denoting a person who has converted **to** a personal faith in Christ. **2.** showing the great enthusiasm of a person newly converted to a cause _born again environmentalist._ **(Me)** also: _born again Christian_ Jn 3:3 - Jesus answered and said unto them: _**Verily, Verily, I say unto thee, Except a man be <u>Born Again</u> —he cannot see the Kingdom of God.**_

Jn 3:5 - 7 - Jesus answered: _**Verily, Verily, I say unto ye, Except a man be born of Water, and of the Spirit, he cannot enter into the Kingdom of God. That which is born of the flesh is flesh. And that which is Born of the Spirit is Spirit. —Marvel not that I said unto thee, Ye must be <u>Born Again</u>. "The Wind blows where it listeth (wishes), and thou hear the sound thereof: but cannot tell from whence it comes, and where it goes". So is everyone that is <u>Born of the Spirit</u> (<u>Born</u>**_

Again) — *1 Pet 1:23 - Being* **Born Again**, *not of (A) Corruptible Seed, but of incorruptible* —by the Word *of* God, which Lives and *A*bides *forever...*

Examples: Here, we will show **Seven** examples of what being **Born Again** looks like from God's Perspective —

1 Jn 2:28,29 - And now little Children, abide in *Him*: that when *He* shall Appear, we may have *Confidence*, and not be ashamed before *Him* at *His* coming. If you know that *He* is Righteous, you know that everyone that does **Righteousness** is **Born of Him**...

1 Jn 3:9 - Whosoever is **Born of God**, does not Commit Sin: *for His* seed remains in *him* and *he* Cannot Sin, because *he* is **Born of God!**

1 Jn 4:7 - Beloved, let us Love one another: For **Love** is *of* God; and everyone that Loves, is **Born of God**; and knows God.

1 Jn 5:1 - Whosoever *B*elieves that Jesus is *the* Christ, is **Born of God**:

1 Jn 5:4 - For Whatsoever is **Born of God**, overcomes the World. *A*nd this is the Victory that overcomes the World, even our **faith** —

1 Jn 5:18 - We know that Whosoever is **Born of God** Sins not. But *he* that is *B*egotten *of* God keeps **himself.** (Note: **Work out your own Salvation with fear** (*Reverence*) **and trembling - Ph 2:12**) ...

New *(Web)* **adj. 6.** Strange; not familiar **8.** Beginning again; starting once more.

New *(Oxf)* **adj. 5.** Reinvigorated, restored, or reformed **New** —

2 Cor 5:17 - Therefore if any **man** *be* in Christ, **he** is a **New**

Creature: *Old* things have passed *Away* —*Behold,* **all** *T*hings have become **New********

Gal 6:15 - For in Christ Jesus *neither* Circumcision avails anything, nor **uncircumcision** — but a **New** Creature...

Eph 2:15 - Having *A*bolished in **His–** **flesh** the Enmity, even the Law *of* Commandments contained in *O*rdinances; *for* to make in **Himself** of Two, *One* **New** man. So, making Peace *(Please also read verses 11 through 22, this will keep it all in context)* ...

Eph 4:23,24 - And be **renewed** in the Spirit of your Mind. And that you put on the **New** —*man:* Which after God is *C*reated in *R*ighteousness and True Holiness ***

Col 3:10 - And have *P*ut on the **New** —*man:* Which is *renewed* in Knowledge, after the Image *of Him* that *C*reated **him...**

Newborn *(Web)* **adj. 2.** Born again; revived, *(newborn courage)*

Newborn *(Oxf)* **adj. 1.** Recently born **2.** Regenerated. — **n.** a newborn child, etc.

Newborn —

1 Pet 2:2 - As **Newborn** Babes, desire the *S*incere *milk* **of** the Word, that ye may *G*row thereby.......

Newness —

Rom 6:4 - Therefore **we** are Buried *with* **Him** by Baptism into **death:** That like as Christ was *R*aised-**up** from the **dead** by the Glory *of* the Father — *E*ven so **we** also should walk in **Newness** *of* Life.

Rom 7:6 - But now **we** are Delivered *from* the **Law:** That being dead *How* **we** were held; that **we** should Serve in **Newness** *of* Spirit —*A*nd not in the Oldness of the *Letter!*

Pure *(Web) adj.* **1.** Not mixed with anything else **2.** Not having anything dirty in it; clean **3.** Not bad or evil; morally good; innocent.

Pure *(Oxf) adj.* **1.** Not mixed or adulterated with any other substance or material

Free of impurities **3.** Innocent or morally good **4.** Complete.

Pure —

Ps 18:26 - With the *Pure* —thou will show Yourself *Pure* ......

Ps 24:3,4 - Who shall Ascend into the Hill of *the* Lord? Or who shall Stand in **His H**oly Place? *(Answer)* He that has **Clean-hands** and a *Pure* Heart....

Prv 21:8 - The *way* of a **man** is Forward and Strange: *But* as for the *Pure, his* Work is Right....

Mt 5:8 - Blessed are the *Pure* in Heart, *for* they shall See God —

1 Tim 5:22 - (:) — **K**eep Thyself *Pure* ***

2 Tim 2:22 - Flee also *youthful* Lust: — But *follow* Righteousness, *faith*, Charity, Peace. With them that call on *the* Lord out of a *Pure* Heart.

Tit 1:15 - Unto the *Pure* all Things are *Pure:* But to them that are **Defiled,** and **un**believing is Nothing *Pure*..............

1 Jn 3:2,3 - Beloved, now are *we* the Sons *of* God: —And it does not yet Appear what *we* shall Be: *But we* know that when *He* shall **Appear, we** shall be like **Him,** for *we* shall see **Him** as **He** is. And *every man* that has this Hope in *him &(Him)* Purifies *himself* — Even as *He &(he)* is *Pure*...

Purge (Now we will examine this Word in a *twofold* context. One: In its usage as a **Verb** — *and* Second: In its usage as a **Noun.**

I will attempt to show its usage by **us** and by God for **us** and to **us**. And this for our **Spiritual** Benefit, as pertaining to Holiness (**For without which no man shall see the Lord - Heb 12:14**). And to the Work of the Ministry, for the Harvest of the Kingdom. So here we will find <u>**Purge**</u> as attached to the Word <u>**Purged**</u> as defined. Supposing that to <u>**Purge**</u> must indeed come first. So that the evidence of being <u>**Purged**</u>, for the Saint, will be witnessed more clearly.) —

Purge *(Web) v.* **1.** to make clear or pure by getting rid of things that are dirty or wrong [*to purge a city of slums*] **2.** To make the bowels move.

Purged *(Web) n.* **1.** the act of **purging 2.** anything that **purges**, especially a Med. that moves the bowels.

Purge *(Oxf) v.* **1.** rid [*someone or something*] of people or things considered undesirable or harmful **2.** evacuate one's bowels, especially as a result of taking a Lax. (**atone for, wipe out**)

Ps 51:7 - <u>**Purge**</u> me with *hyssop*, and I shall be clean: wash me and I shall be whiter than snow. (**Commentary** - *This is of course, a personal prayer by King David for God to do the* <u>**Purging**</u>, *which is a request for something that could only be performed by God at the surrender of the man or woman. Since, at that time, we did not have the power to sanctify, by our own obedient act, to purify or* <u>**Purge**</u> *ourselves as Holy People. So, we see* <u>**Purge**</u> *here being used as a* **Verb**)...

1 Cor 5:7 - <u>**Purge**</u> out therefore the **old** Leaven, that *ye* may be a New lump, as ye are **un-leaven**. For even Christ our **Passover** is **sacrificed** for Us. (**Commentary** - *Now here we see that this Word demonstrates, for us, how we, by way of our New Birth in Christ, now have the Power to not only be able to* <u>**Purge**</u> [**noun**] *ourselves from whatever needs to be* <u>**Purged**</u> [**verb**]. *But we are now able to target whatever the stuff is, whatever the leaven might be* [**and of course all the stuff, matter, issues, being excreted is done so as a noun**]...

2 Tim 2:21 - If a *man* therefore <u>*Purge*</u> *H*imself from *T*hese: *he* shall be a *V*essel unto Honor —*Sanctified* and Proper, for the Master's use...

<u>*Purged*</u> —

Heb 10:2,3 - For then would *they* not have *C*eased to be *offered?* Because that the *W*orshipers once <u>*Purged*</u> —should have had no more *C*onscience of Sins. But in those *sacrifices*, there is a *R*emembrance *again* of Sins, every Year. (***Commentary*** - Here, <u>*Purged*</u> demonstrates for us the <u>*Verb - action*</u> *N*ecessary to <u>*Purge*</u> out the <u>*Noun-stuff*</u> of Sin.)

2 Pet 1:7 – 9 - And to Godliness, brotherly kindness, and to *brotherly* kindness Charity. For if these things be in *you*, and *A*bound they make *you* that *you* shall neither be <u>Barren</u> nor *unfruitful* in the Knowledge of our Lord Jesus Christ. But *he* that lacks these things is ***blind and*** cannot see ***afar-off*** and has forgotten that *he* was <u>*Purged*</u> *from his* <u>old-sins</u>. [*these verses here show us that we should already be* <u>*Purged*</u> *from our sins if we have fully confessed Christ as Savior. But if we have not been cleansed of our* <u>*Noun-stuff,*</u> *as the* <u>*Verb*</u>*-action denotes: —then we are still as defiled, and filthy as before—just as **2 Peter 2:21,22** declares:*] Quote: ***For it had been better for them to not to have known the way of Righteousness, then after they have known it: To turn from the*** <u>***Holy Commandments***</u> ***delivered unto them— But it has happened unto them according to the True Proverb: "That the Dog is turned to his own vomit again — . And the Sow that was washed, to her wallowing in the mire".*** [*and as also confirmed in **Hebrews 6:4 - 6** - **For it is impossible for those who were once informed and have tasted of the Heavenly Gift, and were made partakers of the Holy Ghost, and have tasted the Good-Word of God, and the Powers of the World to come: if they should fall away, to renew them again unto Repentance; seeing that they Crucify to themselves the Son of God — Afresh, and put Him to an open Shame**]. —*

So, you see, I believe that it is of dire necessity for us to get to the place of knowing, and comprehending by revelation, that our **New-Birth** in Christ, comes already equipped with every weapon, and tool that we need to be Free. So that just as a **_Newborn_** Child, we are once again Born without the knowledge of Sin, therefore allowing us to begin **_again_** to learn Righteousness instead of Sin, thus eliminating as much of it from our everyday Life as much as we're able to do in this Human Life. I believe that One of the main **Keys** _to_ this Process [_at least for me_] is the ever Cleansing and highly **_accentuated extirpation_** that daily **_Purging_** can Produce. Of course, — **_Scripturally speaking_** to my under-standing — it is better known as simply a **_"daily act of Repentance"_**. And it really doesn't matter which terminology you use, they're both one in the same and will accomplish in us the works of **_Purification_** unto the Sanctifying of our Souls. —

BUILDING BLOCK #2 CONCLUSION: _CONFORMED_ TO A HOLY TRANSFORMATION — (_SPIRITUAL INSIGHT —_ OCTOBER 30TH, 1992)

Philippians, **C**_hapter 3:13-16 - Brethren, I count not myself to have Apprehended: but this_ <u>_one-thing_</u> _I do, forgetting_ <u>_those things_</u> _which are behind, and reaching forth unto_ <u>_those-things_</u> _which are "In front of Me" — I press toward the mark for the Prize of the High-Calling of God in Christ Jesus. — Let us therefore, as many as be_ <u>_Perfect,_</u> _"In this Way". And if in_ <u>_anything_</u>_, ye be otherwise minded: God shall reveal even this unto you. However, to which we've already Achieved, let us walk by the same Rule, let us mind the same thing. —_

Insight (A)

Now that we have already received Christ in our **_lives_**, let us remember as well: That in the **_Holy Ghost_**, we must walk, as our

Spiritual Fathers did in Victory. For example, we have Apostles, Paul, Peter, John and James, who by their Testimony, demonstrated to us that we have no excuse as to neglect so *Great a Salvation* as we have. Since we, like they: also have at our **sides,** that same Holy Ghost. And by *Him,* they were able to leave us a Traceable Legacy *of faith.* A *faith* that gave us a map of **all** the Great **sacrifices,** each of them contributed to our own <u>*faith-walk*</u>. And this was included in the Perpetual Will and testament of our Savior. As they — **the Apostles;** also dying in Christ, became a part of **His Will** and Testament, as Living Epistles of **His** Goodness. Amen! And so, they were Examples for us, to show us a clear path, not just to **Holiness**: but even more for our indissoluble pursuit to also Please *the* **Father.** *A*nd just as they were transformed day by day into the expressed **Will** of the **Father** *(In the Newness of their Minds, as they put on the Mind of Christ),* Likewise we to must be Transformed. And being Transformed, we should know by now that we're no longer to run after **worldly** **C**onformities, **anymore:** Seeing how such Great a Price was paid to commute and dissolve at hand our **S**entence of **death.** And so, we must be vigilant, to not let slip *"So Great a Salvation"*!

Prov, Chapter 3:6 - *In all thy ways acknowledge Him, and He shall direct their Paths.*

Insight (B)

As a <u>**New Creation**</u> in Christ, learning the ways *of* **R**ighteousness through Self Denial and other **Purification** Processes: —we must, always, be acutely aware of the nature of **worldly** **conformity,** with its destructive **A**genda and intentions. Intentions that are diametrically opposed to all that **R**epresent the Order and Will *of* God in the Life of **His** **children.** Hence, it is therefore, **solely** our responsibility, as Blood-**B**ought Saints, empowered by the *Spirit of* God, to resist all *worldly - inclinations.* Since we know that their hot pursuit is to pollute; at all costs —the Mind *of* Christ in us, if Possible. But here is Wisdom: The *Spirit of* God is in us, reminding us that it's the Expressed Image of Jesus in us, showing forth by us the Evidence that we've been <u>***Transformed***</u>. And as a result, we do strive with great Joy and Confidence, even in *"The Valley of the Shadow of Death",* or wherever our path and Destiny may lead us. Preaching to *all* that Christ is the *only* Way and our *only* **Hope. And it** is our *only* avenue to the Father. Now because of the Finished Work of the Cross, we now have *Access* by our <u>*own faith*</u> to the Abundance that *His S*acrifice has won for us. Now, for *me* to accept this *new* Reality is *T*ruly a *manifested* Confirmation: *Affirming* in Me that I have been *Transformed* — And I, yes; even I, *A*m now with the Brethren, *"Past, Present, and Heavenly Bound"* In a Place of **Prominence.** As *Hebrews 12:1 - 4 - Wherefore seeing we also are compassed about with so great a Cloud of Witnesses, let us lay aside every weight, and the Sin which doth so easily surround us, and let us run with Patience the Race that is Set before us. Looking unto Jesus the Author and Finisher of our Faith; who for the Joy that was set before Him — endured the Cross, despising the Shame: and is set down at the Right Hand of God. For consider Him that endured such Contradiction of Sinners against Himself, lest ye be wearied and faint in your own Minds. (For) Ye have not yet resisted unto Blood: Fighting against Sin.*

Resist the Devil, and he Will Flee from You! (James 4:7)

Isaiah, Chapter 42:16 - *And I will bring the Blind by a way that they <u>know-not</u>: I will lead <u>them in</u> Paths that they have <u>not-known</u>: — I will make Darkness <u>Light</u> before <u>them</u>; and Crooked things Strait. These <u>things I</u> will do for <u>them and</u> not forsake <u>them</u>. —*

Insight (C) —

Here, I hope to show, with *Spiritual C*larity, the Prophecy given by God to the Prophet Isaiah: pertaining to us *(The Body of Christ)*, more so than to those of the Law. For a People *W*rought by the hand of *faith*, even before we were known as a <u>*New-Creation*</u>.

And by this Evidence, we know, *through* our *Transformation* by the *Holy Ghost*, we can Discern more clearly those *things R*evealed, wherein before we were not able to *S*ee. And now because of this, we have hope, where none *existed B*efore. But by the renewing of our Minds. And the willful <u>*Purging*</u> of our Souls, unto *R*ighteousness. We are now able to be Led, seeing that we've been Sanctified by *His B*lood. O yes, because of our *Trans-formation*, to Commit Daily, to the Commandments *of* God, which have been *Summed up* into Two: and they are these: *"Love the Lord God with All your Heart, and with All your Soul: and the second is like unto it. Love your Neighbor as Yourself"* on *these Hang All the Law and the Prophets – Mt 22:40"*! And so, as the Light of the **Word** begins to Illuminate our *P*aths, helping *Us* to be <u>O</u>bedient *Servants, 'As we are wont to be'*. Giving all Praise to God as we continue to be *O*bedient in this: our *'Good Fight of Faith'*. Being always Victorious over the Powers of this *world* that try *M*ightily to *C*onform us.

BUILDING BLOCK #3 — *RE-ACCESSING MY* RELATIONSHIP *WITH* CHRIST

The Twofold Purpose of Our Relationship:

The Gospel unto Salvation & To Be a Witness of The Power of the Gospel. So, here's a most relevant question that's Contextually Conducive to the Twofold Purpose aforementioned, and it's this: *"After being Born Again, and our Lives Transformed, into a New Mind of Confidence: Then What? —*

Answer: *" Ye shall receive Power, after that the Holy Ghost has Come Upon You– and You shall be Witnesses unto Me both in Jerusalem, and in All Judea and in Samaria– And to the Uttermost Parts of the Earth (Acts 1:8) -- But as Many as Receive Him, to Them – gave He The Power to Become the Sons of God. Even to Them that Believe on His Name* (St John 1:12)

<u>**Memory Break:**</u>

The Gospel unto Salvation: *All About relationship -- (A Spiritual Checkmark)* —

Here, I'll take a moment to **R**eflect on the last (*Thirty-four plus Years*): — And how many times, during those years, I've been stopped by a **C**heck in my *spirit*, or I was stopped by the *Holy Spirit*, to **R**eassess— and **C**heck to make sure that my relationship with Christ was still on par to where I was heading. And often, I failed to do so. Not realizing that I hadn't been sensitive to *His* guidance — until I looked up from a *place* that I had no business being in *(By my own Wisdom)*. And once again, crying out like the Babe I no-longer thought I was, but I was wrong. *And* like always, *He* came to my rescue, though not as quickly as I'd wished. Nevertheless, *I* was always delivered. — Now, of course, whenever I would be mature enough to hear what the *Spirit* was trying to show me, regarding my relationship with Christ. I would then begin to ask myself a few questions, like: Lord, where are you in this situation? Lord, am I where I need to be? Lord, am I headed in the right direction. And lastly, *as* a Husband to one Wife *(and vice versa)*, are *we* where *we* need to be in Oneness with each other and *with You*? If not, what do we need to do to improve? Now, as for *you*, the Reader, *Marriage* might not be where you are at this time in your life, *and* as well; none of these Questions may be yours. Nevertheless, I have no doubt that *you* do indeed get my point. But whatever your Question might be, stop put a Checkmark on that spot, and seek the Lord well before trouble. Perhaps in doing so, you'll be spared. So, at the Beginning of whatever it is we need to do for the Lord and for our relationship with *Him (Even if it's a Holy Idea).* We still need to Check with the *Holy Spirit and* not Run ahead on our own. Now let me return a moment, back to the 'Oneness of Marriage'. There, I will speak from a place of experience, whether good or bad. It has taken me over *(Thirty-four plus Years -- from 1990 to the Present)*, to fully realize, by *revelation*, that instead of my Wife being *second* in importance to my *Spiritual-E*valuation: she has to be 'dead center' of everything Relative to the evaluation of my Relationship in Christ, and all that is important to the summary of who I am, or might ever be. *(And my Sheila was just that, Second to no other than Christ all the way to her Departure into the presence of the Lord on June 29th, 2024).* And she was there not because I emotionally desired her to be there, but rather because the Word *of* God bears witness to that Reality. Now, let me reiterate what I previously wrote. Whether Married or Single, we must live *by faith*, Discernment, and *revelation*. There's just no other way for us to Live. Now! Of course, for us to Live in the fulness of what I just mentioned, we must, *by way* of our faith, create a connection with the Son and stir up the Gifts. *Gifts* freely offered to us *by* the Father; on behalf of the *Son [Behold what manner of Love the Father hast bestowed upon us that we should be called the Children of God - 1Jn 3:1].*

Checkmark *(Continuing with Marriage & Other Relationship)—*

Now, before I continue further on Relationships in general, let me go a little further on the topic of Marriage, which is one of God's Greatest and most extraordinarily phenomenal *Achievements* in all of Creation. It is the only *one* that can achieve both Spiritual and Natural Unity. Or let's say it this way: A Godly *Marriage* truly represents the full intent of God's creative Genius, *for* it is the only Relationship that in its' <u>True</u> Purpose, has the Power to accomplish God's Plan. A plan that no individual or no One group's agenda can accomplish. And that Power, simply put, is the Reproductive System of the Male and Female. And there's no invention or Lofty thought of Man, able to accomplish that Great *feat.* "For **He** said to them, *"Be fruitful and Multiply"*. Now please understand this writing is not just about the Conjugal *relationship but* is about the importance of it. And in my opinion, I will always believe that Marriage is the model by which all relationships find their balance, starting with siblings, and from siblings to friends. And so, based on the plan of God with the advent of Family *(beginning with Adam & Eve)*. We now have functional Societies everywhere. Oh, and like everyone else, I've witnessed it play out in my own family for better or worse. Therefore, I know that however a person starts out in Life, it is always relative to their environment, and therefore whatever *relationships* they develop through encounters is always a snapshot of their family environment *(for good or evil)*. And so, because this book is about my life, and my experiences in my *faith walk*, and my *spiritual* Journey with my *Wife, Sheila.* -- Who, because of Christ, is the greatest human Relationship that I've ever had the pleasure of knowing. And next to Christ, she is the *One*. Notwithstanding the fact that I was blessed to have three of the Best friends in Life that any one person could ever hope to have in a lifetime, namely Jacob & Paul Dawkins *(Brothers)* and George Thompson. I can honestly tell you, with their approval, we have not, till this day; ever become *One*! It's only by the *Spiritual & Natural Union* of Man and Wife, in Christ, that Two could ever become as *One*. — But when it comes to *relationships* that are found in the *Spirit of* Agreement, then they too, can become 'As One' in the Unity of the *Spirit*. Hence, we are then able to become Spiritual Friends and Workers together for the Benefit of the Kingdom, whereby fulfilling *(if necessary) the Words* that Christ spoke unto *His D*isciples, saying *Greater Love hath no one than this, than to Lay-Down his Life for his Friends*. And so, here I stand with confidence in saying that the <u>Relationships </u>that have been nourished in Christ are those who are on the same journey as myself, and at different storied moments must be engaged, not just for the strength of each other, but for the different roles we play to the Benefit of the Kingdom. But I must confess to you, even as I realize these *truths*. Sometimes, the Battles of Life distract me into thinking that I'm all alone in the fight. Until I cry out for help and hear the Voice of the Lord, saying: Call Jacob... and then afterward, I am refreshed. As I mentioned earlier, for *Thirty-four plus* Y*ears*, I've been on the Battlefield, and Building <u>***Relationships***</u>, and this Process ain't easy. But neither is the *walk of faith.*

And so let us, while in the process of building-up one another, keep putting <u>Check</u> *<u>marks</u>* on our Progress, *R*eassessing and *R*eevaluating where they are and where they should be in regard to our Fellowship with the Father.

<u>*Taking Inventory of My Relationship with Christ*</u>:

(A)- When I accepted Christ in my life *it* was with a sincere heart. And so, I began to study with great vigor. Hungry for what I needed to know, not knowing all that I needed. And for over Seven Months, I lived the Word I had to have it. I was ravenous for *It*. Then, after 7 months, while channel surfing, I stumbled upon a Tele-Evangelist, and from his fiery message I was filled with the Holy Ghost. Of course, the measure of how much Holy Ghost I didn't comprehend (**not** *knowing at the time that I was filled with the full measure of who He is)*. But nevertheless, after being filled, using an old Basketball <u>cliche</u>, *"The Ball was now in My Court."* In other words, I reckoned my body as that Court —The Temple of the Holy Ghost and a House for the

Lord's Good Pleasure. But it was solely my responsibility for what I used *His Court* for and how I respected where the Lord dwelt. And yes, it's my choice as to how Clean I want the House of the Lord to be. But of course, without real Revelation on the Role that the Holy Ghost would play in helping me to keep <u>*His*</u> *T*emple clean, the Task of it would be impossible. Because it's only by my *will* to be Teachable or *Coachable* that the *Spirit of* Truth can *breathe* its **Breath** *of* Life into the Catacombs of my once *dead* Heart. And once done, then the Temple is made Holy and fit for the Master's use, as the *"Gospel unto Salvation" is made Prevalent in my Life.* [**Scriptures Ref: *2 Cor 5:1,2 Heb 3:6 / 1 Pet 2:5 / Jer 17:9 / Eph 2:1-6*].**

A Witness to the Power of the Gospel: <u>*"I Surrender"*</u>

(B)- Now, if we try to accept Christ in a Halfway manner, then we do so to the deception of our own self. And likewise, unknowingly *(**Because** we have deceived ourselves)*, we begin to operate in the ***unholy-Spirit*** of *Anti-Christ*. And eventually, the evidence of our pretense will be revealed. And that either, to the Benefit of our Soul, or unto our Repentance: or unto everlasting damnation. Our choice: *"**Choose you this day whom you will Serve**"* [Josh 24:15]. You see, no matter how smoothly deceptive you are, there's no such thing as a Fake New Birth: only a Tare in the midst of Wheat. It can also be called lukewarm. Because anytime we do anything *half-heartedly,* whether Spiritual or Natural, we've really become what I call an *"<u>Either, Or Creation</u>"*. A Creature scripturally speaking, better known as a "double<u>*_minded man*</u> [Jam 1:1-8]". Now, as I sit down in the quietness of my Soul and with a prayerful evaluation of my own Heart. I must search my soul to consider whether or not I'm truly committed to my own <u>*faith walk*</u>: Which, in literal and Spiritual reality, is not so much about me but is truly all about Jesus. The Author and *finisher* of all that I am and all that I desire to *poseur* upon the Lord as a Witness to the Lost.

Now, even though I did witness for the Lord, as often as the opportunity presented itself. Yet, somehow, it still wasn't with a whole heart. And I knew it: Now let me explain. You see, even though I was a strong witness for the Lord when testifying of how *He* delivered me from the throes *of* Hell. I still was not fully committed to my *faith walk*, why? Because I was subtly and unwittingly caught off guard. I was distracted by a type of self-righteous busy-ness. As I busied myself casting out demons, anointing babies *(Which I believe I was led to do)*, and accomplishing all manner of outwardly Holy displays, yet God Honored my *faith*. **He** did not punish me for my naivety. But it was the complacency of that **naiveness** that caused Us to falter in our *upward* pursuit of the Lord. It cost us our first Home, and to this point, it might be the only One we'll ever own unless God reveals to us another One: *"There's always Hope."* nevertheless His will be done. And so, it took me over Twelve years to finally understand what complete and total surrender is. And since 2014, I've been endeavoring to press on into the place of Wholeheartedly *serving* the Lord, till I get to the place where I know that I'm *His* Friend and not just *His* Servant. And so, the obvious lesson that must be learned, and hopefully a lot sooner for many who might read this Book. And that is That there is no way *One* could ever approach A **Holy God** in such a Half-Hearted and Haphazardly way: to then expect to withdraw anything of any substantive Value from the Kingdom. You see beloved, *"it's either all, or it's Nothing"*. — And so, after a deep and penetrating Probe, considering all the Years that are now behind me. I now relentlessly pursue and seek to always know, daily, By My *faith* whether I'm truly 'Sold-Out' to my God, no longer as just a Bondservant, but indeed a Friend. And at this time, I can honestly tell you I'm Both. And because of that Spiritual fact, 1 am entrenched even more with an intense desire to live Holy. And to do so with much more fervency and vigor of *faith* than I ever lived for Satan. You see, the *life* I now live, in

Christ: I live to the *Glory of* the Father. And with every fiber of my being, I intend to expend in the *fierceness* of Now. With the shrewd **Efficiency** of a Marksman: I won't miss as I become One with the Mark: *Who* is Christ, my Lord. And whatever way *He* chooses to **E**xploit *me* for *His* Gain, <u>**I Surrender**</u>. And there will be no Haphazard or *lukewarm* Compromising of the Gospel [**Scripture Reference:** *Heb 12:2/ Phi 2:12 / 1 Jn 3:8 / Gal 2:20.*] ...

Epilogue *for* **Building Block #3:** To all Born Again Christians, and even to those who might still be on the fence of indecision, though still contemplating what the Answer might be for your Life: please understand. You should never, at any time, entertain Questions That would have you measure yourself against how someone else may or may not serve the Lord. No! When you are at the crossroads that leads you to Repentance, you should simply seek your Answer in the only place it can be found: The Word *of* God. The Holy Bible *(**Kings James Version - it's my Choice, it is God's Answer to Us**)*. — It's the Answer for every area of our Lives.

And every Answer that it delivers to you will always trend toward Life. Because it has no **answers** for self-willed Pleasures or any other type of Vanity. No, not any: it won't make room or give an excuse to your ***"Saintly Mama"*** who just might slip up every now and again. And it won't make room for your ***"Godly Daddy"*** to cover up the slip of his tongue of a swear word or two: Cause Mama and Daddy both gotta Repent, if they wanna see Heaven **through.**–So if it's truly Answers for your Life that you're in search of, then indeed; it's the Holy Bible. But I must warn you. The Answer that you'll find for each area of your Christian Walk — can only be found when First *things* become First. God First, and His Will (for *us*), through Christ First, just as Christ stated in ***"St John 10:30 (saying)- I and my Father are One"***. Now for me, this is *an* Awesome Revelation, as I view it through this Truth: ***"But Seek ye <u>First</u> the Kingdom of God and His Righteousness, and All these Things will be <u>Added</u> to you - St Matthew 6:33"***. Now, I don't know about you, but for me, this is Very Clear: — "God is the Kingdom, and Christ is the Righteousness of His Glory, and they are One". Just as Jesus declared in: ***"St John 14:10 - I am in the Father, and the Father is in Me."*** So please, I implore you to seek God, to seek Him in **His** Word, and **His** Word will reveal ***Himself*** to ***you.*** And ***He*** will deliver unto ***you*** the Father's Will for your Life, which is the Answer that we Seek. For His Glory, **Amen!**

Building Block #4: *"Again I Say, <u>Be Not</u> Conformed"*

First, before we discuss further the Act of ***"Non-Conformity"*** Let us discuss the Power of this Word **<u>Be</u>**. For me, it is one of the Keys to my Personal Daily *decision* on how to allow *faith* to operate in my Life. Here, I want to show the <u>importance</u> of its meaning in the development of the New Man I am and am becoming unto the necessary place of Maturity. Now of course, if we start from the premise that **<u>Be</u>** is the Instrument by which we become New Creatures, then as seekers, servants and even Friends *of* God, we have to accept that the Righteous living that we are after is truly and totally our Responsibility. Because we, through the Power *of* **<u>Be</u>** and by our surrender to it, can choose to **<u>Be</u>** Transformed and die to Self. Or instead, live by our own Reasoning and continue to *be* shaped and formed into the perpetual degradation that death requires, even unto its own demise. A demise as described in *1 Corinthians 15:54,55* (saying) ***"Death is swallowed up in Victory." – "O Death, where is your sting? O Hades, where is your Victory."*** But of course, the <u>power</u> to be One or the Other, Light or Darkness, Good or Evil, is a Choice given to Man by design: Right in the middle of *his* Garden, in the middle of *his* Peace.

But *his* propensity to *be* evil was obviously much greater than *his* desire for Good. So, you see, the Choice for either Place *of* **Being has** always been ours. But now you see, if the Choice we make is that of Good, then " Praise Be to God" since we now have a *Helper,* and He is the *Holy Ghost.* [**See Genesis 1:26-28,** *and* **St John 14:26/15:26 /16:7**] — But mind you now, He will not choose Righteousness for us, since He is, Himself, the very Righteousness of Christ on display. But rather, He will assist us with making. Choice.

Even as *Shakespeare* so eloquently voiced it, in Hamlet, spoken *by Hamlet:* and I quote, *"To Be, or not to Be, that is the Question: Whether 'tis nobler in the Mind; to Suffer the Slings and arrows of outrageous Fortune, or to take Arms against a Sea of Trouble?"* —Now that same Question, by paraphrase is asked of Us: and so which one do we choose: To **be** Conformed, or not to **Be**. This is a great dilemma, and the greatest Spiritual Battle that will ever be fought is the one of Choice. And so, we wrestle over choosing the more self-centered One, the One that keeps us in constant turmoil, to the detriment of our Soul. Fighting a war that one way or the other we're doomed to Lose, looking up from the bowels of Hell, as we make it our eternal tomb. Just because we decided to surrender to the lesser, and more base **Be**, the **Be** of Conforming to the Flesh. No, we cannot, we dare not Choose Suicide, not when we can choose to be Victorious in the middle of a Fight that has already determined our Victory. Not when we can choose to become defenders of our Right to not Perish and determine that I am the Righteousness *of* God in Christ Jesus. I am a *Spiritual Weapon* of War, and I will engage the enemy on the Battlefield *by My faith.* And by my Choice to **Be Not Conformed,** I will defeat the enemy on the Field of *My* despair and will not cease to engage *Him* upon the Sea of Iniquity, I will not *fear.* Yes indeed, I emphatically Choose the **Be of Transformation**, for it is the Power and the Secret to "<u>Working out your own Salvation</u>". But like was mentioned by *Hamlet but* Paraphrasing by Me: *"To <u>Be</u> Not Conformed, or to <u>Be</u> Transformed, that is the Question!"*

Conclusion to a Spiritual Etymological Revelation: Of the Importance of this *Word "<u>Be</u>"* The very Foundation of My *(Our)* Transformation!

(Now, I know that this may seem to be a little more than Redundant, but this is how I was led by the Holy Ghost to relay this Powerful Word to whoever will read this Book). — So, I will try to define in more depth this Word <u>*Be*</u>. Since I now have a better opportunity, according to my Newfound comprehension *(by revelation),* how to <u>*Be Transformed*</u> by it. So, we may as well glean all that we can absorb from "<u>Webster's and Oxford Press</u>." Let's see what they so kindly have to *reveal* to us: *f*rom their didactical, exhaustive explanation of this most powerful Word of Choice. Since they've done the research for us, let's peek in on their discovery.

Webster's New World Dictionary:

<u>Be</u> *v.* - <u>*Be*</u> is used to join a subject with a word or words that tell something about it. It is also used to tell that something exists or takes place, <u>***and is a helping verb***</u>, with other <u>***verb forms***</u>. In the present-tense, '<u>*Be*</u>' has these forms: *I am; he, she– or it is; we, you– or they* are. 1. '<u>*Be*</u>' may join a subject with a *noun, adjective, or pronoun* [*Ed and Lois are students. Mary is pretty. Who is he?*] '<u>*Be*</u>' may mean '<u>*to live*</u>' '<u>to happen or take place</u>' or '<u>to stay or continue</u>'

<u>Be</u> *a prefix meaning* 1. Around [*To <u>beset</u> is to set around, or surround*] 2. Completely [*To <u>be-smear</u> is to smear completely*] 3. Away [*To <u>betake</u> oneself — is to take oneself away*]

Oxford University Press:

Be *verb (singular: present* **am;** *are;* **is;** *pl. present* **are;** *1st and 3rd singular. past* **was;** *2nd singular past and pln. past* **were;** *present subjunctive* **be;** *past subjunctive* **was;** *present part.* **being;** *past part.* **been)** 1. *(usu.* **there is/are)** *exist* **be present.**

2. Occur; take place. **3.** Have the specified state, nature, or role. **4.** Come; go; visit. **auxiliary verb** –1 used with a <u>present participle to form continuous tenses.</u> 2 used with a <u>past participle to form the passive voice</u>. 3 used to <u>indicate something that is due to, may, or should happen</u>. PHRASES - **the be-all and end-all,** informal the most important <u>**aspect of Something**</u>. <u>**to-be of the future. His Bride-to-be**</u>.

(Me) - Be is establishing prophetically what <u>Now</u> is, in the Reality of Faith

<u>**4. Be**</u> **prefix** forming **verbs**: 1. All over, all around: **bespatter.** 2. thoroughly; **(and)** excessively: **bewilder.** 3. Expressing <u>transitive action</u>: **bemoan.** 4. Affect with or to cause to **befog.** 5. *(forming adjectives ending in – ed)* having covered with **bejeweled.** ORIGIN Old English, related to <u>**bypreposition**</u>. 1 <u>through the agency</u> or means of. 4 indicating <u>**the end of a time period**</u>. 6 <u>past and beyond</u>.

The **Be** *of* Transformation —

As we continue to delve into the power of this truly **dynamic** Word (<u>**Be**</u>), we will discuss in this Part *both* its **Spiritual** connotation in association with its natural meaning. And its natural Application in regards to our **Spiritual-Walk:** Asserting with great **profundity** our position as Servants, and Friends of the Most High God. And we do so rightly by dividing the Word *of* **Truth.** Walking daily in effectual joy and the Confidence that it brings. And to (<u>**Be**</u>) Transformed by the renewing of our **minds** is the first place we really begin to see the power of the Word. Because as we do so: To **Be** lays within us the Foundation that will become the platform by which all of our *Spiritual* **G**rowth will spring from. And in its purest form, for me, the Power *of* **_(Be) can't_** *be* more Profoundly described than the **_(Be) atti-tude:_** When Jesus revealed it for the *first* time to virgin ears. It is for me, the **Precursor** to **_Romans 12:2_**. Since it shows an example of limitless possibilities of having a *Spiritually* **T**ransformed Mind. And without this New and Living way of thinking that was established in your decision **_(Be) Transformed_** **_(by putting on the Mind of Christ)_**. We would not be able to **_Be_** or have any of the **_"9 Beatitudes"_**. Okay, *wow*: Now, that's a **T**enaciously *Powerful* **Revelation:** at least it is to **me**. So, I'll take a break here to hear and reflect on how *Webster's* define this **Word:**

<u>**THE EPILOGUE:** *(Deeper Depths)* Daniel 2:22</u>

<u>**Beatitude**</u> *n.* complete happiness, bliss: **the Beatitudes,** the part of the Sermon on the Mount, in the Book *of **Matthews,*** which begins: **_Blessed are the Poor in Spirit._** **The Beatitude —** *Matthew,* **C**hapter *5:1 thru 12:*

— And seeing the multitudes, *He* went up on a Mountain, and when *He* was seated *His* **D**isciples came to *Him*. Then *He* opened *His* **M**outh and **T**aught them, *S*aying:

(1) **_Blessed are the Poor in spirit, for theirs is the Kingdom of Heaven._**

(2) **_Blessed are those who Morn, for they shall <u>Be</u> Comforted._**

(3) **_Blessed are the Meek, for they shall Inherit the Earth._**

(4) **_Blessed are those who Hunger and Thirst for Righteousness, for they shall <u>Be</u> filled._**

(5) **_Blessed are the Merciful, for they shall obtain mercy._**

(6) **_Blessed are the Pure in Heart, for they shall See God._**

(7) *Blessed are the Peacemakers, for they shall <u>Be</u> called Sons of God.*

(8) *Blessed are those who are Persecuted for Righteousness' sake, for theirs is the Kingdom of Heaven."*

(9) *"Blessed are you when they Revile and Persecute you and say all Kinds of Evil against you Falsely for My sake —Rejoice and <u>Be</u> exceedingly glad, for Great is your Reward in Heaven, for so they Persecuted the Prophets who were before you."*

To complete this *Spiritually Illuminating* and illimitable Teaching on this Word, and so that I won't begin to sound too Magniloquently pompous. I will give a few Scripture references as evidence *(if further evidence is needed)* to confirm, without a *shadow of a doubt (in modern Christendom)*, just where we stand, relative to the <u>Beatitude,</u> in regard to our *faith-walk* today. And how the *Blessings* we now have access to, by the Process of our *Salvation,* — relate to those ancient *Blessings* Promised in the <u>Beatitudes</u>. And so, as we continue on, in our everyday transitional Transformation, meditating upon the Word of God, and with whatever weapon that might assist us in our upward mobility, as we're Transformed *from Glory* to *Glory.* And yes, I do believe that this Book will become an awesome Accessory if you include it in your Arsenal *of faith.* To the Renewing of your Mind, as it has been: Is, and will continue to be for Me: *"As We all come to the Unity of the Faith, and to the Knowledge of the Son of God." —*

Philippians, Chapter **3:13-16** *Brethren, I count not myself to have apprehended: but this one thing I do, forgetting those things that are behind and reaching forth unto those things that are before. I press toward the mark for the Prize of the High Calling of God in Christ Jesus. Let us therefore as many as <u>Be</u> Perfect, <u>Be</u> thus minded: and if in anything you <u>be</u> otherwise minded, God shall Reveal even this unto You. Nevertheless, whereto we have already* *attained, let us walk by the Same-Rule —let us Mind the Same Things.......*

Ephesians, Chapter **4:22-24** *That you put off concerning the former Conversation the Old Man, which is Corrupt according to the deceitful Lust; and* <u>Be</u> *Renewed in the Spirit of your Mind; and that you put on the* <u>New Man,</u> *which after God is Created in Righteousness and True Holiness.*

<u>Spiritual Reflection [A]:</u> — (<u>Philippians 3:13-16 and Ephesians 4:22-24)</u>— *Now that we've already received Christ in our Lives, as our Life, let us duly; with fervor relinquish our past and present Conformities, which are all detrimental to our future. And let us move with determined stealth, into the Newness of Hope. And in the process of working out our own Salvation, we will move into the realm of the Beatitudes of Blessings. And so let us remember, that it's through the help of the Holy Ghost that we've obtained the Transforming Power of* <u>Be</u>*, to the settling of our Soul with Renewed Minds.* (Matthew 5:6 "He who **Hungers** and **Thirst** after Righteousness shall be *filled."*

Isaiah, Chapter 42:16 ***And I will bring the blind by a way that they knew not: I will lead them in paths that they have not known: I will make Darkness Light before them — and crooked things Straight. These things will I do unto Them and not forsake.***

<u>Spiritual Reflection [B]:</u> —(Isaiah **42:16**) *Here we see the Plan of God unfolding in its Perpetual Guarantee, as* **He** *calls into existence by* **His** *faith a People not yet Born: Who would spring forth from the Seed of* **His** *Dear Son, destined to come fully Clothe*(Nothing Missing— Nothing Broken). *And only by His coming will Transformation* <u>Be</u> *made, as old things are passed away, no longer standing in the way of New Things. For this is indeed the Promise of the Father, as* **He** *reaffirms for us All our Promised Hope in Abraham* (Genesis 22:18 "And in thy **Seed** shall All the Nations of the Earth be **Blessed**): *And so here we are, not just Connoisseurs of a Blessed Earth, but rather Partakers of a Heavenly Transformation, into the fruit of all that is in Christ Jesus,*

thereby <u>*Bearing more Seed toward the Harvest of the Kingdom.*</u>
<u>*Hallelujah, and Amen!*</u>

FINAL CONCLUSION:

So now, if we are to __Be__ triumphant in all that we put our hands to do concerning the Splendor of what the __Beatitudes__ accomplishes for us, as an instrument given to us, so that we can get a correct measurement of what it takes to __Be__ Blessed. Hence, through the process and power of our Salvation that we work out for ourselves, the Benefits produced by the __Beatitudes__ are immense. And do show unto us the Measure of the Father's Love shown unto us, by the Grace of our Lord, Jesus Christ. Thus, we are set up as Witnesses of the Glory of the Kingdom: and Praise be to God, that none of our past Conformities, which were damnable, can now at any time separate us from the Love of God, in Christ Jesus. And because we now have our desires corrected. We can now willingly submit —

You see, we no longer need the coercion of a Pastor, or a Teacher, or Mother, for us to know the Word of God. Because of the Transforming Power that has shown our Mind a New and Living Way, we have no more need for any to tell us that we need to know the Lord. Because of the Holy Ghost and the __Be__ of Transformation, __Jeremiah 31:34__ - has come alive, Saying: (__No longer will they Teach their neighbor, or say to one another, 'Know the Lord,' — because they will all know Me, from the least to the Greatest," declares the Lord. — "For I will forgive their Wickedness and will remember their sins no more"__) Yes indeed, because of this great Truth, we can now, with great Joy, activate all the Gifts within us as the Fruits, from the Prophetic Seed of the Beatitudes, we are, for sure —the __Blessed,__ if we believe. And so, we must indeed Praise the Lord, with the Highest of Praise, as we shout Hallelujah. Knowing that we can now, with Purpose, choose to independently, apart from another Human Being, work out our own Salvation to the end, that the __Beatitudes__ are Alive and thriving in the Church. As the Saints of God, seek the Kingdom with a New Mind. Dispelling the wantonness' of "__filthy Lucre,__" according to

(__1 Peter 5:2__): and chasing after, but to do the Father's Will.

Now, one more time, and once again: and over and over again. We must learn what this place in God is all about, always casting aside distractions that try to detract us from the Purpose of God. We must fight the good fight of Faith — *with intense fervor, to the End that Christ be magnified in the Father. And in this, we will find, that we shall never again* **'be conformed to the things of this world. Being well able to prove, with our New Heart, what that good and Perfect Will of the Father is. Amen.'** *(Romans 12:2) ... And as I reflect on the* **Words** *of my Dear Apostle Paul, as he vaunted to us; in these* **Words: "But this one thing I do, for- getting those things which are behind, and reaching forth to those things that are before. I Press toward the Mark, for the Prize** —*of the* **High Calling of God in Christ Jesus** *(Philippians 3:13,14)."*—*And again I say, "Be Ye Transformed."*

CHRIST *our* Transformer, Transforming *Us from Glory to Glory...*

— *The* **HOLY GHOST** — **Our** Sealer, Sealing **Our** Transformation, *According to His Will in Us!...*

PRELUDE: THE BEGINNING —

The Trials *of* Transformation

(This Testimony is as True to the Gist of my Memory as I can recall) Looking into the rear-view mirror at the beginning of my New Birth in Christ. I'm reminded of how simple it was as a Babe *(at least it seemed simple)*. And how sure and confident I was, as I believed that God would always come through for us no matter what. I believed that all we had to do was Trust Him, and it would somehow work out. And in those early days as Babes in Christ, He did see us through. And in the **spiritual naiveness** of my adolescence "and just in the nick of time" He never failed us. And always make away of escape for us. That was in the early 90s before I complicated things. And in those days, I didn't know that once you were Born Again, there was a process called: — *working out your own Salvation (Ph 2:12)*. And since I didn't accept Christ at Church, and no one led me to Christ, I was on my own. So, I thought that all I had to do was to read and study my Bible every day, try to do good, and not disrespect my wife. You see, I really didn't know how to seek or receive the Holy Ghost or that I even needed such a thing. Therefore, I didn't know that an exchange of minds had to take place. My <u>old one</u>, for a **New One.** And being ignorant of all that needed to transpire. I surely didn't know that on the day of my own ***deliverance***, by the Miracle of God in Christ, my **Transformation** had begun.

Shortly Before My Desperately Needed New Birth Transplant: One month or so before I surrendered my Life to Jesus, and six months after marrying the Love of *my* Life. (*I almost succumbed to the pressures of lust within me. I almost became my earthly father, a man who was once upon a time my hero of the flesh. Until I was old enough to see first-hand the harm, he was causing my Mother as I came face to face with his adulterous ways. But that's a story for a different Book*). I met a woman at the Community Bar. And when I first met her, there was nothing special about her, only that she was black. We were usually the only blacks in the Bar, every now and again, other blacks would come in, but mostly just her and myself. She always came with another young lady (of *course, white*). So, we got to be friendly with one another as we talked. We sometimes shot a round or two of pool, nothing more (*by the way, they were both Military*). But like I mentioned earlier, we were only Bar friends, and cheating on my wife never entered my mind (even *though I was still a heathen*). And so often, after a round of pool, we (*all three of us*) would find a table, have a few drinks while enjoying the music, and shoot the breeze. Now, this went on for at least a couple or three months. And not once did I ever inquire about their living arrangement. I wasn't interested.

It was early June 1990. The particulars of that day escape me here. But it was on a Friday. I'd worked that evening with my landlord, as usual. But it was still a nice evening. So, I felt I needed to unwind, and a nice game of pool and a few drinks would do the *trick* (so *I conned my mind into believing*). A few minutes after I arrived, the 'black one' walked in; we acknowledged one another, and that was it.

After a few hours had passed, somehow, we'd navigated into the other's space. Her friend wasn't with her. And so, for the first time since our first meeting, we found ourselves alone. And our usual conversation about *life* ensued. We talked for probably a couple more hours. It was around 7pm, summertime just breaking dusk, when I felt I had accomplished what I set out to do, and that was, (*to get a nice buzz on*), to chill and then head home. (*That was my plan.*) And so, as we wrapped up our conversation, I gathered myself and was about to say: ***"See you later,"*** when she simultaneously gathered her purse, got up with me, and asked if I would walk her home. I was somewhat caught off guard (since *I'd never asked her where she lived*).

And then my stumbled response was: "O, you mean you live around here?" She laughed and said, yes, I live right around the corner. Okay, sure (*I clumsily said: now, before I go any further, let me tell you, she always knew that I was married, but she was single*), not a problem. But it was a problem, I was just caught up in *me* at the moment. The *me* before I met my wife came flooding back. Before her, I was always bold in whatever I wanted to do, whether married or single. When I was in that mindset and *somewhat* intoxicated, I had no regard for anyone. So, as we headed to her Condo, she suddenly wanted to walk to the Park. ***(But to do so, we'd have to walk by my house: the third house from the corner, with my wife possibly in her flower garden.)*** And without a second thought, I didn't hesitate, and with my chest out, I simply said: why not. After our careless interlude in the park, we ended up back at her Condo. And I knew why. It wasn't long till we were comfortable on her couch to get to know one another. And of course, it was the usual conversation that had no other agenda but sex. But before things could get too heated (*Thank you, Lord*), she suddenly got the munches: "AND, WHEW — SO DID I."

Hindsight is 20/20: — Away *of Escape*

Once she got to the kitchen and looked in her empty refrigerator, it dawned on her: she hadn't done any shopping *(and of course, she hadn't, when most of your time is spent on Base, you don't buy groceries too often, so she claimed)*. And with that, she returned with a drink for me as she sighed. Oh well, I'll have to get something later, *(she said, or something to that effect)*. John: Go ahead and get comfortable while I go upstairs and slip into something a little more relaxing; "I will be right back." Now, as I sat there, with my chest out, gloating over the fact I still had it (*whatever it was*). All I could think about was what came next: as I sipped my *drink*. "My Score." And while sitting there with that thought on my mind and a big grin on my face, I suddenly felt the Presence of God. And I knew that I was in trouble as my countenance changed. You see, at that point in my life, I was a *backslider,* but I still knew **His** *Spirit (as I believe all backsliders do)*. And **His** *Spirit of Conviction* stood me straight up. And my knees began to quake as the *Spirit* spoke to me, in a clear and *Audible Voice,* Saying: — **"Didn't I tell You that Sheila's Your Wife"!** And as the *Holy Spirit* spoke to me, her <u>right foot</u> cleared the rung of the bottom step. But before she could take her next step *(in her sexy gown)*, I abruptly interrupted her next move *(while still trying to maintain my Suavity)*.

You know what... "I -AM - STARVING." And ain't no need for you to go out later. If you don't mind, I'll run down to 'Piggly Wiggly' and get us something to eat. (*She agreed, with a big smile, saying: that'll be great)*. And as soon as her door closed behind me, my feet hit the pavement. And I ran as fast as I could, barely able to contain myself *from* the *Holy fear* that had fallen on me. And I ran almost faster than my heart could beat. —That was the last time I ever laid eyes on that Woman. And because a way of escape was provided for me, through *Awe and* Trembling, I have never battled with that kind of Lust again. –

"Fast Forwarded" One month later, On July 13th, 1990, I went to jail. After a two-day stay I was bonded out by my wife and land-lord. Once home, like a *chastened child* sent to his room. Hence, I headed straight to mine, subdued like a harmless dove. Later on, that day in the quiet of my room, I surrendered my lawless Soul to the Lord. With everything in me and with all my might, in humility, I *R*epented. And from that moment, my <u>*New Birth*</u> ignited the *Transformation* of my Soul.

Early Evidence *of* **My** *Transformation* —

Now, after My <u>*New Birth*</u> had taken place. The *Transformation Process* was becoming more apparent. Approximately One month later and learning how to be sensitive to the *Spirit of* God. I began to see in a New Light the importance of my Sheila *(My Wife)*. As I begin to realize her place is beside me, and not behind me. I slowly began to see how I'd been mistreating her. Now, at this early stage of my Transformation, I was still smoking cigarettes *(Though I was completely delivered from Alcohol and all Drugs)*. And as I was yet to be freed from the *filthy* habit of smoking. Still, I was beginning to see how insensitive I'd been to Sheila, even though I knew she was a God send. I showed little to no respect knowing she had asthma, it didn't matter about me smoking, as long as I didn't blow the smoke intentionally in her face.: after all *(this was my selfish nature revealed)*, *"I'm the man of my house, and I'll smoke wherever I want to."* But slowly I began to have a conscious about what, and how I did things toward my Wife. *(this was truly the Lord's doing)*. Soon my wicked way of thinking slowly began to dissipate. The more I studied my Bible, the cleaner I began to think. Not because I was suddenly mature enough to know better on my own. But because the *Holy Spirit* was beginning to lead me more and more into surrender through humility. And because of His patience, I began to be led outside on the Patio to smoke *(rain or shine, cold or hot)*. I was no longer punishing my Wife for my slothfulness. "Wow, I was growing Spiritually," and it was exciting. I began to desire to be on my knees *(with an imminent urgency, both literally and spiritually, as a Quick work was taking Place)*. A day didn't go by where I didn't go before Christ. And one day, while I was seeking *Him*, my *father* began to stir in my *spirit*. I began to reminisce how abusive he was in his speech to my Mother, a woman of God who never deserved his ridicule. Who was always humble toward him and would cry to keep from speaking a railing accusation of any kind against him. And I remembered at 16 years of age, when he put his hands on her, how she stopped me from killing him: saying, don't do it: — "He's your Father". And here, 1990 —Thirty-Two years later, and I was still reeling from the *effects* of his <u>Marital</u> *anarchy*.

Now, please believe me when I tell you: I do not use this word ignorantly, nor do I do so *lightly*. Not when I know the full measure and extent of its derogatory term. But to qualify my statement in layman's terminology, I'll simplify it, it's a *Lawless Person not adhering to the Rules of Engagement as agreed upon Contractually by the Parties involved.* Hence, when he abused my Mom, his Wife: and lawlessly committed *Adultery* on her, *he* became an <u>*anarchist*</u> —against the very laws that he, as a Servant of God, was called to uphold, according to the sacred Vows of *Holy Matrimony*. Yet because of his surrender to the *flesh and* showing blatant disregard for his Covenanted Vows. Vows he confessed before God to his Wife. And being ignorant of the consequences of his **_anarchy_**. He unwittingly opened the gates of Hell upon his Children (**"But That's a Story for Another Time"**).

Therefore, as flesh of his flesh, and bone of his bone, and as his son, I too begin to act as a lawless bastard in the same areas of weakness. Though, I thank God that it was not under the *guise* and similitude of **Holy Hypocrisy**! But instead, it was in me a curse. Now, once the **Holy-Spirit** revealed this Truth to me, I then knew *'beyond a shadow of a doubt'* that my Mind was being Changed... I felt my *spirit* being **Transformed.** —

And while in this **Spiritual Place** *of* Reflective **Transformation**, I began to cry out and repent from all the pain that I'd already caused my Wife. In just six months of marriage, I'd caused her a lot of anguish. So, in my praying and crying out to God, I pleaded with the Lord to remove all the degenerative aspects of my *father* from me and to purge me of his negative and ungodly infection. For the first time in my life, and in my marriage, I truly desired for good to come from me on behalf of another Person, boy this was big. Cause me "John Roberts" wanted to be the best Husband that any man could be. And I knew *(in my spirit, that I needed help)*. Because there was no way that I could ever achieve such a lofty order, accepted by the **Holy Ghost** *(A Friend who is closer than a Brother in all situations according to Holiness)*.

And even though, at the time, I really didn't comprehend fully the *position* and place of the **Holy Ghost** in my Life. And to tell the Truth, I had no knowledge of how to submit to His Way. Nevertheless, I was determined to Learn. And then a miracle happened: one day, as I was studying the Book *of* Job *(later in my maturing process, I would learn that those kinds of spontaneous Spiritual interventions were called 'being led' or moved by the Holy Spirit)*. As I continued to read Job, I came across a passage that simply **blew** *my mind,* and as I read it, it screamed out at me; "THIS IS FOR YOU" And immediately I knew, somehow, I knew, that this Verse *of S*cripture was the key to unlocking the door of my Captivity to Lust, which is always introduced to the heart through the *eye gate.* And as I gazed upon it, I felt its Power invade my *Soul.* It was the One Verse that would open my eyes to see freedom from the despair and shame of my *father.* The Bars to my *spiritual Anguish* would soon be broken down. And *my* pathway to a New Start would begin. *Hallelujah, and Glory to the Lamb...Amen!*

Yes, there it was: right there in Print —*my* Deliverance *(Job 31:1 - I made a covenant with my eyes, why then should I look upon a Maiden?)* And as I pressed on, being urged to read further, I would soon understand, by Revelation: with caution. How the <u>Number 3</u> would somehow play a pivotal role in my life. And always as a witness of confirmation to whatever God was doing, or about to do in my Life. With this <u>*first*</u> Verse God disclosed by Job, it was my first Insight into Fidelity and the role it plays as a *faithful tool* in marital servility. And this powerful verse was the one that started the ball rolling: showing me the <u>*first step*</u> to closing the door to Lust. And the <u>*second*</u> revelation, which consisted of <u>*Two Verses*</u>: that for *me* became the Seal that locked the door of Lust behind me then. *And* even now, that door is still Sealed. For over 34 years, those *'Verses'* are still in me: As strong today as when I first *Received* them in my *spirit.* O yes, these <u>*Two* Verses *of*</u> Scripture, *Job 31:9-10* linked together with *Verse 1 of Chapter 31.* Made for me a Threefold Cord, not easily broken. And those three *Scriptures* would be used *in me,* by the Authority of my *faith*: to confirm my Covenant *of* Deliverance. — Setting me free from the *curse* of <u>*marital -anarchy,*</u> which my *father* unwittingly imparted to me. So, let's read <u>Job 31:9,10</u> and listen to what the *Spirit* is saying: *'If my heart has been enticed by a maiden, or if I have lurked at my neighbor's door.*

Then let my Wife <u>grind</u> (Commentary based on my own Worldly Lexicon in **1990**: *At this time, I interpreted this word <u>grind</u> from gutter slang: it was a word whose meaning and use for me was explicitly sexual. It was used especially when slow dancing. Hence, I didn't know the Biblically Correct use of the word, which was that of a grinder in a mill. And at the time, I was a Spiritual Babe, and didn't have the tools that would acclimate me to the proper uses of the Greek / Hebrew languages and terms. And I'm still educating myself*). **Verse 10: Then let my Wife grind to another, and let others Bow down over her** (*Let her act as the Wife of another Man, and let him give her over to many Men* **[Please read verses 11 and 12 for a complete understanding of the seriousness of breaking the marital covenant, if you have one based on Christianity]**. Now, when I read these Verses of Scripture, I was **blown away** and immediately I received Revelation. But my **understanding** was that of a Babe. And when the impact of it hit me, I fervently and vigorously repented. Right then and there, I committed my **soul** to that Covenant. And was set on a course toward my full and complete deliverance in the area of Lust. As I began to measure the gravity of what was at stake, I knew then without a doubt that I needed to be Trained in the Art *of* **Spiritual Warfare.** As those Scriptures began to burn within me, a yearning for **perpetual** freedom in this area of my **Walk of Faith.** Because I knew within myself that there would never come a day that I'd ever voluntarily give my wife over to another man. Voluntarily, because **sinning** is a choice. And of course, (*Spiritually Speaking: Choose Wisely: So, "I set before you Life and Death, Blessings and Curses: Choose Life." (****Deuteronomy 30:15 thru 19****)*

As I begin to revel in the opportunity of my Newfound Freedom. I knew then that the course of our Future together as One was Sealed on that *faithful* day. Because of my Newly discovered Liberty in the Truth of the Marital Covenant. And now I know, that if **men** would begin to Covenant their whole mind and heart to God, Then Covenanting with their Wives would not be such an undisciplined enterprise. Not when it's orchestrated by our surrender and submission to doing it God's way. As He ordained it to be! We must receive Revelation, just as Job did. I guarantee you that most *men (Christian Men)* would sit down and visualize *(like I did)* another man on top of his Wife and her willingly giving herself over to him as if she had no choice in the matter. Willingly, because the Covenant you made with your Eyes, *"when you broke it, with the Lust of your Eyes [Matthew 5:27,28], you simply handed her over to the other Man."* — So let me be very clear with the way I understood Job's Covenant with his Eyes. You see, I don't believe that Job didn't think much of his Wife or that his Covenant was a slight against her, but instead, I see him as a Man *of* God taking his rightful place as the Priest and Head over his own House. He was not a *wuss*. And he understood what his reason for living was all about: it was to bring Glory to God in every aspect of his Life. It was all about Relationship: *"God first — all else in its proper Order."* And just as Israel was the Apple of God's *eye*... Job's Wife was the Apple of *his*... And he knew that his passion for her could only be relegated *properly* in its righteous Order. The Order that flowed from the Throne of Heaven. After this awesome Revelation was delivered to me by Job, *My* Life was Transformed. And so, I experienced for the *First* time what I've heard others describe as a Quick Work. It had only been one month after my New Birth, and I was in the middle of one of the greatest *Transformations* of my Spiritual Journey. My mind was being renewed. I was given the tools by the *Holy Ghost (Though I was not yet filled) and* was shown by **Him** how to work out of me, those things and thoughts detrimental to my Marriage. Hence, as of June 29th, 2024, 8:30 AM, I was still **maritally faithful** to Sheila, even until that faithful day, she was escorted into the presence of the Lord, **truly as my Gift from God**. And now, I'm still Trusting God as I strive to walk in integrity, in all the other areas pertaining to my Life now as a widower. Life still *lived out* in the Power of One. And all Praise to the Father, our *Covenant* is still Sound. And my mind is continually being *renewed. Amen!*

FINAL WORDS: A Word *of* **Encouragement** *from (1991)*

Now, as you Read this Book: — *about* 85% of what is written in it comes from the *"Summer of 1991* —Charleston, SC. — I was unemployed for the Bulk of that Year. And with Time on my hand, and at the *Beginning Stage* of my Walk with the Lord. *He* began to Impart into my Life through the *Holy Ghost (The Gift I'd Received by then)*. And this Book is the result of those *Deep Things***:** As *Deep calls me unto the Deep.* And so, in Closing, I believe that this Book is written by the hands of a Surrender Sheep who still can't find his way Home on his own: *"But with God, all things are Possible."* AMEN!